Horseracing
and the British
1919–39

MANCHESTER
UNIVERSITY PRESS

STUDIES IN POPULAR CULTURE

General editor: Professor Jeffrey Richards

Horseracing and the British 1919–39

MIKE HUGGINS

Manchester University Press

Manchester and New York

distributed exclusively in the USA by Palgrave

Published by Manchester University Press
Oxford Road, Manchester M13 9NR, UK
and Room 400, 175 Fifth Avenue, New York, NY 10010, USA
www.manchesteruniversitypress.co.uk

Distributed exclusively in the USA by
Palgrave, 175 Fifth Avenue, New York,
NY 10010, USA

Distributed exclusively in Canada by
UBC Press, University of British Columbia, 2029 West Mall,
Vancouver, BC, Canada V6T 1Z2

British Library Cataloguing-in-Publication Data
A catalogue record for this book is available from the British Library

Library of Congress Cataloging-in-Publication Data applied for

ISBN   0 7190 6528 3   *hardback*
        0 7190 6529 1   *paperback*

First published 2003

11 10 09 08 07 06 05 04 03   10 9 8 7 6 5 4 3 2 1

Typeset in Adobe Garamond and Gill Sans by
D R Bungay Associates, Burghfield, Berks

Printed in Great Britain by CPI, Bath

STUDIES IN POPULAR CULTURE

There has in recent years been an explosion of interest in culture and cultural studies. The impetus has come from two directions and out of two different traditions. On the one hand, cultural history has grown out of social history to become a distinct and identifiable school of historical investigation. On the other hand, cultural studies has grown out of English literature and has concerned itself to a large extent with contemporary issues. Nevertheless, there is a shared project, its aim, to elucidate the meanings and values implicit and explicit in the art, literature, learning, institutions and everyday behaviour within a given society. Both the cultural historian and the cultural studies scholar seek to explore the ways in which a culture is imagined, represented and received, how it interacts with social processes, how it contributes to individual and collective identities and world views, to stability and change, to social, political and economic activities and programmes. This series aims to provide an arena for the cross-fertilisation of the discipline, so that the work of the cultural historian can take advantage of the most useful and illuminating of the theoretical developments and the cultural studies scholars can extend the purely historical underpinnings of their investigations. The ultimate objective of the series is to provide a range of books which will explain in a readable and accessible way where we are now socially and culturally and how we got to where we are. This should enable people to be better informed, promote an interdisciplinary approach to cultural issues and encourage deeper thought about the issues, attitudes and institutions of popular culture.

Jeffrey Richards

To Jeff Richards, John Walton, Jeff Hill and Jack Williams,
for kindly introducing me to the fascinating cultural world of
interwar leisure and sport

Contents

Tables

General editor's foreword

Traditionally known as 'the sport of kings' – and famously patronised by the House of Windsor, horseracing was also the people's sport and that long before football acquired the appellation. In this welcome follow-up to his award-winning *Flat racing and British society 1790–1914*, Mike Huggins explores the paradoxes thrown up by that conjunction of classes in the hitherto under-researched interwar period.

Drawing on an impressively wide array of primary and secondary sources, he summons up a vivid and vibrant world of owners and breeders, jockeys and trainers, bookies and tipsters, on-course and off-course gamblers, racegoers and race gangs. It was a world in which the Grand National, the St Leger and the Derby were major national events; Aintree, Epsom, Ascot and Goodwood familiar places in the imaginative geography of the populace; and owners like the Aga Khan, Lord Derby and Tom Walls, jockeys like Steve Donoghue and Gordon Richards and race-track characters like Prince Monolulu, legends in their own lifetimes.

But along with his richly detailed narrative, Mike Huggins explores every aspect of his subject. He analyses and evaluates the structure and nature of the racing industry. He uncovers all the nuances of class and gender integral to the sport. He assesses the role of the mass media in promoting horseracing, with cinema and broadcasting joining the previously dominant fields of journalism and popular fiction. He explores the appeal of betting and measures the impact of the anti-betting campaigners. His consistently subtle and sensitive analysis reveals a sport which at the same time mirrored the structures and snobberies of a class society and helped to promote cross-class harmony and a sense of national unity. His book constitutes a major advance in our understanding of the role of sport in British society.

Jeffrey Richards

Preface

The interwar period is now emerging as the new era for investigation by sports and leisure historians. My earlier interest has been in Victorian and Edwardian leisure, but the high quality of much recent work has prompted me to move tentatively forward chronologically. I have long been an admirer of the work of Ross McKibbin, and his comments on racing, with which I sometimes disagreed strongly, first gave me the impetus to write this book. It depends heavily on source material gathered in the British Library, Newmarket Library, York Racecourse Museum and Cambridge University Library, although library staff at Newcastle, York, Leicester and Liverpool also deserve acknowledgement. So do the many county archivists and racecourses whose racing material I consulted, although space precludes naming them individually. Martin Johnes, Wray Vamplew, Jack Williams and Tim Cox read and helpfully commented on earlier drafts.

In due course I hope to produce a cultural analysis of the place of sport in British society between the wars. This book is a first foray into that exciting field.

Price conversion index

Year	Index	Year	Index	Year	Index
1918	100.0	1926	92.3	1934	79.1
1919	109.6	1927	90.3	1935	79.6
1920	126.5	1928	90.3	1936	80.6
1921	115.8	1929	89.3	1937	83.2
1922	99.5	1930	86.7	1938	84.2
1923	93.9	1931	83.2	1939	87.2
1924	92.9	1932	81.1		
1925	93.4	1933	79.1	2001	3206.1

This index is provided to help readers convert spending between the wars to modern equivalents. To ascertain this for any year compared to (say) 2001, the index for 2001 (i.e. 3206.1) should be divided by the index for the year in question. So to find out how much £1 in 1920 was worth in the year 2001 you would divide 3206.1 (the index for 2001) by 126.5 (the index for 1920), giving the answer £25.34. (All long-term price indices should be treated with caution because the nature of goods purchased has changed over time.)

Introduction

Horseracing has a powerful claim to be Britain's leading interwar sport. Cricket had its adherents; indeed, Jack Williams, the historian of interwar cricket, shows that its supporters presented it as the English 'national game'.[1] But British racegoers claimed that racing was 'our real national sport'.[2] On the basis of active *participation*, cricket was certainly superior with somewhere between 200,000 and 400,000 playing each week in the early 1930s, although football had even more participants, with 37,000 clubs affiliated to the Football Association by 1937, and many others unaffiliated. In terms of *spectatorship*, First Division soccer attracted average crowds of over 30,000 in 1938–39, but cricket only got large crowds for test matches and a few important county matches, and these probably never exceeded 50,000 in a single day. Such figures were dwarfed by the crowds attracted to racing's 'national' events: the Grand National, the Derby, 'Royal' Ascot and the Doncaster St Leger. Even small race-meetings got higher crowds than most country cricket games. If a third criterion, interest in betting on the sport, was included, horseracing was supreme, although football pools and greyhound racing were also important. It was racing, not cricket or soccer, which really sold newspapers across Britain. Widespread public interest in results, longer traditions, its year-round season and largest crowds, all support racing's claims as Britain's leading national sport.

Yet Ross McKibbin's critically well-received book on classes and cultures in England between 1918 and 1951 marginalised racing, arguing that:

> Horseracing was a national sport only by a somewhat skewed definition of 'national'. What made it 'national' was popular betting which linked a mass of working-class betters to a sport which was, in fact, aristocratic-plutocratic. Without betting it would have been no more national than 12-metre yachting or deer hunting … many had little interest in horses or horseracing as such. The middle class as a whole and the sober, serious working class were even more indifferent, even hostile.[3]

Elsewhere McKibbin argues that cricket could claim to be England's 'national' sport because it was 'the only major sport which had real support among all social classes', and because its internationals 'held more significance'.[4] McKibbin's treatment of social classes and cultures is usually subtle and persuasive. Here his analysis is less sure. It ignores the many racegoers drawn to racing by a passion and appreciation for those highly-strung equine aristocrats, thoroughbred horses, those enjoying the races but not the betting, and those going for social reasons, the enthusiastic fans and racing addicts drawn from *all classes* which cultural anthropologists have shown are still central to the racing world.[5] Second, the strong attachment to racing amongst sections of the *middle* classes is left unappreciated. Third, the results of key races like the Derby created far more national (and international) interest than those of cricket test matches.

Study of racing thus sheds light on a leading national sport which played a key role in how the British imagined their social world. Admittedly, racing aroused strong feelings and divisions across class, culture, gender and religion, creating significant cultural dissonance even within classes, although these too show its importance. In part these were related to the politics and cultural conformity of broader British society. Horseracing had been a central feature of both urban and pastoral British life since far earlier that any of the other major sports, yet across Britain and across the social classes, attitudes to racing and betting after the First World War also lay along a major fault line dividing British society, representing a struggle for ascendancy between competing value systems.

Some sports were closely linked to debates about 'respectability'. Academic historians of leisure have been slow to explore and foreground those many hugely popular activities, such as racing and betting on racing, that were ambiguously respectable, and sometimes seen as morally problematic or illicit. Unconscious puritanism or careless cultural myopia has wrongly presented them as marginal to popular culture. By the interwar years, the appeal of such disreputable pleasures was spreading more widely. The balance of power was shifting. Racing illustrates this well. Over this period the formerly vociferous opposition to racing and betting from the more sober and serious was in clear decline. Racing followers dismissed them as 'joy-killing faddists'.[6] Anti-racing successes were rare, although at Southend, for example, women successfully petitioned against proposals for a new race meeting.[7] Occasional opposition to the treatment of horses in steeplechases continued. There were, for example, 'the usual' RSPCA attacks on the Grand National, led by Lord Lambourne, in 1922, with letters to the press.[8] They were ineffective. Evangelical Christianity was strongly anti-racing but its numbers, never large, were dropping, while the Church of England was divided and the Roman Catholic Church showed little opposition. Although Labour and Liberal activists and politicians were generally negative, racing was popular amongst many of their voters. The Civil Service, formerly opposed to betting, was split. The Home Office was opposed, but the Customs and Excise and Post Office departments both encouraged it as a useful source of revenue. As the popularity of betting and racing rose, debates over their meaning and importance faded. By the 1930s interest in and support for racing could be found right across the social scale. Increasingly it seemed exciting yet safe. Those worried about class revolution entered racing in large numbers because it had traditional and conservative features. This fascinating variation of views provided a starting point for this study.

Popular images of the interwar years have focused largely on mass unemployment, the General Strike, increasing government control, or improved welfare and education. Yet the period also saw a major spurt of growth in leisure, recreation and sport. Mass unemployment and business depression coexisted with increased standards of living within some sectors and for some social groups, creating tensions and opportunities which heightened and transformed social attitudes to leisure. Britain was the originator of much modern sport, and in turn sport was a paradigm of British culture. Historians have been slow to develop an understanding of the way sports influenced and were influenced by the cultural, social and economic changes of the interwar years, a sporting era aptly described by Sir Derek Birley as 'confusing and sometimes contentious', with key continuities alongside a strengthening of professionalism and commercialism.[9]

This ambiguity about the treatment of interwar leisure and sport as a whole has not been aided by the potentially problematic role of social class in sport. Sports were differentially presented as 'upper class', 'middle class' or 'working class' in different social contexts. Sport could both unite and divide. Professionalism and amateurism, gender roles, commercialism, and the extent to which physical violence or active support was acceptable were all issues of debate. Sport was popular throughout the class structure of much of Britain, although some of its manifestations were very unpopular with a minority. Class as culture is a complex manifestation, and its visions were socially constructed. The picture sports provided was highly complex, subtle and more nuanced than historians have admitted. For example, some at least amongst the middle classes were always attracted, for a variety of reasons, to more supposedly 'working-class' sports, including those sports like racing associated with drink and gambling. This could be due to earlier working-class origins, the attractions of 'slumming', or the cultural hedonism of a homo-social subgroup. So while some middle-class people saw attendance at a race meeting or a bet on the Grand National as danger zones, to be avoided, for others they offered key sources of pleasure. Racing was a game of wits, often much less gentlemanly than it appeared. As Larry Lynx of *The People* remarked, 'I learn a lot of things from certain followers of the noble sport of racing who if they had their just dues would be languishing in one of the hotels which HM the King provides for those of his subjects who blatantly break the laws'.[10]

This book does not attempt a full history of racing, or an account of major races, horses and jockeys. It has two major focuses: an examination of the relationship between racing and British society, and an exploration of the cultural world of racing itself. Racing both influenced and was influenced by the social and economic changes of the interwar years. Racing was riddled with paradox, and this book helps to disentangle both the complexities of the ways the sport was organised and its social and cultural resonances. Even those who never bet, never went near a racecourse, or actively opposed the sport could hardly avoid meeting the racing world if they opened a paper, went to the cinema regularly, or even looked at newspaper advertisements and cigarette cards. The sheer variety, substance and character of racing's visual, linguistic and oral images have much to say about the culturally-complex role of British racing and betting. It is perhaps not unsurprising that racing has given names to more public houses than any other sport: interwar horses like Golden Miller, Brown Jack or Windsor Lad, or races like the St Leger, were all commemorated. But racing's influence spread much wider. Racehorses gave names to railway engines. Streets were named after racecourses or racing towns. Racing was a major industry, generating significant annual turnover, upon which the economic difficulties of the 1920s and early 1930s had only limited impact. Racing was sufficiently popular for many people to use their excess income to enjoy spectating, betting or owning racehorses.

Racing reflected the economic and social inequalities and snobberies of its time, and made them manifest in racing architecture, the racing clubs, the deference given to owners, or the distinctions between amateur and professional involvement. It also helped to sustain the essential harmony and cultural conformity of broader British society. Yet its opponents associated racing with those lacking in culture, given to greed, rapacity and depravity, involved in clearly illegal acts. Racing therefore provides a case study which helps us unpack, examine and begin to understand the cultural values and assumptions that helped to fashion wider economic and social relationships.

More importantly, it helps to move forward our understanding of the ways in which social class, gender, culture and leisure related to each other during this period. McKibbin argues that interwar Britain was characterised by a major divide between manual and non-manual workers, and that leisure, lifestyle and employment created subcultures which he calls 'working-class culture' and 'middle-class culture'. Yet at the same time he accepts that 'England had no common culture, rather a set of overlapping ones', although the sports played and watched were partially at least self-enclosed and determined by class.[11] The social theorist W. G. Runciman sees the cultural gulf between the two major social groups, the working and middle classes, as important in terms of self-ascription, but he attaches more importance to employment conditions and self-ascribed status.[12] In leisure terms, Cunningham's picture of overlapping leisure cultures in the nineteenth and early twentieth centuries is potentially useful, discriminating as it does an upper-class 'leisure' class, 'urban middle-class' and 'artisan' cultures, separate 'religious' and 'rationalist' 'reformist' leisure cultures, 'rural' and 'urban' popular culture forms. But Cunningham has been criticised both for an overly-simplistic picture of middle-class leisure, and for under-estimating the extent to which cultural roles in particular leisure contexts were fluid.[13]

It is becoming increasingly clear that while social distinctions were still expressed in class terms, social roles were increasingly dependent on *leisure contexts*.[14] A polarised dichotomous view of class might be embraced at work but not in wider leisure relationships. There might be strong consciousness of status divisions within a middle-class group, yet the group might present a solid face to the world. The spatial aspects of class, expressed in the more middle-class ethos of the suburbs, and the more working-class feel of terraced city streets or newly-built council estates, clearly had their effects. But there were manual labourers in the suburbs, and clerks in city streets, embracing or standing against locally dominant cultural practices like betting.

Racing has often been seen as a sport which united the top and bottom of British society. Certainly in part, but only in part, racing was a sport which relied on the continued persistence of working-class deference, and a strong emphasis on rank and status within the sport, helping it sustain a clear rear-guard defence of hierarchy. Runciman has presented powerful arguments that fundamental, societal-level changes in social, economic and political practice, and resultant shifting patterns of class, were a result of the First World War, arguing that notions of natural hierarchy were under attack from 1915 onwards.[15] Yet gentlemanliness, and its characteristic sporting amateurism, still enjoyed strong, although not unanimous, support among commentators on national character.[16] Within racing it was the claims of inherited rank, title and status which conferred on its ruling bodies, the Jockey Club and National Hunt Committee (henceforth NHC), their right to rule, to call recalcitrant jockeys before them on the real-life 'carpet', to demand that jockeys employed their titles or military rank when they addressed them, and to use their surnames in return. It was deference too which allowed trainers to remain remote, to rule their stables with firmness and authority. It was the claims of hierarchy which allowed the royal family to repackage the ceremonial trappings which ensured they continued to receive acclaim at Ascot, Epsom, York or Newmarket, a manifestation which David Cannadine has noted in other contexts too.[17] Within racing some tried to put forward the view that such hierarchies were natural and preordained, and that social perception and behaviour should reflect such views.

Views amongst the wider public were more mixed. Racing certainly appealed to working-class conservatives, but such beliefs in deference can be overdrawn. Working-class racing heroes were always popular. In 1923 when a relatively poor owner won the Derby with Papyrus, his win was well-received. The press headlines like the *Daily Mirror*'s 'Tenant Farmer Beats Millionaire Owners' reflected a delight amongst some sections of the population that racing's biggest race could be won by the 'little man', a 'struggling farmer'.[18] Equally, the most popular jockey of the period amongst the public at large was Steve Donoghue, born into a poor Warrington family of Irish descent, someone who regularly broke agreements with upper-class owners, and won regularly. Even the differences between amateur and professional were different in racing, with 'amateur' steeplechase jockeys often eventually joining the professional ranks, and 'gentlemen' setting up as professional trainers.

More research has been carried out on working-class leisure and sport than on the middle-class sporting world. The picture drawn of the latter has been over-broad and over-inclusive, creating a highly inaccurate impression of a relatively homogenous middle-class, amateur, respectable sporting culture. Yet as David Cannadine has recently stressed in his revisionist attempt to rehabilitate 'class' as a legitimate subject of historical enquiry, by the Edwardian period the middle class was already 'protean, varied and amorphous'.[19] It was divided in a whole variety of ways: horizontal divisions of income, property, status, social leadership or education competed with vertical divisions such as religious/denominational allegiance, political affiliation and splits between manufacturing, commercial and professional groups. There were also the more complex geographical divisions between north and south, and between the middle classes in competing regions or cities such as Liverpool and Manchester. So in what ways were the middle classes involved in racing? Were they, as McKibbin has suggested, indifferent or even hostile?

Not so. In fact the middle classes were increasingly supportive, taking part as spectators, owners, trainers and investors, occupying professional roles in racing's administration, placing bets or heading bookmaking firms. For some, with anti-working-class attitudes, often coupling snobbery and wish-fulfilment, it was the upper-class owners from which they took their model. Others were prepared sometimes to move across what were in reality by this period, highly porous divisions between classes, and between 'roughs' and 'respectables', to enjoy racing's liminal pleasures. Betting could be presented as essentially modernistic, and the reliable, known salary of the middle classes, stepped by age and promotion, allowed them to indulge betting, ownership or spectatorship as a leisure habit. Although the separation of suburban home and work sometimes confined sociability, people in many middle-class occupations, from industrialists to merchants, lawyers to shopkeepers, were able to attend nearby race meetings a few times a year. The bulk of racehorse owners were middle class. Others derived substantial incomes from economic activities which ministered to the needs of the racing world.

In terms of academic racing historiography the interwar period has been addressed only *en passant* in histories covering longer time periods and emphasising economic rather that cultural features. Wray Vamplew's well-researched *The Turf* focused on regulation of the sport, changes in transport, betting and bookmakers, ownership and breeding, and the lives of jockeys and trainers, covering the last two hundred years.[20] It could profitably be read in conjunction with my recent culturally-oriented study of flat racing from 1790 to 1914.[21] The economic historian Roger Munting has provided insightful studies of steeplechasing and betting.[22] Working-class betting and bookmaking have been better explored, and books and articles by Dixon, Chinn, Clapson and others have made major contributions here.[23]

Yet while interwar football, cricket and even speedway have attracted detailed research, racing has not.[24] In works focusing on twentieth-century culture and sport, racing has received limited attention. Three examples by leading writers make the point. McKibbin's book devoted twelve pages to football, eight to cricket, four to rugby and only three to racing, although he devoted a further seven to working-class betting. Jeff Hill's work on sport, leisure and culture gave little consideration to racing, excusing his lack of coverage by claiming that 'horse racing is much less a sport' than cricket, football or rugby. His brief discussion focused on the strong working-class appeal of betting.[25] Stephen Jones's overview of working-class leisure between 1918 and 1939 provided limited reference to racing in an otherwise wide-ranging discussion.[26]

Previous studies of racing have relied on a relatively limited range of primary sources. This study breaks new ground by using parliamentary papers, the records of race companies, films, photographs, cartoons, cigarette cards, oral evidence, national, local and sporting newspapers, fictional accounts, annual racing publications, and more. It consciously attempts to cite sources from across Britain to show regional and local variations, the different ways in which racing sheds light on communal and regional identities, and the ties which linked different parts of Britain together.

The first chapter provides an overview of racing between the wars, covering flat racing, National Hunt, point-to-point and pony racing. It examines the distribution and differing statuses of courses, and the financial challenges they faced in terms of attendance and income. It also gives details of the meetings themselves, including the types of races, ages of horses and prize money offered. Betting was important to racing, so a short guide to the varied legislation relating to betting is provided. More importantly, this chapter analyses the extent to which the ruling bodies of racing were able or willing to use their power. The sport was run by two semi-aristocratic amateur bodies, the Jockey Club and the NHC, whose membership was a relic of the nineteenth century and had changed little since in either attitude or composition. Yet the racing world, and the racing press, generally accepted their rules happily enough. The rule of 'the only efficient self-elected body I could name' was indeed claimed as an extra virtue, while *The Times* claimed of the Jockey Club that racing 'is safe in their hands'.[27] Both bodies were socially elitist, with a predominantly upperclass, landed or military membership, and exercised rule-making, authoritarian leadership. The acceptance of their established amateur authority in a deeply conservative sport illustrates the strength of tradition and conservatism in British society.

Such respect for tradition within racing was reflected in the reception given to Lord Derby, a leading member of the Jockey Club, when his horse Sansovino won the Derby in 1924. His family had founded the race in 1780 yet had never won it. 'At Last!', exclaimed the *Daily Graphic*, and others followed the same line. His was 'a popular victory', given a 'rolling torrent of cheers', with Lord Derby 'overwhelmed with congratulations'.[28] Yet such social conservatism was problematic. Britain was slow to copy American track and training innovations.

Equally, while many of the Club bet, at least on their own horses, they only reluctantly accepted government attempts to make betting contribute to the sport via betting duty, despite the economic problems as costs rose and owners increasingly paid for their own prize money through entry fees.

The sport appeared wealthy yet was actually poverty-stricken, heavily reliant on owners' conspicuous consumption to bale it out. The power of both the Jockey Club and the NHC was more apparent than real. Their rules were only partially obeyed. Horses would be deliberately held back to increase future chances; horses in selling races were rarely sold. Equally, the apparent respect paid to the upper-class owners could be a matter of form. As one turf correspondent observed in 1937, 'most trainers and jockeys still doff their hats to a patron or an honorary steward, but it is the custom and not the humility of the servant'.[29]

The next three chapters have a macro-focus, providing new and important evidence of the key place of racing and betting on races in British culture. Racing possessed its own subculture, explored later in the book, but racing impacted even on those who never went to a race meeting and never placed a bet. Given its media coverage, no one could ignore it. Racing was the leading cultural manifestation of sport. Chapter 2 explores the sometimes ambiguous, often complex and always interdependent relationships between racing and the mass media. It examines the ways in which racing was presented, packaged and imagined, from the racing pages in the sporting, national and regional press, to cigarette cards, advertisements, film, drama, novels, non-fiction, radio and television. Together these provided a cumulative cultural validation of the sport in British society, helping both to define the collective identity of the British and to shift their interests more towards the affluent consumption of sporting experience and a franker enjoyment of betting, contributing to the development of a culture of hope and consolation even in bad times. Most images were positive, showing successful owners, trainers and jockeys, honest bookmakers and lucky punters.

Chapter 3 explores betting, the 'lifeblood' of racing. Betting was found across class, gender and generation. Illegal off-course cash betting was tacitly accepted, and led to widespread corruption of the police force. The interwar period was one in which spending on betting went up faster than real wages, occupying an increasingly-higher proportion of household expenditure. Writing just after the Second World War, Seebohm Rowntree, with pardonable exaggeration, estimated that 'between 300,000 and 400,000 people were gainfully employed in the betting industry'.[30] While most of these would have been part-time workers, betting came second only to the cinema as a leisure interest, leading to the inextricable entanglement of racing, betting and the mass media. Even at the height of the Depression, the assessment of one social historian of unemployment is that 'gambling, generally for very small amounts, remained as popular as before'.[31] Betting was part of a wider popular culture in which the views of anti-gamblers and 'respectables' had limited relevance. In its own way, the perception that cash betting was illegal as part of a class conspiracy, and the homogeneity of cash betting patterns in particular areas, must have helped to unify skilled and unskilled working-class groups, and aided the broader process of working-class formation and solidarity.

Yet many historians still neglect the centrality of betting and gambling to much interwar leisure. For example, recent revisionist attempts to demonstrate that a modern 'teenage' culture already existed between the wars stressed their leisure activities such as cinema-going but failed to ask questions about the extent of teenage betting.[32] The intellectual life of the British working classes, a section of society not necessarily expected to think for themselves, has been largely confined to discussion of working-class auto-didacts with more respectable interests in the world of the arts and literature, as for example in Jonathan Rose's work. Rose fails to recognise the potential intellectual challenges of betting.[33] McKibbin's emphasis on English betting's 'markedly intellectual character', although overdrawn, is not yet widely grasped in academe.[34] His arguments for the rationality of betting need to be tempered with a recognition of the perennial appeal of the occasional long-odds bet, relying on luck and chance, across *all* classes, as the all-pervasive dream of the Grand National 'sweep' win made clear.

Illegal working-class cash betting was almost universal: legal middle-class credit betting was almost invisible, leading to an under-estimation of its extent. Modern cultural theorists like Bourdieu have adopted a over-simplistic model of respectable bourgeois life.[35] So have most social historians. McKibbin was confident that 'the middle classes rarely betted on sport'.[36] This was to accept a carefully constructed middle-class myth. Chapter 3 brings forward evidence to support a revisionist view that for significant numbers of the middle classes, betting was far too resilient a pleasure to be avoided.

Some media presentations of racing and betting painted a more negative picture: of criminality, dishonesty or betting addiction. Bookmakers could be presented as dishonest, corpulent and 'flash'. The pools and greyhound racing were legal, cash 'street betting' on 'the horses' was illegal. It was the latter upon which the anti-gamblers most firmly fixed. Chapter 4 explores the beliefs, work and anti-betting activities of that minority of the British population who disliked racing and that even tinier minority who opposed betting, and supported state action against it. Anti-gamblers were well organised, vociferous and able to generate publicity for their arguments. Even if found annoying, they could never be ignored. Support for them, like racing support, crossed class boundaries. Active members of the Liberal and Labour parties or the Nonconformist churches often played key roles. The arguments, language and discourses through which such anti-gambling views were expressed influenced the debates about betting, and the chapter explores these in some detail, before examining the variety of ways in which active opposition was mounted. What is clear, however, is that the anti-gamblers' actions and arguments were ever-increasingly failing to sway public opinion. They had lost the battle before the Second World War.

Those who opposed betting probably knew little of racing's own cultural world, its own complex set of social and cultural inter-relationships. The next three chapters move to a micro-focus, exploring the internal culture of racing itself, the course and course life, trainers and jockeys, owners and breeders.

Most courses only had one or two annual meetings and many people only went to a race meeting once a year, yet the densely-textured culture of the racecourse lay at the heart of racing. Chapter 5 begins by exploring the change from rail to motor transport to the races, with its implications for sociability, speed of access and freedom of movement. Social relationships, behaviour and attendance are next discussed in relation to social class and gender. The races themselves were only part of the enjoyment of racing, so changes and continuities in the comfort and facilities of courses, and in the ancillary activities such as sideshows, food and drink provision, tipsters and bookmakers are next explored. Race meetings varied. Some, like Ascot and Goodwood, played a role in the 'society' calendar; others, like the Pitman's Derby at Newcastle's Gosforth Park or the St Leger at Doncaster, were key events in regional popular calendars. The chapter concludes with an assessment of the 'moral panic' associated with the racecourse crime of the early 1920s.

Chapter 6 has a more rural focus, exploring the micro-culture of the stables. It covers their distribution, and then examines the lives of jockeys, stable lads and trainers. Key indices include their differing social status, income, social relationships with others in the racing world, and attitudes to betting. The chapter also explores some of the concealed and unspoken divisions in racing. Amateur and professional jockeys shared dangers and camaraderie yet were in competition for scarce rides. The leading high-status trainers and jockeys had similar incomes to many owners, and away from the course enjoyed a similar lifestyle, yet stable lads could be badly-treated and underpaid casual workers. Attempts at unionisation faced real difficulties in a conservative world.

Chapter 7 examines those who bred and owned racehorses. Some just bred, some just owned, some did both. Only some breeders bred for sale. Owners and breeders occupied an ambiguous status within the sport. They were not in practice treated with huge respect, but regarded themselves as socially-superior amateurs, although they came from a wide variety of social backgrounds. Many were obsessed with winning and some spent huge amounts in consequence, employing highly-paid professionals to help them do so.

The Conclusion links back to the Introduction, beginning with further discussion of the class relationships within and surrounding racing. It also draws out three key themes running through the book: racing's innate conservatism and reluctance to change or innovate, its role in the establishment of regional and national culture, and the part played by racing and betting in the lives of women across the social spectrum.

Over the interwar years the racing journalist 'Hotspur' discerned continuities and changes in racing's robust identity. Racecourses changed little over the period because 'they are ancient institutions that make the ideals of centralisation … difficult of achievement'. Four changes were that 'breeders give more thought to their problems … The standard of training is higher … More of the public know something about horses since the war than before it … The news mind and outlook had to be readjusted'.[37] This book seeks not just to explore the changes and continuities in racing between the wars, but to 'readjust' the mind of the historian to the integral place of racing in British interwar culture.

Notes

1   Jack Williams, *Cricket and England: a cultural and social history of the interwar Years* (London: Frank Cass, 1999).

2   Jack Fairfax-Blakeborough, *The turf who's who* (London: Mayfair Press, 1932), p. xxi.

3   Ross McKibbin, *Classes and cultures: England 1918–1951* (Oxford: Oxford University Press, 2000), p. 353.

4   Ross McKibbin, 'Class, politics, money: British sport since the First World War', in *Twentieth century British history*, 13:2 (2002), 191.

5   See, for example, Kate Fox, *The racing tribe: watching the horsewatchers* (London: Metro Books, 1999).

6   Turf Guardian Society, *Directory of turf accountants and commission agents* (London: Turf Guardian Society, 1921), p. iv.

7   *The Times*, 1.1.1922.

8   *The Times*, 30.3.1922. *ibid.* 1.6.1922.

9   Sir Derek Birley, *Playing the game: sport and British society 1910–1945* (Manchester: Manchester University Press, 1995), p. 3

10 Arthur J. Sarl, *Horses, jockeys and crooks: reminiscences of thirty years' racing* (London: Hutchinson, 1935), p. 69.

11 McKibbin, *Classes and cultures*, pp. 527–8.

12 W. G. Runciman, *A treatise on social theory: volume III, applied social theory* (Cambridge: Cambridge University Press, 1997).

13 See Mike Huggins, 'Culture, class and respectability: racing and the middle classes in the nineteenth century', *International journal of the history of sport*, 11:1 (1994), 1–35.

14 See Mike Huggins, 'More sinful pleasures? Leisure, respectability and the male middle classes in Victorian England', *Journal of social history*, 33:1 (2000), 585–600.

15 Runciman, *A treatise on social theory*, pp. 135–6.

16 Marcus Collins, 'The fall of the English gentleman: the national character in decline, 1918–1970', *Historical research*, 75:187 (2002), 90–9.

17 David Cannadine, *Class in Britain* (London: Yale University Press, 1998), pp.137–43. See also David Cannadine, *Rituals of royalty: power and ceremonial in traditional societies* (Cambridge: Cambridge University Press, 1987).

18 *Daily Mirror*, 7.6.1923.

19 Cannadine, *Class in Britain*, p. 121.

20 Wray Vamplew, *The turf: a social and economic history of horseracing* (London: Allen Lane, 1976).

21 Mike Huggins, *Flat racing and British society 1790–1914* (London: Frank Cass, 2000).

22 Roger Munting, *Hedges and ditches: a social and economic history of National Hunt racing* (London: J. A. Allen, 1987); Roger Munting, *An economic and social history of gambling in Britain and the USA* (Manchester: Manchester University Press, 1996).

23 David Dixon, *The state and gambling: developments in the legal control of gambling in England* (Hull: Hull University Press, 1981); David Dixon, *From prohibition to regulation: bookmaking, anti-gambling and the law* (Oxford: Oxford University Press, 1991); Carl Chinn, *Better betting with a decent feller: bookmaking, betting and the British working class, 1750–1990* (London: Harvester, 1991); Mark Clapson, *A bit of a flutter: popular gambling and English society, c.1823–1961* (Manchester: Manchester University Press, 1992).

24 Football has received the bulk of attention. Nicholas Fishwick, *English football and society, 1910–1950* (Manchester: Manchester University Press, 1989) was an early contribution. Martin Johnes, *Soccer and society: South Wales, 1900–1939* (Cardiff: University of Wales Press, 2002) covers the interwar period well. For cricket see Williams, *Cricket and England*; for speedway see Jack Williams, 'A wild orgy of speed: responses to speedway in Britain before the Second World War', *Sports historian*, 19:1 (1999), 1–15.

25 Jeffrey Hill, *Sport, leisure and culture in twentieth century Britain* (Basingstoke: Palgrave, 2002), p. 38.

26 S. G. Jones, *Workers at play: a social and economic history of leisure, 1918–1939* (London: Routledge and Kegan Paul, 1986).

27 'The Scout' (Cyril Luckman), *The Scout's guide to racing 1937* (London: Daily Express, 1937), p. 8; *The Times*, 21.3.1938.

28 *Daily Graphic*, 5.6.1924.

29 'The Scout', *The Scout's guide to racing 1937*, p. 8.

30 Asa Briggs, *A study of the work of Seebohm Rowntree, 1871–1954* (London: Longmans, 1961), p. 325.

31 John Burnett, *Idle hands: the experience of unemployment* (London: Routledge, 1994), p. 239.

32 See David Fowler, *The first teenagers: the lifestyle of young wage-earners in Interwar Britain* (London: Woburn Press, 1995).

33 Jonathan Rose, *The intellectual life of the British working classes* (Yale: Yale University Press, 2001).

34 McKibbin, *Classes and cultures*, p. 371.

35 Pierre Bourdieu, 'The aristocracy of culture', *Media, culture and society*, 2:3 (1980), 235–53.

36 McKibbin, *Classes and cultures*, p. 371.

37 Sidney Galtrey, *Memoirs of a racing journalist* (London: Hutchinson, 1934), p. 10.

1

The racing business between the wars

The racing industry was amongst the largest and most sophisticated of leading British industries between the wars, yet was also highly conservative, and often unprofitable for its investors. Racing contributed significantly to national economic turnover, and in turn wider British economic pressures impacted on racing. It was cosmopolitan, with horses, owners, trainers and jockeys coming from or going to countries across the globe, although most especially the English-speaking world. Very large numbers were involved in British racing as at least occasional spectators and betters. In London alone over 500,000 copies of racing editions of evening papers were sold daily. The industry employed full-time trainers, breeders and their employees, racecourse employees and jockeys. Thousands of bookmakers took racing bets. Racing also supported a wide variety of ancillary trades, including not only local saddlers, suppliers of racing breeches and silks, blacksmiths, farmers who provided forage and veterinary surgeons, but also horse photographers and artists, jewellers who designed and made racing cups, and specialist bloodstock insurance firms.

With the conspicuous exception of Aintree's hugely popular Grand National meeting, flat racing had longer meetings, higher status, far bigger crowds and generated far larger amounts of betting than National Hunt racing whose steeplechases and hurdle-jumping events, some held in winter, overlapped with flat racing in autumn and spring. National Hunt racing was portrayed as a 'poorer relation', or 'an inferior and uncouth offshoot of the true sport', attended by 'the needy and greedy', although this was inaccurate.[1] Steeplechases, the most dangerous form of racing for horse and jockey, were especially popular between December and April. Courses had to be at least 2 miles long and have at least twelve fences, all at least 4½ feet high. Hurdle races often made up half the races at jumping meetings. Their maximum height was only 3½ feet. They could still be hazardous since the pace was faster and inexperienced horses often tried to go through hurdles instead of jumping. In 1928 a subsidiary type of meeting, the Bona-Fide Hunt or Military Meeting, was introduced, giving army officers in places like Aldershot opportunities to take part, and the 1930s became a golden age for military steeplechasing.

Point-to-point races, increasingly popular, were amateur steeplechases. By the late 1930s there were nearly two hundred fixtures. Some were on circular courses across natural country and 'natural' obstacles like fences, ditches and walls rather than on formal racecourses; some had artificial 'made' fences. A tiny few retained the older straight-line courses as late as the mid-1930s.[2] They relied on landowners and farmers' goodwill and had obstacles and courses marked with flags. Courses could be very stiff and challenging: High Peak in 1936 had a members' race over 4 miles with thirty-six stone walls to jump. Held annually, point-to-points were often associated with particular hunts, mostly foxhounds, and were run to raise funds towards the end of the hunting season. Others were military meetings, although there were also Oxbridge point-to-points, and the Pegasus Club for judges and barristers. Most point-to-points were raced for by both heavy and more lightweight riders, and there was often a mixture of 'open' events, and others restricted to members, local farmers or members of adjacent hunts.[3] Mounts varied from farmers' cobs to hunters and thoroughbreds. They were local, fun events, not charging gate money: days out for the local agricultural community. After 1928, under qualified hunters' rules, professional jockeys were banned. Below this level, and largely lost to history, were the rural races at local fairs and fetes, and the many unlicensed and unregistered trotting and 'flapping' events, unreported in the *Racing Calendar* or *Ruff's Guide*, like Hendon or Greenford Park, described by one jockey as 'great fun ... and I suspect, very crooked'.[4]

While any form of betting on-course was legal, as was credit-betting off-course, off-course cash betting was illegal, but popular. Ross McKibbin suggests that before the Second World War 'it seems reasonable to conclude that about four million people bet regularly on horses, and perhaps double that number – those who liked a "flutter" – less frequently'.[5] This figure was only challenged by football pool betting, where ten million were having a weekly flutter by the late 1930s, and was well ahead of greyhound racing.[6] During this period the amount spent on legal gambling in general tripled, rising from an estimated £63 million in 1920 to £221 million in 1938, when it was 5 per cent of total consumer expenditure.[7] Racing offered a wide range of betting permutations. Each meeting offered six or more races in an afternoon. National racing ran from Mondays to Saturdays, across varied distances, on highly idiosyncratic flat and 'sticks' courses, offering left or right hand, tight or slow turns, undulations, and varying going to challenge the most expert gambler.

Geographical distribution of courses

Entertainment and sport were amongst the most powerful of Britain's civil cultures. Cricket was played and followed throughout the country by all social classes. Football, 'the people's game' and greatest winter sport, had its professional heartland in the North and the industrial Midlands, while the South had a disproportionately high number of recreational sides. If racing was as aristocratic-plutocratic as McKibbin has claimed, one might expect racecourses to be particularly clustered in the South-east of England, with its higher proportion of the wealthy. Of the national total employed in sport and entertainment industries more generally according to the interwar census figures the South-east had 40.6 per cent in 1921 and this had risen to 42.7 per cent by 1931. In fact, however, race meetings were well distributed throughout Britain, with significant regional variation. In the early 1930s there were twenty-two courses with flat racing only, sixty-five courses with National Hunt racing only, and twenty-six courses with both forms of racing. The seven counties of the North, where flat racing was most popular, had fifteen different flat meetings, with the majority in Yorkshire, rather than the North-west, which might have been expected looking at broader patterns of sporting activity. The South-east had twelve courses close to or easily accessible from London, together with the more distant Bibury Club course at Salisbury. Scotland had five courses (Irvine's Bogside, Hamilton Park, Edinburgh, Ayr and Lanark) but flat racing was not popular in Wales, which had only Chepstow.

Of the far more numerous National Hunt courses spread across the country, only eleven were in northern England, indicating that this form of racing was less popular here, perhaps because of the winter climate. There were many more in the South and Midlands. Metropolitan courses attracted London and sub-urban visitors and were 'socially rather smart', while the Midland courses at Birmingham, Leicester, Worcester and Warwick attracted 'very fair crowds from the big industrial centres'. The small country meetings in the South and West of England attracted 'mostly country folk, keen on horses, not gambling'.[8] Scotland had only three courses (Bogside, Kelso and Perth) yet in Wales, which in 1932 had five courses (Bangor, Cardiff, Chepstow, Newport and Tenby), National Hunt racing appeared more popular than flat racing.

In 1923 there were still at least twelve pony-racing meetings in the South-west of England, but most of these died out. By the 1930s the Pony Turf Club controlled two major courses at Portsmouth (founded 1928) and London's Northolt Park (founded 1929). Chelmsford left steeplechasing to reopen as a Club course in 1936, and there were minor courses in the 1930s at Southend, Worthing, Swansea and Lilleshall.

Racing was a traditional sport with long-standing roots in local communities, and many racecourses were of ancient date. Newmarket, Epsom, Doncaster or Ascot had used their moor or heath courses for hundreds of years. Courses shut during the First World War slowly came back into use in the first post-war years. Between 1919 and 1939 some twenty-five, mainly minor, courses were forced to close at least temporarily, but overall there was little change in numbers, since some completely new meetings entered, including Chepstow, laid out in 1926 in a 400-acre park, and the attractive steeplechase course laid out by former trainer Alfred Day on his Fontwell Park gallops in 1924.

The majority of the larger racecourses were run by the directors of racecourse and grandstand limited companies. Nottingham, for example, was run by Nottingham and Colwick Park Racecourse and Sports Company Ltd. Share ownership varied, but was broadly similar to that of the later nineteenth century, and as then was dominated by the middle classes.[9] Even at Leicester, where shares were relatively expensive at £50 each, only approximately 40 per cent either had titles or had no occupation, implying living on private means. Another 31 per cent were more clearly middle-class males, including solicitors, auctioneers and pawnbrokers, a company secretary, steel manufacturer, butcher, decorator and tobacconist. There were also nine married women, five widows and an unmarried woman who held shares, and this growing female share ownership marked a change from the earlier period.[10] Epsom was run by predominantly middle-class members of its Grandstand Association, who were still buying up the Downs in 1925 to ensure control.

There were several other forms of ownership. Given the traditional support for racing right across classes it is perhaps unsurprising that, as in the nineteenth century, some courses were owned by local corporations, although their actual management varied. Doncaster and Yarmouth were run by special Corporation Race Sub-Committees. At Brighton the council granted to the supporting three-quarters of its members a lease of the ground and buildings for a short period of years, and they managed it and reported back, a strategy designed to keep the minority who opposed racing from active interference.[11] York and

Lincoln leased their races to voluntary, unpaid Race Committees, composed mainly of middle-class private citizens. Chester was leased to a limited company, at a percentage of gross income, and gained significant revenue from the races. In 1932 Chester received the equivalent of a two-and-a-half-penny rate.[12]

Other courses were privately owned by upper-class groups and individuals. Newmarket was owned by the Jockey Club, Ascot by the Crown, and Goodwood by the Duke of Richmond. Privately-owned courses increasingly became incorporated. Lewes, formerly run by solicitors Verrall and Co., became Lewes Racecourse Company Ltd. in December 1930.[13] Epsom's middle-class-dominated Grand Stand Association became a limited company in 1932. The Association of Racecourse Executives (aka Racecourse Association) was formed in 1920 to look after the interests of all course managements.

Meetings varied significantly in social status. 'Royal' Ascot was a highlight of the London 'season', with Goodwood or York August Meeting not far behind in attracting the 'county set', while many of Newmarket's meetings were largely for Jockey Club members and serious racegoers. Races like the Epsom Derby or the Doncaster St Leger were hugely popular, cross-class occasions, attracting vast crowds, although the days before or after might be quieter, only for more regular racegoers. In National Hunt racing the Grand Military Meeting at Sandown and the Household Brigade Meeting at Hawthorne Hill were particularly high status in terms of those attending. Cheltenham was growing in national popularity in the interwar years, and in the 1930s the Cheltenham Gold Cup, based on weight for age, became regarded as the 'chasers' Derby', attracting fans from across Great Britain and Ireland. The Aintree Grand National Steeplechase was hugely popular both in terms of numbers attending and in terms of national betting interest.

Regular racegoers saw each of the courses as having its own individuality. Ascot was 'the aristocrat of English racecourses', with 'wonderful paddock and lawns'. Liverpool was 'a splendid course, with excellent stands and paddocks', Lingfield was 'lovely', and Brighton 'jolly', but at Lincoln there were 'never very many people' so the 'rather scanty accommodation is usually adequate'.[14]

Economic problems of racing: under-use and attendance

The public, and many in racing, failed to realise that beneath its fun-loving facade, and its rhetoric of modernisation, commercialisation and the triumph of capitalism, interwar racing was characterised by amateurism, inefficiency and ineptitude. It was hopelessly uneconomic and unviable at almost all levels, sustained only by those loyal lovers of racing prepared to give generously of their time, effort and money. Racing's costs rose significantly over the period. In the early 1920s payments for police, gatemen and paddock supervisors rose dramatically in response to the moral panic associated with racecourse crime. The costs of entertainment tax (applied to racing from 1919), advertising, and income tax schedules A and D rose steadily. Facilities increasingly needed updating, especially when compared to the far more up-to-date facilities of the new cinema chains and theatres. They seldom were.

One reason for such lack of investment was the limited income each meeting generated. Newmarket had more than twenty days of annual racing but most flat and National Hunt racecourses were conspicuously under-used. The five large dual flat and National Hunt courses round London did reasonably well, each having between twelve and sixteen days' racing a year. Similar levels of dual racing also took place at Manchester and Haydock in the North-west, and at Nottingham, Leicester, Birmingham and Wolverhampton in the Midlands. Liverpool had just ten days' racing a year. Many other long-standing flat-racing courses had four or fewer days' racing a year. Their facilities usually lay idle the rest of the time, and some courses, like Epsom, which were only partially enclosed, could not maximize admission fees. Many National Hunt courses were even less used, having only one short annual meeting.

This pattern was very different to racing elsewhere. In France racing took place more regularly, but at a far smaller number of courses. The Santa Anita track at Los Angeles was fairly typical of the USA in having fifty-three days' racing, while in India Calcutta's Turf Club had twenty-eight days' racing each year.[15] In 1919 a Jockey Club committee recommended that some courses should amalgamate, to create more races at fewer courses, with the aim of reducing overall costs, providing better accommodation, and increasing attendance and revenue. However, little was done as a result. The Jockey Club was unwilling to incur local and national anger by shutting down courses. Even if courses were more regularly used, as at Northolt Park, which had fifty-four days' racing in 1934, the need to find sufficient prize money to attract runners, and to invest in the course itself, could still make for difficult economics. In 1938 when attendances dropped, prize money was reduced so the number of ponies in training dropped, then entries to races suffered, making races less attractive, a vicious circle leading to receivership.

In 1925 37 per cent of flat racecourses, and 65 per cent of National Hunt courses, only had one or two annual meetings. Meetings lasted from one to four or more days but the pattern was somewhat different for the two forms of racing. The two-day event was the most common in both, although slightly more common on the flat. But generally about two-fifths of National Hunt meetings were only of a single day. For some like Bungay this could be their only meeting. Alexandra Park, a London flat-racing course, had six meetings, each lasting only one day. This was uncommon on the flat.

Table 1.1 Percentage of British meetings by length of meeting in days, 1921–39

Racing year	1 day Flat (%)	2 days Flat (%)	3 days Flat (%)	4 plus Flat (%)	1 day N.H. (%)	2 days N.H. (%)	3 days N.H. (%)	4 plus N.H. (%)	Total number of meetings
1921	14	64	14	8	39	60	1	0	281
1927	10	69	14	8	45	53	1	1	322
1933	18	64	12	6	43	56	1	1	326
1939	20	61	12	7	47	51	1	1	329

Source: *Ruff's Guide to the Turf*

Attendances at recognised race meetings, despite the infrequency with which they were held, were still higher than at other 'national' sports. At the great popular festivals at Epsom or Aintree, an estimated 300,000 might be expected to attend on the big day, although precise figures are difficult to determine because these courses were not fully enclosed. More money was spent on going racing too. In 1937–8 expenditure on admissions to racecourses totalled £3.1 million compared to £2.7 million for professional football matches, and even less for cricket.[16]

Peak total national figures for racing attendances were highest in 1919 and 1920, and then dropped, but remained well above pre-1914 levels. While the majority of crowds were still largely local, railway companies still found it economic to lay on special excursion trains from a wide hinterland for 'racing men', while the growing use of cars amongst the wealthier ensured that all courses had to provide motor parks. British attendances fell steeply between 1925 and 1927, by about 16 per cent according to statistics supplied by the various racecourses to the Jockey Club at the request of the stewards.[17] Flat racecourse receipts had been £838,764 in 1925 but were only £712,220 in 1927, while they were even poorer in 1926 thanks to the General Strike. Views differed as to the causes of this decline, with many arguing that 'there could be no doubt that chief among them was the Betting Tax', although one usually well-informed contemporary commentator blamed this more on 'bad times and strikes'.[18] By

1928 the continued decrease in the number of people attending was causing concern, and in 1929 several courses, including Newmarket and Thirsk, reduced entrance charges in an unavailing attempt to increase attendance. The economic difficulties of 1931 saw a further significant drop in attendance, racecourse receipts and prize money, and during the first six months of 1932 attendances at race meetings in Britain were down on the previous year by a further 9.5 per cent.[19] By the mid-1930s receipts were rising again, though partly due to increased charges for grandstand facilities. More modernised London courses for a while got better crowds, yet still well below the peak years of 1919–21. But in both London and some other major towns they soon started dropping away once more, perhaps due to increased competition from the greyhound tracks. The very full Epsom records, for example, indicate decreases in attendance in 1938 and 1939 compared with the average for 1934–37.[20] In the countryside, by contrast, 'greatly increased attendances' were already a feature of National Hunt racing by early 1938.[21]

Strikes and other trade disputes from outside the industry, and the broader economic Depression, all had significant economic effects on some individual meetings. As early as 1920 an October coal and railwaymen's strike forced the abandonment of some meetings. In 1921 another coal strike brought out railway and transport workers, and the government banned racing as a temporary measure. In May 1926 courses as far apart as Bath, Haydock and Ripon were abandoned as a consequence of the General Strike, while at other meetings attendances and the numbers of horses engaged were reduced. At Epsom, the building of new grandstands was delayed, and they struggled to finish it in time for the 1927 Derby. At Ascot in the early 1920s there had been huge house parties, local houses were let at 'the most astronomical prices' and there were eleven luncheon tents organised by the top military regiments, but the 1930s Depression reduced rents and the numbers of luncheon tents halved, while the roads surrounding the course were plagued by bands of ex-soldiers and other beggars.[22] Courses in the South generally survived the economic vicissitudes better. North of England courses were more adversely affected, although Yorkshire courses, with their long tradition of flat racing, did less badly. In Scotland, Hamilton Park near Glasgow only reopened in 1926, and even then, as one investor bitterly complained, was 'a white elephant', with poor crowds, regularly failing to provide a return.[23]

While flat racecourses had a measure of continuity, the under-capitalised National Hunt courses, many of which only reopened in the early 1920s, found conditions less favourable, and a number closed over the period, often selling on payboxes, rails or parts of stands.[24] The local competition, high costs or the weather could all be problematical. Banbury Hunt closed because of the competing popularity of local point-to-points. Bournemouth opened in 1925, but spent £70,000 on its construction, a capital cost it could not recoup, especially with vociferous local opposition and poor crowds. It shut in 1928. Plymouth struggled financially through the 1920s, and the floods of 1931 which forced the meeting's abandonment were the last straw. Retford closed in 1929 when the 8th Viscount Galway had to sell off the estate to meet deepening debts. Cardiff closed in 1937 when its stand burned down.

Racing was generally conservative and unprepared to innovate. Programmes changed little over the period, putting the needs of racing insiders above the general public. A *Times* writer in 1933 argued that at National Hunt races they served up a 'monotonous programme' week after week, with the same names of events, same lunch and tea, the same entrance charges. He felt that 'what was good enough forty or fifty years ago may possibly not be good enough now'.[25] Most writers agreed that for the general public 'the attractiveness of racing in England has fallen far behind that in the countries in which it is of more recent origin', and that 'race-course executives . . . have shown little disposition to cater for the individual man or woman outside the fringe of those directly concerned with the business of racing'.[26] Entrance costs were high, and accommodation for the general public, especially women, was poor. Most courses were unprepared to change the pricing, type of race or prize money to bring more people into racing.

Although shareholders in some of the major meetings certainly expected to receive a dividend, the moderate rates of return even here suggest that most investors were motivated as much by love of racing and a desire to ensure their meeting's survival as by cash. They were thus seen, in economic terms, as utility more than profit maximisers.[27] This was particularly so in many of the smaller, one- or two-day annual National Hunt meetings, where most race committees gave their services free, and which relied partly on subscriptions. At Cartmel, for example, all the profits went back into racing or charity.[28]

Races, prize money and horses involved

Each day of a meeting had 5, 6 or more races and in 1934, a fairly typical year, there were over 8,000 National Hunt races on 91 courses and somewhat more flat races on the 48 higher-status flat-racing courses. In 1934 there were 269 days' racing on the 22 courses with flat racing only, 166 days' racing on the 26 courses with both forms, and 151 days' racing on the 65 courses with National Hunt racing only.[29]

Total prize money in British flat racing first exceeded £500,000 in 1898, and peaked in 1913 at £573,498, but it reached a new and much higher peak in 1920, totalling £704,564, before beginning a temporary drop.[30] By 1930 it had risen to £823,770 in England, Scotland and Ireland and then fell steadily through the next few years to £726,603 in 1934 before rising again.[31] English races always dominated, and in 1937 the value of prize money to winners on the flat amounted to £730,282 in England, £39,789 in Ireland, and £27,844 in Scotland. It was unevenly distributed, and highest in major weight-for-age races like the Ascot Gold Cup (where a sliding scale ensured older, usually stronger horses carried more weight than younger ones), and in the classic sweepstake races for three-year-olds, like the One Thousand Guineas or the St Leger. Such races were run at the more prestigious courses and owners contributed nearly all the prize money. Handicaps, races where a handicapper allocated weights differentially to horses depending on their age and previous form to help equalise their chances, had lower prize money. Even the bigger handicaps had prizes of only between £1,000 and £2,000 in the later 1930s.

Prize money in National Hunt racing was even less. In 1929/30, for example, the only major prize was the Grand National, which earned the winner £9,800. In general steeplechasing was over-dependent for its reputation on this race, which drew huge entries, including some poor-quality horses who could not jump Aintree's demanding fences. The next five highest prizes were from £2,000 to £1,000, and the sport's small rural meetings generally had very low prize money. A sample of balance sheets suggests that middling National Hunt races mostly had prize money between £100 and £150, of which entrance stakes contributed about half. Small meetings usually had least prize money, were rarely well organised, and had a significant proportion of results which could seem suspicious to well-informed onlookers. Point-to-point prize money could not exceed £20 in cash, in order to keep the sport essentially amateur, and professional jockeys, and thoroughbred horses which had been trained, were banned. In 1935 total prize money at the three leading pony courses amounted to £43,470 spread over eighty-one meetings. Pony races at Northolt Park had the highest prize money with a £1,050 Northolt Derby and seven others of £500 or more, but most prizes were less than £100.

In Britain racing was very costly for owners compared to France, the USA or the rest of the world, where prize money was mainly offered by course executives. Sir Abe Bailey claimed that in South Africa it cost an owner only £1 to race for a stake of over £400.[32] In Britain owners largely raced for their own money, contributed through entry subscriptions and forfeits, with course executives providing very limited added money. The leading 1929 flat race for two-year-olds, the National Breeders' Produce Stakes at Sandown Park, offered over £6,000, but £5,000 came from owners. The Derby, for the top three-year-olds, offered the winner over £9,000, but owners contributed over £6,000. The leading weight-for-age race, the Sandown Park Eclipse Stakes, offered over £9,000 to the winner, with more than £2,000 in further prizes, yet only £1,500 was from the race fund.

The long-term trend of flat-race runner numbers was rising over the interwar years, although the difficulties of the early 1930s very temporarily cut back total runner numbers.

Table 1.2 Numbers of horses racing at different ages, 1919–37

Year	2-year-olds	3-year-olds	4-year-olds	5 and above	Total
1919	1,293	816	457	703	3,269
1924	1,561	1,191	709	1,125	4,586
1929	1,562	1,295	752	993	4,602
1934	1,619	1,194	764	983	4,560
1937	1,740	1,323	769	1,163	4,995

Source: Ruff's Guide to the Turf

In racing's early history most races had been for older horses, but the interwar years continued the trend towards increased opportunities for the racing of two- and three-year-olds: 60 per cent in 1924, 62 per cent in 1929 and 62 per cent in 1934.[33] Associated with the increased opportunities for two-year-olds were the changes in racing to incorporate more sprints of under a mile, while older horses, with more stamina, ran the longer-distance races. In 1936, for example, when there were 606 races in Britain and Ireland for two-year-olds, 499 were run over the shortest distance (5 and under 6 furlongs), and only 16 of the races were at a mile and over. The number of races for older horses was dropping, partially because owners of successful horses were keener to put them to stud while they were still successful, so it became increasingly uncommon for classic winners to race as four-year-olds.

Races included not just sweepstakes, weight-for-age races and handicaps, but also selling races where the winner had to be offered for sale, although the latter two sometimes overlapped. In 1937 there were 335 selling races for three-year-olds and upwards, of which 240 were handicaps. Even for the younger two-year-olds there were 229 selling races. These gave owners opportunities for racing and selling on poorer horses.

The racing labour force

Although without the horses there would be no racing, racing was an industry very dependent on people. But establishing a soundly-based impression of the real numbers involved is difficult. Published lists of owners, for example, cannot be relied upon, since some owners were no longer racing. In national census figures, grooms working in racing stables or in studs but residing elsewhere would often be allocated to other industrial categories. Many people involved in racing, from breeders to gatemen at meetings, who worked only in a part-time capacity, were also not categorised. The census figures therefore only provide minimal estimates of racing occupations. In England and Wales in 1921 there were 4,377 males and 108 females employed in racecourses and racing stables, with this being 0.04 per cent of the occupied population. In 1931 there were 5,336 males and 93 females, still 0.04 per cent of the occupied population. In Scotland there were only 93 males and 2 females in 1921, or 0.01 per cent of the total occupied population. In 1931 there were 177 males and 1 female, also 0.01 per cent. This implies that racing was less popular in Scotland than further south.

Some data on the numbers of breeders, owners, jockeys and those involved in the training of racehorses are collectable, however, and are dealt with in subsequent chapters. The main background data given here, therefore, are on the various occupations associated with the courses themselves. For each course a clerk of the course handled the business side, the drawing up of the programme, its conditions, advertising, entries and forfeits, engaging of officials, and policing the meeting. Clerks were key employees, and their abilities were crucial, helping to determine the eventual number of runners, the attendance and the course ethos. William Bell's takeover of the clerkship of Gosforth Park in 1932, for example, made it seem better managed, and those connected with racing were made to feel welcomed, appreciated and cared for.[34] The clerk of the course was appointed and paid by the meeting executive, an appointment which formally had to be ratified by the stewards. Some clerks ran several courses as a result. W. E. Bushby, who had started as an office-boy at Hurst Park racecourse, was later clerk at up to nine courses, and left an estate of £40,900 on his death in 1933.[35] The clerk of a single-day National Hunt meeting could earn about £50.

The day-to-day running of various racecourses was in the hands of secretaries, who sometimes ran several courses. In 1921, for example, Messrs Weatherby, who held stakes and ran Newmarket for the Jockey Club, also acted as secretaries at Ascot, Bath, Bibury, Epsom, Brighton and Goodwood. Messrs Pratt and Co. ran four southern courses, and J. W. Ford three in the Midlands. The secretaries of small National Hunt courses seem to have earned about £100, the secretaries of larger flat races proportionately more.

A number of officials, including in order of importance the judge, handicapper, starter, clerk of the scales and veterinary surgeon, fulfilled the other major functions at the meetings. These had to find their own work, although they were licensed by the ruling organisations of racing, the Jockey Club and NHC, and were appointed separately by each course. After 1936 they were appointed by the Jockey Club, and paid from the contributions paid by racecourses to the Race Course Officials Fund. Major courses contributed £110 for each day's racing to this; minor ones £90 a day. The Jockey Club stewards now appointed handicappers to specific courses, and the NHC followed this some years later, with one of the eight handicappers being an assistant, engaged in learning the skills. Fees in the 1920s for a handicapper at 'glorious' Goodwood could be as much as £130 for a single meeting, but were about £40 for a more ordinary two-day flat meeting and over £30 for a two-day steeplechase meeting, and they rose somewhat in the 1930s.[36] The handicapper at a smaller Hunt meeting might get 10 guineas a day. Thomas Dawkins, who was handicapper to the Jockey Club from 1912 to 1931, and then became concerned with racecourse management, left an estate of £30,674.[37] Although numbers varied somewhat it is clear that both racing organisations limited the number of licences for particular posts.

Table 1.3 Numbers of officials licensed by the Jockey Club and NHC, 1921–38

	1921 flat	1938 flat	1921 N.H.	1938 N.H.
Clerk of the course	26	29	49	41
Handicapper	8	8	10	8
Stakeholders	–	–	24	26
Clerk of the scales	12	9	25	27
Starters	9	5	15	21
Judges	7	5	16	17

Source: *Ruff's Guide to the Turf*

The table above somewhat exaggerates the numbers involved. Some officials, especially clerks, fulfilled several roles simultaneously at one meeting, or had different functions at different meetings to maximise their income. Throughout the period, for example, S. B. Ford was qualified as clerk of the course, clerk of the scales and judge at both flat and National Hunt meetings, and stakeholder at National Hunt meetings.

Minor employees included full-time licensed gatekeepers who travelled from meeting to meeting, controlling turnstile entry to the owners' and trainers' stand, the weighing room, the horse gate or the paddock. There were also specialist plain-clothes racecourse police, watching for welching bookmakers or well-known criminals. Courses required some full- but mostly part-time staff. Epsom maintained a between-meetings staff of around fifteen, but on Derby Day employed almost one thousand people. Because there were few full-time workers, their salaries were a relatively small percentage (*c.* 5–10 per cent) of race-meeting expenditure. The 1921 census identified 1,369 full-time course staff in Britain, but this number would be extended by a wide range of part-time workers, including jockeys' valets, veterinary staff, number-board telegraphers, stewards' secretaries, declarations officials, local gatemen, checkers, attendants, catering staff, police, programme sellers, and many others. In terms of cost to the proprietors of smaller courses, officials' salaries were the main item of expenditure, followed by the costs of gatemen, police and detectives. For larger courses this was reversed. Specialised full-time racing journalists followed the meetings and commented on the sport for both the specialist racing press and the national newspapers.

Control and administration of national racing

De facto control was in the hands of formally-separated self-elected bodies, who tried both to maintain the good name of racing and to protect the welfare of the British thoroughbred. The senior and most high-status body was the Jockey Club, founded *c.*1750, which from the later nineteenth century controlled all the top flat racing events. This long period of power aided the acceptance of its role. The NHC, founded in 1866, controlled steeplechases and hurdle races, and had a watching brief over the Master of Foxhounds Point-to-Point Committee (whose Association was founded in 1913). The Pony Turf Club controlled races for ponies which were no more than 15 hands and 2 inches high. As the youngest and most junior member it tried to ensure that meetings did not clash with Jockey Club dates, and generally its rulers felt that they had a sympathetic working relationship.[38] The two senior authorities were responsible for rule-making, the agreeing of fixture dates, and overall control of recognised British courses.

Messrs. Weatherby, the private publishing and financial firm, provided a secretariat and day-to-day administrative services for the Jockey Club and NHC, publishing the *General Stud Book* every four years, acting as general stakeholders, collecting and distributing prize money, entry fees and forfeits, and managing riding fees for jockeys and similar disbursements. They also published the Club's official weekly sheet newspaper, the *Racing Calendar*, which was a communique of rule changes, results and entries for owners, trainers and officials. To a large extent Weatherby's was the real power behind the racing throne. As a turf civil service, they provided continuity, especially given their knowledge and experience of racing people, racing practice and racing law, helping to guide the stewards and enable them to carry out their wishes more effectively.

The Club and Committee had power to 'warn off' and exclude wrongdoers from all the courses they controlled. The various racing bodies cooperated, acted on information from Tattersall's Committee (which oversaw British betting), and also tried to ensure that sentences passed by foreign turf authorities also applied in Britain. They had the power to regulate the conduct of officials and others such as owners, jockeys or trainers involved in British racing. However, this was a power only reluctantly and often belatedly exercised. The Jockey Club, for example, was well known to be less harsh than authorities abroad. As one turf insider explained, 'The Turf is essentially a sport where one lives and lets live. I've known many a slippery customer enjoy a run that wouldn't be permitted in say Australia'.[39] Even a journalist defender of its 'conservative', 'high-tone' rule in the face of 'agitation growing up', admitted that it did not 'smell out abuses'.[40]

Membership of both authorities was by ballot, all-male, almost entirely middle-aged or older, and generally very conservative in attitude, a benevolent autocracy. The Jockey Club membership, some fifty or sixty, was dominated by the exclusive, wealthy, aristocratic and landed gentry groups. About three-quarters of the elected membership usually possessed titles, and most others held military rank. They were closely linked with the political and social establishment, and were usually extremely wealthy. Probate inventories show that of those members of the Club who died between 1930 and 1939, almost all left over £100,000, and many over £1,000,0000. A significant proportion of the membership was relatively inactive. Sir Waldie Griffith, a member of the Club since 1897, ceased racing from 1914 when his coalmines in Bohemia were taken over, and on his death left only £1,495. Captain Homfray, who 'never had a horse of merit', seemed content with the 'moderate performers that came his way'. Lord Abergavenny, who registered his colours in 1927, and became a member of the Club in 1933, only raced 'on a modest scale'.[41] The elitist social distance and intolerance of pre-war years was changed only slowly. Even the Jockey Club historian Roger Mortimer, writing of the first decades of the twentieth century, suggested that 'it needed no particular brilliance to shine in the Jockey Club', which was characterised by 'an elderly, staid aloofness'.[42] After the war a few older, wealthier and socially-accepted businessmen and merchants managed to secure election, usually well after being knighted. Wray Vamplew rightly sees these occasional aberrations as 'only minor chinks in the otherwise impenetrable armour of the Club, only slight exceptions to the age-old prescribed channels for its recruits'.[43] The shipping magnate Lord Glanley (1868–1942), for example, was only elected in 1929 after twenty years of high-spending turf involvement. Sir John Rutherford (1854–1932), the Blackburn brewer, was elected in 1924, after being in racing since 1896. The well-respected trainer Fred Withington was unique in being elected to both the Jockey Club and the NHC in late middle age (in 1931). The son of a parson, he had ridden as an amateur, began training in 1899, and had retired in 1930.

As Paull Khan has demonstrated, for most members the Club's function was social, not administrative.[44] It was a social club for the aristocratic, the autocratic and the intransigent. The senior supervisor of racecourses between the wars, William Bebbington, claimed that the Club was 'very conservative in its ideas', and when they introduced anything new, 'the older members seemed thoroughly ashamed of themselves'.[45] They distanced themselves from and thoroughly disliked the press. Two stories told by 'Robin Goodfellow' of the *Mail* illustrate their attitude. When the press began to report criminality on London courses in the early 1920s the Club were unhappy at the adverse comments, so when he reported a Newmarket racecourse robbery the stewards, including Lord Lonsdale, were 'inclined to discredit' his story and treated him 'like a court-martial'. When the stewards invited the press to a luncheon to celebrate the new Newmarket stands in 1935, Club members dined at a separate table.[46]

Club members were sensitive to attacks, and intensely disliked what Lord Londonderry, in a 1920 York Gimcrack speech, called the 'baseless criticism' he felt was 'so often levelled' at the Club.[47] When the northern journalist and racing judge Jack Fairfax-Blakeborough wrote a novel, *Warned Off*, published in 1934, which criticised the indefinite period of 'warning off' meted out to offenders, his judge's licence was not renewed and he found himself for a while under the 'pained displeasure' of the Club. He felt that the inertia of the 'Racing Top Table' meant that necessary reforms never got off the ground or were delayed.[48]

Yet Lord Derby claimed in 1937 that 'the Jockey Club has never stood higher in the opinion of the racing public'.[49] The racing press was generally supportive. Many commentators, like the journalist Sidney Galtry, were 'deeply impressed by the loyalty of the Press to the Jockey Club', claiming it had been 'unswerving'.[50] In part this may have been because much of the racing press came from middle-class backgrounds, often having been educated at public school, was conservative in outlook and steeped in conventional racing attitudes from childhood so there was much common ground. In part too it was because much press information was based on ties of sociability and access and both could be withdrawn by the Club.

The NHC was only slightly less exclusive. Of the forty-four elected to it between the wars thirty-one had titles, including the Dukes of York, Gloucester, Norfolk and Windsor, and Earls of Cadogan, Derby, Gowrie, Haddington, Harewood, Londesborough, Rosebery and Sefton. Eighteen held military rank. Usually over 20 per cent of its members were also members of the Jockey Club. Membership was relatively old. Lord Coventry, who had been a founder member in 1866, continued to serve until his death in 1930. Amongst men of ability there were Lord Gowrie, a very able administrator, and Brigadier-General Ferdinand Stanley, who invented the criteria for Bona-Fide Hunt or Military Meetings. The Pony Turf Club stewards, including the Earl of Harewood, Sir William Bass, Sir Delves Broughton and the Earl of Carnarvon, were of similar background, but rarely actually visited the pony races.

By the interwar years both major authorities provided a generally acceptable racing autocracy. Tradition was important to most racing people and they were seen as part of racing's unbroken continuity. Unfortunately 'a break with tradition' was often an argument against the desirability of change.[51] They were highly unrepresentative, reactionary and exclusive, but were looked up to socially, and put money into the sport rather than taking it out. They relied heavily on the persistence of deference amongst other social groups, and hierarchical claims of birth and status. Their services were provided without fee or expenses, and, generally carrying out their work with urbane dignity, they were never likely to cause waves within racing by introducing sudden and major innovation. There was a predilection to leave things as they had 'always' been, to exercise power with extreme circumspection. Their unrepresentative nature was a common complaint but was made largely as a matter of form. Certainly a *Times* call for a more representative body of owners, breeders, course executives, trainers, bookmakers and the press to be formed, running alongside the Jockey Club, but presided over by one of its stewards, received little or no support.

The three organisations licensed racecourses, officials, jockeys and trainers, and could withdraw this at any time. This threat, although very seldom exercised, was the real basis of their continued control. This was consolidated in the Jockey Club ownership of the 3,500 acres of gallops, course and farmland at Newmarket, the main racing, breeding and training centre. At 'exclusive' Newmarket, the Club did not allow bookmakers' or professional backers' horses to be trained.[52] Furthermore, some Jockey Club and NHC members were always amongst the leading owners and breeders so they exercised a hidden economic power over other racing insiders. Their views, opinions and approval directly impinged on all those they employed, while more indirectly, their refusal to send horses to a meeting could have a major effect on entries.

Actual power rested with a small group within each organisation. In the Jockey Club, the three stewards, elected for three years at a time, provided leadership, and usually had more racing knowledge, understanding and experience. Their social background, reputation and wealth within the London 'establishment', and their influence, tact and wide-ranging social contacts all helped their exercise of power. Some had government experience. Most writers agreed that the stewards carried out their duties with great integrity and their motives were rarely questioned. The racing historian Bland, for example, praised their 'wisdom and ingenuity' and their ability to conduct 'negotiations of a supremely delicate character' with governments.[53] The owner Sir John Jarvis described them as 'a benevolent autocracy we could trust'.[54] Stewards settled racing disputes and appeals, and could withdraw or refuse licences, all without explanation. Disciplinary meetings were held in secret, with no press present and very little opportunity to appeal, except to the courts of Britain, giving rise to occasional suggestions of parallels with the Star Chamber. Any warning off could be without time limit. So while the press were usually supportive there were occasions when the stewards' sometimes high-handed and arbitrary actions seemed unfair.

One example was the case of a young Sussex trainer, Charles Chapman, who won a Kempton race with the horse Don Pat in August 1930. A dope test showed positive, and though the Jockey Club stewards, on examining the evidence, accepted that the trainer was not involved, he was warned off and his licence revoked, on the grounds that he was responsible for the horse's care. Chapman issued writs against the Club and Weatherby's when a phrase in the subsequent *Racing Calendar* implied he had been a party to the doping, and was initially awarded damages by a sympathetic jury. Eventually the Court of Appeal ruled that both were protected by privilege. This further buttressed the Club's authority though it did little for the reputation of racing.[55] Indeed since even innocent trainers could be blamed for any doping carried out by others, either to speed a horse up or stop it, it simply made it less likely that doping would be investigated. The following year Cameronian, the St Leger favourite, finished last, showing a high temperature and strange running behaviour. But his trainer Fred Darling was forced to claim there was no suspicion of foul play to save his licence, and the race stewards declined to ask for a routine test to avoid trouble.

Racing's ruling authorities enjoyed power and status, but were reactive, not proactive, in managing change. Even Lord Hamilton, one of the more imaginative and innovative stewards, preferred to wait until there had been a 'crystallisation of views' whenever the Club was divided.[56] So change was at the pace of the slower, more conservative members. Doping, like the problems of racecourse crime, the introduction of the Totalisator (see p. 36), and the issue of stipendiary stewards, took years of discussion before action was taken. Despite regular calls for stipendiary stewards to provide assistance to the sometimes inexperienced and ill-informed elected local stewards at each meeting, it was only discussed by the Jockey Club in 1931. It then took a further four years before in 1935 the Club passed a scheme, and even then not for paid stewards, but for the appointment of cheaper, lower-status stewards' secretaries, to assist and guide the stewards acting at each course. Stipendiary stewards were first introduced by the more innovative Pony Club. When the NHC thought better control over point-to-points might be needed, desultory discussion took place over the early 1930s, and then there was a period of consultation from January to March 1934 to see if there was consensus, with individual clubs passing resolutions, before the creation of a Joint Advisory Committee. This put point-to-points under the jurisdiction of the NHC, and finally provided a clear definition of professionals: 'paid servants in any capacity in private, hunting, livery, or horse-dealers' stables' or who had 'received payment directly or indirectly for riding in a race' to ensure continued amateur dominance.[57]

The racing authorities cared little for the interests, comfort and convenience of ordinary racegoers. One critic questioned if the Jockey Club 'represented anyone apart from its own members'.[58] The ruling bodies had their own special stands at major race meetings, with associated rooms and dining facilities, so they had little sense of the low level of ordinary facilities. Progress was extremely slow, largely because action was left to the enterprise of individual course executives, and it was well known that facilities in Britain lagged well behind those in other countries. Even though the profits from the Tote were meant to benefit racing, they were often used to raise prize money rather than fund specific improvements.

Racing and the betting industry

By the post-war period the currents and counter-currents of betting support and opposition were highly complex, but attitudes to betting in general were becoming more equivocal, and social opposition was weakening. The laws about betting were confused and confusing, incorporating statute law, judge-made law and municipal by-laws. Betting on the racecourse or on credit was legal, so the better-off could bet freely. Cash off-course betting was illegal but many communities did not see it as a crime or morally wrong. Yet 'Establishment' worries and 'respectable' opposition made changes difficult. The dominant political policy basis was that governments should not be seen to condone or sanction gambling, although the state was moving from prohibition towards an acceptance of the necessity for administrative regulation. By the 1930s it was widely accepted that prohibition of cash betting and street bookmakers was unworkable.

Yet different governments and different departments of state held differing views. The progress towards such realisation was slow and winding, as experts on the history of betting make clear.[59] Within Parliament some were strongly anti-betting, some simply did not want to make betting easier, some preferred to maintain the status quo. Some MPs viewed racing more positively and had fewer concerns about betting. The opinion that betting in moderation within one's means was simply a leisure amusement was also taken more seriously. Sheltered from the realities of the problems that the police faced, many departments and parliamentarians naively believed that the police efforts enjoyed public support. Home Office officials supported the state orthodoxy of prohibition, believing decriminalisation would increase the amount of betting. Meanwhile, other sections of the state were beginning to articulate opposition to this view. The Post Office generated huge revenues from both legal and illegal betting traffic by post, telegraph and phone. Financial pressures and growing unemployment meant that the Department of Customs and Excise and the Treasury were considering betting taxation to help balance the budget.[60] The police were well aware that the 1906 Act was unworkable.

In the early 1920s chancellors began exploring the practicality of a betting tax, and in 1923 the Conservative government established a House of Commons Select Committee on Betting Duty to investigate its desirability and practicability. Its findings were somewhat inconclusive where desirability was concerned, and endorsed the traditional opposition to street betting. It saw the existing anti-gambling laws as confused, class discriminatory and responsible for widespread public resentment. But it treated seriously the possibility of raising revenue from credit and on-course betting, and suggested that a betting tax was 'practicable'.

Although the following Labour administration, party and trade unions had stronger anti-gambling views and felt that betting duty was against the public interest, Baldwin's return to power in November 1924 put betting taxation back on the political agenda. In 1926 a law to tax legal forms of betting and license all bookmakers was introduced. The proposals were clumsy, ill thought out and impractical, targeting only bets made on a racecourse or with a credit book-maker. A duty of 2.5 per cent of the stake was levied on course and 3.5 per cent off course. The bookmaker was expected to recover it, and had to pay a £10 annual licensing fee. Initially the course bookmakers staged a strike at Windsor on 1st November 1926, and then formed a Betting Duty Reform Association. Punters resented paying the extra tax. It worked well on racecourses, being easy to collect and check, and reasonably well with credit bookmakers – Ladbrokes supplied about one twenty-eight of the entire revenue. It was ignored by the vast majority of illegal cash bookmakers. The figures of the Racecourse Betting Control Board (hereafter RBCB) for 1927/8 show £36.75 million was bet on course and £48.75 million off course. Because illegal street bookmakers were not taxed, legal bookmakers began 'laundering' money into illegal transactions, and following a High Court judgment in 1927 the Customs and Excise began taxing illegal bookmakers. Bookmakers, who were increasingly well organised politically, began lending support to Labour anti-gambling candidates, who had promised to repeal the tax, at by-elections, forcing the government to drop duties to 1 per cent on course and 2 per cent off course. In 1929 the incoming Labour government finally abolished the tax, removing the bookmakers' licence certificate charge in 1930. This failure reduced parliamentary interest in legal-ising off-course cash betting, though the Home Office began to accept that legalisation was inevitable.[61]

Mixed views on betting extended to the purchase of sweepstakes, which was, with only a few exceptions, also illegal. The Post Office tried to stop postal pur-chases, and there was particular alarm in the 1930s when the Irish Hospital

Sweepstake became popular. It was large, foreign and resented by some British parliamentarians because British money benefited the new Irish Republic. Others saw the example more positively and wanted to set up an on-going Lottery Commission to administer three or four big lotteries to help fund public works schemes.

To resolve the issue a further Royal Commission on Lotteries and Betting was set up in 1932. But again the Commission's conclusions were ill thought through, and the government did not respond. The issues were complex and contentious, other aspects of betting such as the increasingly popular football pools and greyhound racing were also involved, whilst ritual police action through regular, often prearranged arrests maintained 'effective' crime figures. Widespread betting continued as before. Even so, the report was significant in placing the issue on the political agenda. Legislation was introduced to deal with the Irish Sweepstakes Lottery. In 1934 the Betting and Lotteries Act allowed small lotteries but prohibited the purchase of foreign lottery tickets, the advertising of a foreign lottery or the sending of such tickets through the post. Sales were reduced as a consequence.

Racing did not benefit directly from betting in Britain, where betting was with bookmakers, who made their profit by offering carefully-chosen odds on all horses. In several other countries a system was used which acted as stake-holder for all bets and paid out after the race to winning backers in proportion to the sum backed, retaining a fixed percentage as remuneration and ensuring that a proportion of revenue was ploughed back to aid racing. In France this was the 'pari-mutuel', in New Zealand, India and elsewhere it was the 'Totalisator' or 'Tote'. In most such countries bookmakers were banned or restricted. In Britain, with its emphasis on tradition, there was no political will to introduce this. The on-course and credit bookmakers were able to exercise significant political opposition. The Jockey Club had tentatively approached some owners and trainers during the First World War, but subsequently did nothing.

The situation changed when the tax on betting, and the General Strike of 1926, reduced attendances. In 1927 the Jockey Club set up a committee, with NHC and National Coursing Club representation, to consider 'how betting might best be made to contribute to the maintenance of sport'. It recommended the Tote's introduction. In 1928 the Club arranged to draft a Private Members' Racecourse Betting Bill and found MP sponsors. The government was sufficiently supportive to allow a free vote. As first proposed it would have left the Tote's racing administration, operation and cash in the hands of the Jockey Club and NHC. Anti-betting MPs allied with alarmed bookmaker lobbyists to have the proposals watered down. The RBCB, responsible directly to Parliament, to whom its accounts were annually presented, was created to operate the Tote. Its chairman and four members represented various government departments. The Jockey Club had three seats, the NHC two, while the Racecourse Association and Tattersalls, who managed betting disputes, had one each. Racecourses, the Jockey Club and the NHC were not allowed to operate their own totes as this was seen as a potential conflict of interest. The new Tote was restricted in its operations to racecourses. From money paid to winners, there were deductions for taxation, running costs, and a putative profit devoted to horse-racing, the improvement of horse breeding, and veterinary science and education. Table 1.4 illustrates the grants made to racing by the RBCB in 1936.

Table 1.4 RBCB grants made to racing, 1936

Nature of Grant	Amount in £
Owners of racecourses	72,460
Racing authorities	11,500
Premiums for light horse breeding – thoroughbred stallions	6,000
Promoters of point-to-point and hunt meetings	5,458
Fund to assist reduction of admission charges	5,000
Assistance towards cost of transporting horses to Scottish meetings	3,546
Veterinary science	3,500
Heavy horse breeding	1,000
Pony breeding	300

Source: RBCB annual report

The Tote was unattractive to large betters who preferred the bookmaker's publicly-offered odds. It attracted less than 5 per cent of the betting market, appealing mainly to small punters, especially women, and to backers of longer-priced potential winners, where it offered better odds. The few meetings at each course made it difficult to operate profitably. The staff had constantly to move between racecourses, since individual racecourses could not maintain separate staffs. Some Totes were machine-worked, others were worked manually.

Excessive expenditure and over-estimated revenue ensured that its early operations were unsuccessful, though Tote turnover increased year on year, from £534,000 in 1929, to £4 million in 1932 and over £7 million by 1936. It was only in 1934, when 150 permanent travelling staff were being employed, that all racecourses offered a Tote service. Indeed the Tote was operated at the

Doncaster St Leger meeting for the first time that year. Although it achieved a limited surplus in 1933, and raised £178,000 profit in 1938, it was unable to compete with bookmakers on equal terms.[62] A specialised company, Tote Investors Ltd, set up a credit service to allow clients to bet in London and transfer their bets to the relevant course Tote. By 1939 it had branches in over seventy larger provincial British towns.

Betting divided Britain, so it was perhaps unsurprising that its investigation by both a parliamentary Select Committee in 1923 and a Royal Commission in 1932/3 ended inconclusively. But in doing nothing, governments of whatever political persuasion lagged behind a significant proportion of popular opinion. Indeed, increased interest in betting sometimes boosted attendances at meetings. When the Irish Hospital Sweepstake used the Manchester November Handicap as its betting medium the *Bloodstock Breeders' Review* claimed it had 'given racing a wonderful advertisement' and 'enormously increased' gate money at Manchester.[63] The complex inter-relationships between the presentations of racing and betting in the media, and the ambiguous, complicated and highly nuanced ways in which attitudes to betting on races varied socially, culturally and politically in British society are the subject of the next three chapters.

Notes

1 Michael-Seth Smith *et al.*, *The history of steeplechasing* (London: Michael Joseph, 1966, p. 105; John Hislop, *Far from a gentleman* (London: Michael Joseph, 1960), p. 190.

2 Terence Brady and Michael Felton, *Point-to-pointing: a history, an introduction and a guide* (London: Pelham Books, 1991), pp. 11, 37.

3 See Charles Richardson, *Racing at home and abroad, Vol. 3. British steeplechasing and racing in Ireland* (London: London and Home Counties Press Association, 1927), p. 148.

4 Hislop, *Far from a gentleman*, p. 67.

5 Ross McKibbin, *Classes and cultures: England 1918–1951* (Oxford: Oxford University Press, 1998), p. 373.

6 Mark Clapson, *A bit of a flutter: popular gambling in England c.1823–1961* (Manchester: Manchester University Press, 1992), p. 162.

7 R. Stone and David Roe, *Measurement of consumer expenditure and behaviour in the UK 1920–1938* (Cambridge: Cambridge University Press, 1954), pp. 91–2.

8 T. W. Nickalls, 'The Southern steeplechase meetings', in J. H. Verney, *Steeplechasing* (London: Seeley Service and Co., 1954), pp. 193–4.

9 See Mike Huggins, *Flat racing and British society 1790–1914* (London: Frank Cass, 2000), pp. 76–7.

10 Leicester County Record Office, DE 2805 Leicester Racecourse shareholder list.

11 East Sussex Record Office, DB/B 277/5–8 minutes of the race ground lessees, 1921–39.
12 Captain Heath, *News chronicle racing annual 1934* (London: News Chronicle, 1934), p. 59.
13 East Sussex Record Office ACC 6980/1–2 deeds and partnerships.
14 Captain Heath, *News Chronicle racing annual 1934*, p. 70.
15 1923 Select Committee on Betting, Q7556 (Fawcett); *Bloodstock breeders' review*, 1937, p. 115.
16 Roger Munting, *Hedges and hurdles: a social and economic history of National Hunt racing* (London: J. A. Allen, 1987), p. 51.
17 John Tyrell, *Running racing: the Jockey Club years since 1750* (London: Quiller Press, 1997), p. 90.
18 T. H. Browne, *A history of the English turf 1904–1930, Vol. 2* (London: Virtue and Co., 1931), p. 272; Jack Fairfax-Blakeborough, *The analysis of the turf* (London: Philip Allan, 1927), p. 271; Tyrell, *Running racing*, p. 90.
19 *Bloodstock breeders' review*, 1932, p. 3.
20 Surrey History Service, Surrey County Council, 3434/7/12–29, balance sheets and profit and loss accounts. See also 3434/53/1–2 race meeting statistics.
21 *The Times*, 10.1.1938.
22 Dorothy Laird, *Royal Ascot* (London: Hodder and Stoughton, 1976), p. 201.
23 John McGuigan, *A trainer's memories: being 60 years' turf reminiscences and experiences of home and abroad* (London: Heath Ganton, 1946), pp. 44–5.
24 For example, Essex Record Office, D/Z 54/2 minute books of Galleywood Race Committee, 1922. Chris Pitt, *A long time gone* (Halifax: Portway Press, 1996), provides a well-researched overview of these deceased courses.
25 *The Times*, 6.2.1933.
26 The Jockey Club's Racing Reorganisation Committee Report chaired by Lord Ilchester, 1943, quoted by Eric Rickman, 'The Jockey Club', in Ernest Bland (ed.), *Flat racing since 1900* (London: Andrew Dakers, 1950), p. 28.
27 Wray Vamplew, *Pay up and play the game: professional sport in Britain 1875–1914* (Cambridge: Cambridge University Press, 1988).
28 Jack Fairfax-Blakeborough, 'Northern steeplechase meetings', in Verney (ed.), *Steeplechasing*, p. 190.
29 Munting, *Hedges and hurdles*, p. 59.
30 *Ruff's guide to the turf*, winter 1921, p. xix.
31 Calculations based on analysis of data in *Ruff's guide to the turf* and *Bloodstock breeders' review*, 1930–38.
32 *Bloodstock breeders' review*, 1937, p. 272.
33 Meyrick Good, 'Owners and trainers' in Bland (ed.), *Flat racing*, p. 153.
34 McGuigan, *A trainer's memories*, p. 44.
35 *Bloodstock breeders' review*, 1933, p. 127.
36 Based on a sample of racecourse accounts.
37 *Bloodstock breeders' review*, 1937, p. 111.
38 W. A. Read, 'The popularity of pony racing', *Sporting Chronicle*, 22.3.1935.

39 Captain X, *Tales of the turf* (London: Partridge Publishers, 1943), p. 55.

40 C. R. Acton, *Silk and spur* (London: Richards, 1935), pp. 268–9.

41 See memorative biographies in *Bloodstock breeders' review*, 1934, p. 133 and *ibid.*, 1938, p. 164.

42 Roger Mortimer, *The Jockey Club* (London: Cassell and Co., 1958), p. 145.

43 Wray Vamplew, *The turf* (London: Allen Lane, 1976), p. 108.

44 Paull Khan, *The sport of kings: a study of traditional social structure under change*, Ph.D. diss., University of Wales, Swansea, 1980, p. 27.

45 W. Bebbington, *Rogues go racing* (London: Gooch and Betts, 1947), p. 15.

46 Eric Rickman, *On and off the racecourse* (London: Routledge, 1937), pp. 183, 260.

47 *The Times*, 6.12.1920.

48 Noel Fairfax-Blakeborough, *J. F.-B: the memoirs of Jack Fairfax-Blakeborough* (London: J. A. Allen, 1978), pp. 77–8, 178.

49 Derby's foreword to Rickman, *On and off the racecourse*, p. ix.

50 Sidney Galtrey, *Memoirs of a racing journalist* (London: Hutchinson, 1934), p. 1.

51 See for example Edward Moorhouse, 'the racing year', *Bloodstock breeders' review*, 1938, pp. 92–3.

52 Captain X, *Tales of the turf*, p. 100.

53 Bland (ed.), *Flat racing*, p. xi.

54 'Gimcrack Club dinner', in *Bloodstock breeders' review*, 1937, p. 272.

55 See George Plumtre, *Back page racing: a century of newspaper coverage* (Harpenden: Queen Anne Press, 1996), p. 70.

56 See for example his Gimcrack speech, *Bloodstock breeders' review*, 1933, p. 264.

57 Brady and Felton, *Point-to-pointing*, p. 40. Michael Williams, *The continuing story of point-to-point* (London: Pelham, 1970), pp. 34–5.

58 William Hickey, 1923, quoted in Neil Wigglesworth, *The evolution of English sport* (London: Frank Cass, 1996), p. 11.

59 Key texts include David Dixon, *The state and gambling: developments in the legal control of gambling in England* (Hull: Hull University Press, 1981); David Dixon, *From prohibition to regulation: bookmaking, anti-gambling and the law* (Oxford: Oxford University Press, 1991); Roger Munting, *An economic and social history of gambling in Britain and the USA* (Manchester: Manchester University Press, 1996).

60 Dixon, *Prohibition to regulation*, pp. 188–9.

61 *Ibid.*, p. 295.

62 Vamplew, *The turf*, pp. 224–31.

63 *Bloodstock breeders' review*, 1931, p. 95.

2

Horseracing, the media and British leisure culture, 1918–39

M edia experience was part of everyday activity. It helped make sense of the world and construct cultural citizenship.[1] Reading the racing pages in the sporting, national and regional press or the adverts, novels and non-fiction with a racing theme, provided a temporary escape from Britain's economic problems. Watching breathtaking racing action shots in newsreel and film was enhanced by ever-improving photographic equipment. As electricity and radio became more available, the BBC radio commentaries on the premier races, with their sustained dramatic action, contributed to the creation of an emerging mass culture. In the late 1930s the first television coverage arrived.

The inter-relationships between racing and British culture, society and the media were ambiguous, complicated and subtle. The following sections explore the highly complex, sophisticated and resolutely populist cultural representations of racing and betting in the mass media, whose ideological power and dominant, negotiated and oppositional influences played a crucial role in fostering British sporting identity.[2] They fed off and contributed to an interest in racing, helping to reconstruct social identities and rework norms and values. The media confirmed and reinforced the extent to which racing was part of a common culture, a highly popular leisure form across all levels of British society, and made celebrities out of leading racing figures.

Racing and the media were interdependent, shaping and reflecting the increased interest in racing and betting, whilst at the same time, in fiction and film, presenting a partial, distorted or imagined view of racing culture. Ever more people bought the leading newspapers with their racing pages, watched the last furlong of major race meetings in the cinema, or listened to radio commentaries, perhaps after purchasing sweepstakes or placing a bet. Interest in and support for racing became more widely acceptable, even amongst the middle classes. This contributed to wider changes in social attitudes to betting. Some older racing journalists were less enamoured of such increased attention. J. B. Booth, for example, felt in 1938 that 'modern race reporting has been reduced to an exact science, and like most exact sciences … it is a colourless affair'.[3]

Media coverage of racing

Sports journalism played a key role in the wider construction of racing ideology, and located it within wider structural and ideological constraints.[4] For racing insiders and regular punters, detailed racing coverage was found in the specialist racing press. Its writers provided informative, forward-looking and vital data on horses' form, weight carried, jockey, place on the start and similar material, for an audience who needed that knowledge and information for a range of purposes. The tone of such publications was one of camaraderie, implying that the reader, like the writer, was an integral part of British racing. The material appealed most to those who believed in the rationality of betting. But owners could read an expert's opinion about their horse, breeders could enjoy the coverage of stud farms and see how other stud farms were doing, trainers could keep an eye on the progress of two-year-olds at other stables, to help future placing of horses, and bloodstock agents could read detailed reports from overseas correspondents. Pictures could be cut out to decorate the training stable saddle room. Thus different sections might be read by owners, breeders, stable lads, jockeys and trainers.

Journalistic autobiographies show that many built a career in racing.[5] 'Warren Hill' of *Sporting Life* had been in racing for over fifty years when he retired.[6] Journalists had their own organisation, the Racecourse Press Committee. Messrs Weatherby issued about 120 press passes each year. There was a clear hierarchy of status and income, with ability plus the patronage and recommendations of older journalists seen as helpful in building careers. When Norman Pegg (Gimcrack) first entered the racing press he had found it unwelcoming, 'a snooty closed shop', with many poorly paid, earning a precarious living.[7] This changed with growing public interest in racing. Newspapers increasingly wanted a new, well-informed, more journalistic approach, with writers able to tip occasional winners but also to recognise 'stories' and 'news values'. Quintin Gilbey's jobs for the *Evening Standard* and *Daily Sketch* in the 1930s required him to write a diary during big race days, and a short daily article dealing with personalities.[8] The proportion of better-educated, sometimes ex-public-school, professionally literate writers grew, enjoying a regular racing round of contacts, congenial company and pleasant working conditions. Meyrick Good suggested that many had come from the universities.[9] Others were ex-army officers. To develop good relation-ships, they had to be convivial, highly-skilled socially, with appropriate manners. Geoffrey Hamlyn, for example, was always 'polite, courteous … one of nature's gentlemen'.[10] Around 1920 most received minimum starting salaries of 8 guineas a week plus first-class expenses, while leading reporters earned annual salaries of around £1,000. The top jobs, like that of 'Ajax' (Jimmy Park) of the *Evening Standard*, were soon carrying a salary of from £1,250 to £2,000 per annum, with 'an adequate expenses allowance'.[11]

The *Sporting Life* was the widest-circulating London racing newspaper, selling some 100,000 daily 2*d* copies in 1926, providing detailed betting news, 'form-at-a-glance' of previous races, and even details of silks for feature races. Within racing, some of the elite, like trainer the Hon. George Lambton, dis-missed it as 'a paper of no account', one 'looked on with contempt by all racing people'.[12] Others read it avidly. It employed specialised touts who acquired information by talking to stable boys, or observing horses in training, so stable secrets were difficult to keep. Copies of the paper could be found anywhere people gathered: in barbers' shops, in public houses or at the workplace, and it also provided information on theatres, tennis and golf, and stallions at stud, all suggesting a substantial upper- and middle-class readership. Some public libraries stocked it and at least one public school, Charterhouse, carried a copy in the school library.[13] At Dean Close school, Cheltenham, pupils read it.[14] An annual summary, *Ruff's Guide to the Turf*, which gave a complete record of all racing under Jockey Club and National Hunt rules, cost 15*s* in 1921, rising to 30*s* in 1930.

A similar, but slightly more working-class sporting paper, the *Sportsman*, covered racing, football, billiards, athletics, rowing, bowls and boxing, but its circulation was falling and it shut in 1924. The dominant northern daily racing paper was Hulton's *Sporting Chronicle*, printed in Manchester at 2d, which claimed to provide 'the Best and Latest STABLE Information'. With the *Sporting Life* it provided official starting prices.[15] It covered football, cricket, dog racing and other sports, but concentrated on racing.

Before the First World War few daily papers, beyond the *Daily Telegraph* and *Morning Post*, had their own racing representative. Instead the Press Association had supplied a service of racing news to newspapers. The popular press of the interwar years opened up racing and its affairs to wider public view and under-standing, hugely increasing and sensationalising its coverage, a point already alarming anti-betting campaigners in 1923.[16] Each paper had tipsters, pro-viding further betting information and a new lighter touch of incidents, gossip and 'talking points' for the ordinary reader. Despite its Liberal political slant the *News Chronicle* was the first morning newspaper to provide a list of probable starters and jockeys. Others soon followed. Even *The Times* used bolder, larger and more eye-catching headlines in its racing reports, an indication of racing interest amongst its more select, well-educated readership. Racing's international links were catered for by Reuters, who now provided reports and results for the major races on the Continent, Australia and elsewhere.

Racing journalists employed specialist language, written for the supposed racing insider, replete with fairly obscure terms. 'Busy', for example, could mean known to be out to win and expected to do so. 'Ran loose' meant a horse unbacked by its stable. A 'stumer', 'dead meat', a horse not 'trying' or 'pulled' in some way, all suggested a horse not intended by jockey, trainer or owner to win. Racing journalists had an ambiguous relationship with racing, fairly detached, but, as journalist reminiscences show, with a strong sense of group cohesion. They spent much time away from home, and needed to create mutual support systems. As racing insiders, they were always very generous with praise, and avoided direct censure of jockeys, trainers, horses or the Jockey Club or NHC, although betting and bookmakers might come under fire. The obituary of Henry Dixon, one of the best-known journalists on the *Sportsman*, noted his 'smooth and efficient style' and how 'he always tried to avoid hurting anyone's feelings'.[17] Of Quintin Gilbey, the jockey Gordon Richards said 'nothing gave him more pleasure than to write a glowing report'.[18] Such behaviour paid off. They were generally trusted, respected and well liked.

Newspapers printed photographs of racing even before the First World War, but after it there were great improvements in the efficiency and quality of photographic reproduction, alongside new technologies of layout and design. This visual reorientation of the press helped increase circulation and define style and journalistic personality. The cinema created a demand from those wanting to see racing as well as read about it.[19] Papers maximised their audience by increasingly collapsing cultural distances, trying to get consumers to identify with the paper's production team, and rapidly replicating and distributing racing material in ways that brought Ascot to Airdrie, Newmarket to Newcastle and vice versa. The *Daily Mirror*'s expansion of racing coverage helped it become the largest daily tabloid newspaper in the 1930s. Its presentation was highly visual, focusing on racing individuals as much as on racing itself. The *Daily Telegraph*, aiming determinedly at a middle-class readership, had far more racing pictures than before the war. The nature of photographic images newspapers chose varied depending on core readership. In 1927 *The Times* provided occasional, usually staid racing photographs with an elite view of racing: London-based, or from those meetings for which 'society' might organise a visit or houseparty, together with pictures of horses from high-status studs, such as those of Lord Glanley or Lord Derby. By 1937 *The Times*, although still a 'class' as opposed to a mass paper, had almost as much on racing as the *Daily Mail.*

For major races most national papers included a rich mixture of discursive features, detailed race coverage, betting, winner's pedigree and human-interest stories, by their 'Special Correspondent' and 'Own Correspondent', writing in the first person. Reports and tips from such specialist turf writers had turned them into well-known and widely-read figures, although writing still under short, easily memorable *noms de plume* – 'Bouverie' in the *Mirror*, 'Hotspur' in the *Telegraph*, the 'Scout' in the *Daily Express*, 'Robin Goodfellow' in the *Daily Mail*, 'Carlton' in *the Daily Dispatch*, 'Gimcrack' in the *Daily Sketch.*[20] Even the Labour *Daily Herald* had a racing section, and the Communist *Daily Worker* reluctantly included starting-price odds and tips. That papers provided tips across the spectrum of class and politics, illustrated the extent to which the commercial press met a clear demand for racing news.

The cult of expertise had its parallel in racing and the papers fostered this, although only their experts' triumphs and not their failures were trumpeted. Although headlines were still dominated by the name of the winning horse, coverage of major races included sensationalist presentation, human-interest accounts, and interviews with jockeys, trainers and owners before and after important races. The racing journalists were themselves part of the racing world, and the register in which they addressed their readers often showed an assumption that they too were friends, close acquaintances, part of that same world. They were rarely overtly critical. If reviewing runners, something positive would be found about almost every horse. Any controversy, problem or difficulty would be focused on the horses, who were found plausible excuses for failure, such as too heavy or too hard going, or too much or too little racing. Any overt blame for jockeys or trainers was extremely rare, and comments were always guarded. More likely, a trainer would be described as in or out of form, suggesting a large measure of luck. Personal biographies suggest that journalists were largely friendly and positive, and had substantial elements of mutual solidarity.

Local and regional morning and evening papers also covered racing in some detail, with only rare exceptions such as the *Manchester Guardian* which were sufficiently anti-betting to forgo the extra sales that racing information generated. Most morning papers gave lists of expected runners and reports of the previous day's racing, and provided some sort of tipping service; evening papers gave racing results. Any local race-meeting would be given a fuller, more detailed report. In areas where betting was particularly popular, papers such as Liverpool's *Sporting Echo* or *Sporting Express* often had a separate racing-sheet edition of two or more pages. These were first published before mid-day with lists of runners, summaries of tips from the morning papers, reports from the various training grounds, and general racing news, and were followed up by later results editions. In London similar papers like the *Star* or *London Evening News* supplied a large public demand.[21]

The sporting press, national and leading regional newspapers almost all expected their racing columnists to provide tips about potentially winning bets. Although most betting readers took these with a pinch of salt, they provided an extra source of advice. Some readers would have been aware that leading national tipsters' success was highly variable. The *Sporting Chronicle*, for example, ran a Challenge Cup for tipsters, and its data showed clearly that over a season only a small proportion of tipsters showed a profit if all their tips were backed with a consistent sum.[22]

Table 2.1 Turf correspondents showing profit on a season, 1929–31

Year	Total number of correspondents	Number showing profit	Percentage in profit
1929	36	12	33.3
1930	35	6	17.1
1931	43	3	6.7

Source: *Sporting Chronicle*

The frequency of appearance of jockeys' comments in the daily press demonstrates the extent to which these sporting celebrities were of interest to readers. This coverage, together with rarer interviews for the cinema newsreels or wireless, helped to promote the top jockeys even more. Their views on racing prospects were regularly reported and approvingly received. The memoirs of the much-loved jockey Steve Donoghue were serialised in the *Sunday Express* in 1923. In 1927 the *London Midday Standard*, which had contracted Donoghue to write for them, arranged for a fleet of Tiger Moths to fly over London and by means of a series of lights give out his coded 'tip' for the Derby to its readers.[23] The race for the jockey championship was also an appealing feature. Top jockeys became celebrities, gossipy coverage of their social appearances at nightclubs, banquets and other fashionable gatherings now aiding press circulation. The racing industry itself increasingly used jockeys' fame to foster its links with the wider community through specially organised London charity events: annual dinners, cricket matches between the sporting press and jockeys, or football matches between boxers and jockeys. These were mirrored in the provinces, adding to both the work and the pleasure of racing men. In York, for example, in 1932 charity events for the funds of the local hospital included a football match between jockeys representing the North and the South and a recently-initiated (1931) charity golf tournament open to owners, trainers, jockeys, bookmakers and the sporting press. The press also publicised the jockeys' attendance at the York Charity Dance at the Assembly Rooms, where Donoghue presented the prizes.[24]

Ancillary events connected with racing were also well covered. For example, when in 1923 the journalist and crime writer Edgar Wallace became president of the Press Club, he instituted the Derby Dinner, to which top owners, jockeys and trainers were invited on the Monday before the race. This soon became an established and well-reported sporting occasion, the press praising itself. Wallace continued to preside at the lunch, giving the introductory speech with humour, imagination, reflection and sentiment until his death. In contrast, the Grand National Party at the Adelphi Hotel after the race, was well-known as a raucous, uninhibited heavy-drinking celebration characterised by excess behaviour and the occasional fight.[25]

Press portrayal of women's racing involvement expanded. There was recognition that some women liked to bet. More commonly, papers at all levels flattered women readers and boosted their self-esteem by allowing them to participate vicariously in the fashion dilemmas and choices of the upper classes attending the racing at Ascot, Goodwood and other society events. National papers almost all featured occasional racing fashion columns focusing on what the 'top people' were wearing, with titles like 'Dresses at the Oaks: the Royal Party', or 'Gold Cup Day: Ascot Frocks and Colours'.[26] Towards Ascot, the high spot for feminine fashion in the Royal Enclosure, these reports were reflected in London with displays of 'Ascot dresses' in dress shops and costumiers aimed at building up female demand. There were similar features in the provinces, such as the *York Herald*'s column 'A Woman Goes to the Races', which covered in some detail the 'dresses and suits seen on the Knavesmire' or the *Liverpool Echo*'s 'Tweed the Favourite at Aintree: Fashion Today at the Races', suggesting that there was a female interest group more interested in *haute couture* than horses.[27] Public interest in the doings of the wealthy was also reflected in the long lists of aristocratic and gentry guests at racing country houseparties. Such material located racing as part of cultural baggage for the socially aspirant.

For the betting *aficionado*, weekly and annual material was also available. The *Chronicle*'s hugely detailed form guides were popular – especially the bulky weekly *Saturday Up-to-Date Form Book* available on Fridays for weekend perusal. Its annual versions of *Raceform* and *Chaseform* covered flat and National Hunt racing respectively, while its annual *Racing Up-to-Date* at 3*s* was a cheaper version of *Ruff's Guide*. Less popular, but also available in the 1930s, were the *News Chronicle Racing Annual* and *Cope's Racing Encyclopedia*, first published in 1939, for those who were keen without being technically expert. Such summaries provided a compendium of comprehensive, informative and useful racing data and advice, with horses to follow, a basis for analysis and discussion throughout the year. Further books provided useful data on sprint times for two-year-old racing. The sheer number of such publications demonstrates the powerful hold of betting.

Racing also had a broader factual literature. An indication of where racing representations stood in relation to other fields of sporting literature can be found by comparing the number of books acquired by the British Museum on different sports in particular years. Between 1931 and 1935, for example, golf topped the list with eighty-nine books, many being short club handbooks. Angling, perhaps an even more popular participant sport of the period, had seventy-nine, and cricket sixty-two books. Although there were only twenty-five in the racing section, there were as many again relating to betting on racing, and further books on training and riding thoroughbreds. Overall the number of racing books listed was only slightly less than those devoted to cricket, and far more than association football's sixteen books or rugby's nine.

Their style reflected a clear demand for racing information from a more literate middle- and upper-class, and generally older, readership. Literary and subhistoricist approaches pre-dominated. Content was upper-class, romantic and anti-urban in tone, with a highly ambiguous attitude to mass betting, commercialism, course criminality and changing forms of social relationships in its interpretative structure. The writings of Jack Fairfax-Blakeborough perhaps most typified this style. Unlike the moral rhetoric of cricket which was emblematic of honesty, selflessness and upright conduct, his work carried more mixed messages. His *Analysis of the Turf* (1929) looked at 'owners, trainers, jockeys and race officials, with the respective part each plays' and the 'difficulties with which each has to contend'. It claimed that 'sportsmen in the very best and truest sense of the word' followed racing, yet acknowledged its 'supposed rascality', its 'turf rogues and roguery', and 'turf flotsam and jetsam', accepting their existence but minimising their extent. His books coupled an affectionate and nostalgic view of racing's past and fears for the future of rural landowners with a more cautious admiration for the efficiency and innovation of a few racecourse managers.[28] Blakeborough published some 112 racing books, many on the history of northern English racing, alongside short stories, plays and newspaper columns.[29]

A similarly defensively nostalgic view pervades much other published material. The London publishers Hutchinson and Co. were major publishers of racing memories, in which there was significant interest amongst middle- and upper-class readers. Amongst many other books they produced Charles Morton's *My Sixty Years on the Turf* (1930), Sidney Galtry's *Memoirs of a Racing Journalist* (1934), Arthur Sarl's *Horses, Jockeys and Crooks: Reminiscences of Thirty Years' Racing* (1935) and Quintin Gilbey's *Racing for Fun* (1936). Racing memoirs produced by other publishers included C. A. Dighton, *My Sporting Life* (Richards, 1934). Another literary non-fiction form was the biography or autobiography in which the lives of trainers, owners, jockeys or even horses generally received fairly adulatory, non-critical treatment, unsullied by mention of dishonesty or unsporting practice.[30] Racing history texts centred on the racing elite, with histories of 'major' individuals[31] and 'key' races[32] alongside general treatments.[33]

Listeners hoping to hear racing on the wireless were initially disappointed. The BBC, with its dedication to the raising of public taste, at first showed little interest. It only reluctantly broadcast the Epsom Derby result in 1922.[34] It began presenting studio sport in 1923 but maintained an ambivalent attitude towards mentioning racing results. It wished to promote 'correct' social attitudes and enhance its own respectability, and had moral reservations about gambling. It was also concerned about harming the press, since the 1923 Sykes Committee had reported to Parliament that broadcasting racing results would damage newspaper sales. In 1925, the year when the Kentucky Derby was first broadcast in the USA, there were negotiations about broadcasting a 'sound impression' (without commentary) of the Epsom Derby but these came to nothing, partly due to heated press opposition.[35] In 1926 the BBC finally introduced the 'daring experiment' of a Derby outside broadcast to 2LO London listeners. It was not a great critical success. The inexperienced commentators were poor, ending the brief broadcast with a very tentative announcement of the result, 'It looks like 9-5-1', rather than providing the horses' names.[36] The BBC first provided commentary on the Grand National in March 1927. This was taken more seriously, and broadcast on the London and Daventry transmitters. The BBC described it as 'a new and thrilling kind of broadcasting entertainment'. It was the first suggestion of a slightly more popular flavour being given to sport, and a clear recognition of racing's cultural importance. The broadcast lasted over an hour and used five microphones, two of which picked up background noise from the crowd, betting ring and unsaddling enclosure, helping to create atmosphere, as did crowd interviews. Meyrick Good, a well-known racing journalist and expert race reader, provided commentary. His assistant, George Allison, an Arsenal director and future manager, already commentated regularly on amateur and professional football, using a slightly more excited and less detached style of commentary.[37] Good had 'read' the race to George V since 1921, and on this occasion the king stood to Good's right by the open microphone, with Allison providing the 'colour'.[38] Good got over-excited and omitted details of the official placings.

By then an emerging part of the BBC's mission was to cover 'national' sporting events, accommodating quietly to a more genuine national sporting culture and providing a shared frame of reference across widely divergent groups. Both the Grand National and the Derby were always covered thereafter, consolidating them as key features of the national sporting calendar. They became part of an annual core of broadcast national rituals and ceremonies, like the Boat Race, Test Matches or the king's Christmas message. This helped to present the BBC in a more democratic and less elitist light, while conferring increased respectability and status on racing. The two races were the leading betting races of the year. Now even those who never attended a race meeting and had little interest in racing were made familiar with them. Listening audiences were large, and coverage may well have helped to further expand betting on the two events or participation in workplace sweeps. Racing was becoming basic British cultural capital, something almost everyone could anticipate, recognise and respond to. It also spread an image of British culture abroad. The 1933 Derby commentary was relayed to India, Canada, the United States and Ireland.[39]

Technological changes improved the presentation. For the 1927 St Leger, the 'desensitised' microphone that cut out background noise on the commentary was used for the first time. This allowed the use of a separate microphone for atmosphere, the sound level from which could be controlled by an engineer. In 1928 the length of broadcasts was shortened to half an hour, and the approach was tightened up. The broadcasts had some limited negative impact on evening newspaper sales but made the major races ever more popular, attracting excellent listening figures from the early 1930s. The enclosure of courses in the nineteenth century had reduced racecourse attendance, making spectators predominantly adult males, removing racing from the experience of many women and children. The new BBC sports coverage, coupled with the increased popularity of sweeps on the Derby and National, was therefore important in widening access to racing and disseminating interest in its major events on a new and larger scale.

'Mains' valve sets with attached loudspeaker became a common feature in the early 1930s. Hire purchase spread, and radios became smaller and more compact. In 1937 over eight million licences were paid for, and by 1939 71 per cent of all households had a radio, allowing ever more people to experience the entertainment and excitement of racing. Further technical improvements were introduced to outside broadcasting in the 1930s, and by the later 1930s more races, including the Chester Cup, the Oaks, the Cesarewitch, the Eclipse Stakes and the Ascot Gold Cup, were being broadcast. The latter incorporated yet another innovation, a description of women's fashion in the enclosure, by a female broadcaster. To maintain standards, Quintin Gilbey, who had appeared in a divorce case, was formally refused entrance to the Royal Enclosure as a commentator, but was allowed in after being given a footman's uniform, which satisfied all parties![40] Some of the regions began providing race commentaries too.

In the 1920s the BBC had found that racing experts often made poor broadcasters, while those with good microphone technique were generally unable both to 'read' a race and share the information about owners, jockeys, trainers or chances which many listeners wanted. By the later 1930s, however, the BBC had developed the technique of having an expert 'race reader' coupled with a 'microphone speaker', a professional BBC staffer. New commentators like Thomas Wood and Richard North were now more able to provide what the public wanted in terms of race reading and description. The 'reader' gave guidance to the commentator, whose voice was the only one heard, thanks to the desensitised microphone. The scene was now better set, the course and horses were better described, and the pace and pitch of delivery began to match the crowd noise.

Even so, commentating was still difficult. Given the often inconvenient vantage points, accurate interpretations of the race were difficult to achieve, especially in a close finish. At Aintree in 1938, the commentary on the Grand National 'left millions of listeners to the broadcast description of the race uncertain who had won' for just this reason.[41] During the race more information was given about those horses most favoured in the betting market, although the BBC still expressly forbade reference to betting. The starting prices of the winner and placed horses were never given until well after the Second World War. The BBC also gave far less coverage to top jockeys than the press, although when Gordon Richards achieved a record 247 wins in a season in 1933 he made a nervous broadcast from Liverpool's Adelphi Hotel. Steve Donoghue only made his first broadcast in 1935 when he appeared with Noël Coward on Henry Hall's guest night.[42]

The first television outside broadcasting of the Derby was carried out as early as 1931 by the Baird Television Company in cooperation with the BBC, and a lucky few watched it at home in London on primitive 'Televisors'. *The Bloodstock Breeders' Review* was awed. 'Truly,' it admitted, 'we are living in an age of wonders.'[43] Baird claimed that it 'marks the entry of television into the outdoor field and should be the prelude to televising outdoor topical events', but the BBC initially failed to follow it up.[44] A more serious attempt was made in the late 1930s, when the BBC began to develop television coverage in the London region for those few richer homes where a set could be afforded. Outside broadcasts of the Boat Race and Wimbledon were attempted. The BBC considered coverage of the 1938 Epsom Derby, a recognition of the attraction of the event to this wealthier market, and approached the local authority for van space in early January. Before even being approached, the Epsom Grandstand Committee, echoing the opposition of the traditionalist Jockey Club, and perhaps feeling it would cut attendances, issued a press statement, saying that they would 'not in any circumstances give their permission'.[45] As a result the BBC was approached by Leonard Jayne of the Pony Turf Club, offering their 1938 Pony Derby as an alternative, an offer accepted by the BBC, who recruited Jayne as race reader and broadcaster.[46] This forced a rapid change of heart by the Epsom Committee, and both Derbies were shown.

At Epsom two commercial companies used the television transmission 'live' as a commercial 'trailer' for potentially marketing the transmission in cinemas and elsewhere. There was a private showing by Gaumont British at the Tatler News Theatre in London on an 8-foot-square screen. Reportedly the crowd there found it 'as thrilling as being in the grandstand', and could not refrain from bursting into applause during the close finish. The TV presentation tried to create a 'realistic' atmosphere, showing the fun-fair in the valley, the rows of bookmakers, and the king and queen returning from the paddock after inspecting the horses.[47] It was also shown by the Scophony Company to six hundred people at a Kennington department store using a 6-foot screen.[48]

The press coverage of the dispute, good weather and the TV cameras brought large crowds to Northolt for the Pony Derby for the second horserace to be televised in Britain. The entertainer George Robey was introduced to viewers, Freddy Grisewood provided context, and the commentary was given by the official Northolt commentator, Leonard Jayne, perched on the roof of the Tote Stand.

Despite their technical imperfections and limited visibility at Epsom, partly thanks to rain, the broadcasts generated widespread interest and increased audience, resulting in further television coverage of the Derby in 1939. But racing was conservative, and only a minority of racing executives around London welcomed the new medium. When in the same year the BBC approached Sandown Park with a view to producing a commentary on the July Eclipse Stakes, it was turned down.[49] The popularity of TV racing was still well in the future.

The audience for these early television broadcasts was small. By contrast the cinema, the most dominant cultural leisure form of the period, and deeply rooted in the British social fabric, played an especially significant role in helping to stimulate and sustain interest in racing. Going to the cinema was a potent medium of popular cultural practice, providing a powerful illusion of simultaneity, truth and participation, and both confirming and transcending that world. Sport was already a pervasive popular feature of news reporting in cinemas. Indeed, a film of the Epsom Derby had been shown at the Alhambra Theatre, amidst 'wild enthusiasm', as early as 1896.[50] *Pathe Gazette and News* sports features helped to alter ordinary people's views of sport. Fights by top boxers such as Carpentier, Tunney or Dempsey were regularly shown, as were major national sporting events such as the Football Association Cup Final. By 1921 Gaumont Graphic's film of the Derby was quite technically sophisticated, and a hundred or more copies were sent out the same evening.[51] In 1923, when the British horse Papyrus was sent to Belmont Park course in New York to race the American champion Zev, accompanied by top jockey Steve Donoghue, the visit was recorded by *Pathe News*. The 'official film' had excellent pictures of the actual race from start to finish, including slow-motion sequences, and pictures of the crowd, as well as glimpses of Papyrus during the journey and of the training quarters where the two horses did their preliminary work. As these new techniques of recording racing were more generally applied to other races, journalists found their eye-witness, rapidly written and more spontaneous reports sometimes at variance with films, forcing more mature reflection. To quote just one example, a radio commentator wrote, 'the motion picture of the Grand National which I saw yesterday has made me revise some of the views I held before'.[52]

Film sound caught the excitements of the course even more. *Gaumont Sound News* covered the Derby in 1929, the same year that *Pathe Sound Magazine* was introduced. Two American-owned organisations, *British Movietone News* (1929) and *British Paramount News* (1931) also began to compete, soon using a modernised magazine format, with a separate sports section. In 1932 the British Movietone Derby introduction included crowds arriving, the horses, the pearly kings and queens, the real king and queen (a neat social contrast), gypsies and stunt men. Its presentation indicated both the liminal and carnivalesque nature of the course, and its underlying boundedness and respectability, reflecting traditional British social values and characteristics. Then the title was introduced and music started as the race began, with some audibility of thudding hooves and distinct crowd dialogue, perhaps dubbed on later, creating excitement. The finish was shown in slow motion. As techniques developed, big race coverage even occasionally included brief interviews with jockeys, owners and (much more rarely) trainers.

Promoters of race-meetings often sold exclusive rights to one company. *Pathe*, for example, claimed to present 'the only authentic and official pictures' of the 1933 Grand National, which was 'described by Captain G. H. Gilbey, the famous racing journalist'.[53] It had a staff of twenty-six at the course, but had its work cut out to keep opposition cameras out. The 'cinema battle' was a regular occurrence at Aintree in the 1930s. In 1935 'a large balloon was ready to be floated in front of the lenses of the pirates, and while the race was on bright flares shone over the canal bank, presumably to blind the lenses of others, and a smoke screen was set up'.[54]

Selling products

Racing was also used as a powerful advertising metaphor. *Sporting Life*'s advertisements, aimed at upper- and middle-class sporting men, formed a substantial part of the paper. For example, its advertisements during Derby week 1924 included Burberry coats ('a winner all the way'), Austin and Morris cars, car tyres, Schweppes tonic, goldsmiths and silversmiths, makers of racing binoculars, and a number of cigarette firms.

In towns with popular races local advertisers of products with more limited racing connections often used racing in their advertising slogans. There may even have been some external social pressure to do so, a point made explicit in the Liverpool civil, navy and military tailor Albert Henderson's 1922 advertisement, which stated 'somehow it seems customary for the advertisers of Liverpool to get a little topical interest into their advertising during National Week, and to the dictates of this custom we yield'. Other advertisements during that week included 'Monserrat: the Grand National Health Salt', and 'The National Favourite: Barker and Dobson Viking Chocolate'.[55] Betting language was often coupled with the name. In York, for example, you could get 'A certainty for the Ebor Day purchaser. When you purchase at Gawthorne's you are on a sure winner'.[56] Cigarette advertising cashed in on the popularity of racing. J. Player and Sons, for example, had annual advertisements during race weeks in local newspapers, showing middle-class or respectable working-class men smoking whilst watching the races, accompanied by slogans like 'It's a Certainty, Players Please' or 'Horses for Courses, Players Please', picking up on the verbal cliches associated with racing and utilising them in a new commercial context.

Cigarette cards were another potent advertising medium. Their sporting coverage was popular, with football, cricket and then racing themes most popular of all. Racehorses and jockeys were the most commonly produced series. In 1933 alone there were three racehorse sets. Player and Sons issued a set of 'Derby and Grand National Winners', while Ogdens and Hignett Bros. had sets of 'Prominent Racehorses'. No one racehorse seems to have caught the public imagination in the way Seabiscuit did in the USA, although Brown Jack, Golden Miller and Papyrus came close.[57] Series which cover wealthy racehorse owners, like Ogdens' 'Trainers and Owners' Colours', are more from the 1920s, while the 1930s had far more jockey series, such as Gallagher's 'Famous Jockeys'. Richards (thirty-four cards), followed by Donaghue (twenty-six cards), appeared most often.

Racing and betting were also perennial themes for topical popular cartoonists, especially Bill Haselden of the *Daily Mirror*, Joseph Lee of the *London Evening News*, David Low of the *Evening Standard*, George Strube of the *Daily Express*, and Tom Webster of the *Daily Mail*. They often used racing as a cartoon metaphor for commenting on current events, especially politics. Cartoons about racing itself also appeared regularly – clear evidence that readers had sufficient background racing understanding to 'read' their visual humour.

Betting facilities also advertised themselves. Bookmakers receive detailed treatment elsewhere, but 'specialist' tipsters advertised too, implying that they had extra, more secret information at a price. Newspaper editors occasionally pointed out that 'any person who could find winners with regularity would keep the knowledge to himself', but kept publishing them. They brought in revenue.[58] Some cheap newspapers consisted entirely of betting tips, advertising professional tipsters and lucky mascots.[59] Tipster advertisements in the various *Sporting Chronicle* publications usually included lists of testimonials from the successful – not, naturally, from the unsuccessful. Many adverts offered to send cables to racing fans abroad, which implies that a lucrative and perhaps safer market existed where the unsuccessful had less opportunity of complaint. The 'Newmarket Resident Commissioner' suggested he offered 'a splendid opportunity to South African backers', and testimonials from South Africa were common. Lawson of Southport quoted his 'colonial clients', such as the following from Jamaica, 'Received Cables of 20th October! Had £10 on LOVER'S FATE Won 100–8 ... Must REALLY CONGRATULATE YOU ... I am including a PRESENT of TEN POUNDS in my draft'.[60] Some tipsters were frauds. Others did their best to provide reliable information, although often gaining it by spying on trials or bribing stable boys in local pubs. One, who had a hotel bill of £50 a week, claimed an income of up to £2,000 for a single successful major race, paid for by being 'put on the odds to a fiver' by successful punters.[61]

Fictional portrayals of racing

Fictional representations of racing, in films, plays and books, were quite common during the period. Racing films were generally positively described in local papers. One 'Grand Holiday Attraction' at West Hartlepool in 1936 was 'a fine racing story which provides some excellent entertainment'.[62] In the 1920s most were American, largely reflecting American attitudes. *Riders Up* (1924) had many of its scenes filmed on an American racecourse, although the later Marlene Dietrich and Robert Donat film *Knight without Armour*, a good example of the 'Hollywood idea of England' genre, made in England but aimed at the international market, featured a re-enactment of the 1913 Ascot meeting. American films often saw racing as a crooked sport, and many of their plots had some form of racing crime as the main storyline, alongside a romantic subplot. They often assumed that racing attracted criminals who were out to fix races, nobble opponents' horses and run their horses dishonestly, while other owners, especially the hero, were men of integrity: honest and straightforward, never bet and ran their horses straight. British filmgoers preferred more comic American racing films such as the Ritz brothers' 1939 film *They're Off*.[63]

British-made films are more revealing about British cultural attitudes to racing and betting, and recent research has recognised their importance in British interwar cultural history.[64] The 1930s was a prolific period of British film-making, stimulated by the Cinematograph Films Act of 1927, which required a quota of all films shown in Britain to be produced here, rising from 5 per cent in 1928 to 20 per cent by 1936. McKibbin has argued that 'British films were rather disliked' up to the late 1930s.[65] Certainly there was disregard for more 'popular' cinema amongst London critics. Yet the evidence of the exhibition lists of leading London and provincial cinemas listed in *Kine Weekly* suggests that British films were on average as popular as American ones.[66]

Of these British films, a 1973 analysis suggested that between 1929 and 1939 about 1.5 per cent of them were sports films.[67] This was an under-estimate, since a large number of films in other categories, such as crime, comedy, musicals or adventure films, also dealt in passing with various British sports, or gambling on them in the form of racing sweepstakes or football pools.[68] More than half of sports films had a racing or betting focus, although the quality of them in film critics' eyes was often poor.

Research carried out on audience preferences in the 1930s does not suggest that these British sporting films were particularly popular in comparison with other genres – films of plays or books, musicals and dance films, epics, historical and adventure films. Mass Observation in Bolton, for example, found musical romance, drama and tragedy, history and crime the most popular, with male youths being particular devotees of crime films.[69] However we need to be careful in assessing the reliability of this data. Given that the bulk of films were on non-sporting themes it is possible that the questions asked by contemporary interviewers or recent oral historians may have obscured more favourable working-class responses. Women or middle-class interviewers were statistically less likely to be interested in popular sports, and Mass Observation interviewers had manifest difficulties in understanding the languages of popular culture in other contexts.[70] In recent years more women than men have been interviewed about their recollections, and interwar sport was a more masculine interest.

Textual analysis of British films shows how racing was visually represented, imagined and received. Films had to appeal to the needs, wants and aspirations of the audience, and their skillfully-manipulated images showed British filmmakers' attitudes to the way they thought British society perceived the culture of racing and betting. Certainly Elstree producers were 'carefully and successfully evaluating the kinds of films the public wanted to see'.[71] The success and popularity of some of these films suggest that they can provide an insight into the way ordinary people thought about racing.

The cultural meanings underlying these films are complex, subtle and difficult, not least since in films entertainment, ideology and audience came together. A unitary reading is impossible, and they indicate unresolved dualities and concealed conflicts in the thinking of authors, producers and audiences. All played a role in the social construction of meaning. They provide clues to tensions, contradictions and resistances in people's thinking about racing and betting. More generally they defined, mythicised and disseminated attitudes. Some were made to appeal to the working classes, the poor and unemployed through their often realistic elements and settings, their familiar atmosphere and social commentary and concerns, although many of the scenes are broad caricatures. In some of these films the working classes could see working-class environments, characters and conditions, including 'cops' and costermongers, bookmakers and betting, touts and tipsters.

But others preferred to enjoy racing through escapism, comedy, fantasy and wish-fulfilment, winning a big bet, living in a country house and having one's horse winning the Derby, and the audience response to such escapist films, emphasing tradition and social decorum, was particularly positive. This variety of needs was met by a relatively diverse film culture, part of an ideological process of shaping people's thoughts on racing, class, gender and culture. Racing films were capable of being read by audiences in a variety of ways, validating the interests and concerns of women as well as men, rational punters as well as those relying on luck, middle- as well as working-class audiences.[72]

Many films portrayed racing as a suitable theme for comedy. Film audiences always enjoyed 'humour'. In *Up for the Derby* (1933) comedian Sydney Howard played a punter who was lucky enough to pick out winning horses from a paper with an infallible pin, but unlucky enough to always find a dishonest bookmaker to place his bet. Finally broke, he became a stable lad, bought a broken-down horse for fifty shillings and trained it in the back garden of his Downs cottage, hiding it inside when he was pursued by brokers' men. The horse, of course, finally became a Derby winner.

The fast-talking Cockney Max Miller's *Educated Evans* (1936) portrayed its protagonist as a horse-racing tipster, friendly with the nouveaux riche, who becomes a trainer and eventually gets a fortune by backing the wrong horse. It suggested the unreliability of tipsters, and was hugely popular, especially in southern England. Funny and fast-moving, it grossed four times its costs, and was described by one London letter writer to *Film Weekly* as 'amusing, human and plausible'.[73] In a sequel, *Thank Evans* (1938), the tipster has a long losing streak, gets involved with a crooked trainer, and makes money by persuading one of the trainer's unwitting owners to change his horse's dishonest jockey for a 'straight' one before the big race. In the North the leading box-office attraction was singer-comedian George Formby, a former professional jockey famous for cheap, profitable, social-satirical comic films, their popularity enhanced by his risqué, slightly smutty songs.[74] His first film, in 1915, was a horse-racing drama, *By the Shortest of Heads*. In *Come on George* (1939), filmed at the peak of his popularity, he goes on the run after being falsely accused of theft, and shares a horsebox with a hitherto unmanageable racehorse whom he calms. So he is hired as stableboy/jockey to look after the horse and ride him in the big race. Unfortunately he loses his nerve, but is cured by a psychoanalyst and rides the horse to victory, outwitting a stock gang of crooks in the process.

Films were part of a culture of hope and consolation, often portraying cheerfully optimistic characters who craved good luck. Unsurprisingly, many such escapist films featured betting on horses. A successful bet meant happier times and circumstances. It built confidence, provided fortune and wealth. For the audience it anticipated an improvement in their economic circumstances. In most racing films closure was achieved when the horse finally won the big race, fortunes were recouped, the hero's merits were recognised and he got the girl, or the girl got the boy. In *Two on a Doorstep* (1936) a girl has a similar phone number to a bookmaker and begins to take some of the bets, setting up her own betting agency. She takes a big bet on a favourite and finds she owes more than she can pay, but recoups her fortunes by winning at a greyhound stadium. In *Thoroughbred* (1931) a racehorse trainer is suffering from amnesia, his success is disappearing, and as a result his girlfriend is going to have to marry the disagreeable son of her guardian. A racing accident restores the trainer's memory and he is revealed to be a man of considerable means.

An alternative way in which racing films helped deal with people's economic difficulties, impoverishment or decline in status was through plots which implied that wealth bred unhappiness. Purchasers of sweepstakes dreamt of winning and an upward shift in status. Given the long odds, they were almost certain to lose. Films helped them accept that, by suggesting that sudden riches could bring mixed blessings or cause social and cultural embarrassment. In *Spring Handicap* (1937), for example, a miner inherits a legacy and enters the racing world, and is equally unsuccessful at betting, bookmaking, tipping and owning before his wife brings him to his senses. In *Sporting Love* (1936) a couple attempt to cure their financial difficulties by running a horse in the Derby. It ends in disaster and further debt before they finally escape. The underlying message of such films was that if you didn't win the bet or the race, or even find well-paid work, it didn't matter. Success, wealth, status and power had their problems; you were better off even with hardship, pain and poverty. Envy and frustration were a waste of time. Watching such films may have helped diminish radicalism and disruption and contributed to the Conservative dominance of the 1930s.

Attitudes to betting were usually positive. Several films gently mocked the anti-gambling group, or hinted that their attitude was hypocritical. In *Don't Rush Me* (1936) two apparent anti-gambling zealots get themselves deeply involved in greyhound racing. In *The Sport of Kings* (1931) two racing toffs wager that they can get the puritanical anti-betting crank Amos Purdue JP to make a bet within a week. Purdue is soon not only betting on a grand scale, but turns bookmaker to recoup his losses. The presentation of bookmakers varied. Sometimes they are fairly sympathetically presented, indicating that even censors accepted betting as part of the social fabric. In *Be Careful Mr Smith* (1935) the eponymous hero, a retired clergyman, buys a bookmaking business to escape his nagging wife. In the 1938 comedy musical *On Velvet* the Cockney bookmaker and a Jewish punter have enormous losses but recover their fortunes with a television company.

Much more negatively, in *Easy Money* (1934) the two bookmakers are the villains of the comic piece, shady blackmailers whose evil is foiled by their more honest clerk. In the eerie 1933 film *Eyes of Fate* the shifty bookmaker bullies his wife, finds tomorrow's newspaper and wins a fortune at the races, before eventually reading of his own forthcoming death. In *Trouble Brewing* (1939) George Formby wins a bet but is paid with counterfeit money by the bookmaking gang.

News features in the racing press were sometimes recycled in fictional form. The doping or otherwise nobbling of horses, and the difficulty of identifying who was to blame, was one good example. In one of the first racing news films, *P.C. Josser* (1930), a policeman kicked out of the force redeems his reputation, aided by a trainer jailed for doping, by catching the real dopers. In *Don't be a Dummy* (1935), a racehorse owner and jockey are wrongly warned off for doping, but catch the crooks who framed them. In *Dandy Dick* (1935) a country vicar bets on a horse to raise money for his church spire, but has to clear himself of a doping charge before getting his winnings. The suggestion that horses might ever be pulled is challenged in *The Calendar* (1931), based on an Edgar Wallace stage-play, where an ex-convict butler helps a bankrupt horse owner prove he did not deliberately lose a race. Here, as in the case of positive images of bookmakers, racing films sometimes fail to follow conventional 'respectable' narratives about expected social roles, and can be highly subversive of predictable ideologies.

The increased wish of Americans to own the Grand National winner provides a useful vehicle for rounding off *Luck of the Irish* (1935), in which a financially struggling Irish gentry owner whose estates are mortgaged hopes to win the Grand National. Though his horse comes first, ridden by his amateur rider son, it is disqualified. His fortunes are saved only when a rich American buys his horse at a generous price.

What is also interesting is what films did not show about racing, although it should be noted how censorship practices also contributed to presentation. Film-makers were always careful, for example, never to suggest that street bookmaking often relied on complicity between bookmakers and the police. The British Board of Film Censors was quite clear that 'in this country we do not allow our police to be shown on the screen as … accepting bribes from criminals'.[75] Films generally reflected conservative approval of the status quo, social stability and cohesiveness. In racing films only occasional trainers could be crooked, book-makers dishonest or horses doped. This view that racing was generally 'all-square' but had its 'flotsam and jetsam' was the dominant image. The upper classes were sometimes lampooned and their pretensions exposed, yet were somehow usually 'straight' in their racing. Crooks in racing films were almost always working-class.

The quota system also created large numbers of one- or two-reeler British 'shorts'. One producer, N. R. Newman (established in 1929), specialised in horse-racing subjects. One example was his annual series called *Derby Secrets*, another his *Gordon Richards*. Although most 'shorts' were made by professional actors, photogenic Steve Donoghue's popularity enabled him to star in six short two-reel movies made at Islington Studios between 1925 and the 1930s. These linked romance and the turf to attract a female audience, coupled with stock criminal ingredients for the males, in a style reminiscent of Nat Gould or Edgar Wallace. Another, the first of these, *Riding for a King* (1925), starred Steve as a jockey who was the secret admirer of a beautiful married girl to whom he had given riding lessons. He had accepted the ride for the Lincoln Handicap on a horse owned by her jealous husband. The film's premiere, at the Tivoli theatre, drew a wide range of racing personalities, and Donoghue's acting was received with some praise. In 1937 he appeared in *Wings of the Morning*, which told the story of a Romany queen who owned a brown racehorse, secretly trained in Ireland, which won the Derby at 100–1.

Stage drama also drew on racing, featuring stock bookmakers as often as racing itself. Farces or comedies dominated. In the farce *Sporting Love* two owners of a bankrupt racing stable tried to kidnap their mortgaged prize horse. The classic *Me and My Girl* was probably the most successful theatre comedy of the period, starring veteran stage comic Lupino Lane as bookie Bill Snibson.[76] It built on an earlier Lane stage success, a racing comedy called *Twenty to One*, in which the bookie joined the Anti-Gambling League, whose attitudes here again were largely ridiculed. *In Me and My Girl* the bookie is portrayed very positively. Lane inherits a title, and faces snobbery and numerous other class difficulties, before humanising the values and attitudes of his stereotypically portrayed aristocratic relatives more closely to those of working folk. Lane played the role over five thousand times, while it was broadcast on BBC radio in January 1938 and on BBC television at a special performance in front of King George VI and Queen Elizabeth. In *The Naughty Age*, later filmed as *Strictly Illegal* (1934), a street bookie wrongly thinks he has killed a policeman. On the run, he poses as a clergyman, is invited to be a country house guest and prevents a jewel theft. What both these latter plays showed, within an overall context of acceptance of the status quo, was the interdependence of classes, and people's ability to take on role impersonations.

Racing's widespread popularity meant that many fictional books with cultural representations of racing reached the reading public. A large section of the population revelled in romances with racing backgrounds. The public perception that racing was dishonest, coupled with the attractions of the crime novel, a popular interwar genre, provided novelists as diverse as Edgar Wallace, who knew his racing, and Enid Blyton, who did not know hers, with racing themes. Titles like *Easy Money: The Amazing Adventures of Tom Denton, the Raffles of the Turf*, or *The Turf Crook*, convey the sense of this literature. There were even specialist racing imprints. By mixing crime, romance and the turf, the Hornsea Journal Printing Works had published 262 'Racing Novels' by 1938, from small beginnings in around 1927. The Aldine Press began publishing its 'Aldine Racing Novels' in the early 1920s. Many such novels were potboilers, written by people with limited knowledge of racing. Graham Greene's 1938 novel, *Brighton Rock*, with its focus on the violent criminality of racecourse gangs, relied for its background on contemporary newspaper reports. Some authors specialised in racing fiction. Fairfax-Blakeborough occasionally attempted this, presenting 'real live people' and having 'far more intimate and accurate knowledge of racing and its governance' than the leading figure, Nat Gould.[77]

Gould was a Manchester man who had raced in Australia before returning to England and writing novels and plays with racing themes.[78] His books sold at prices ranging from 6s to the more popular 6d. He was hugely popular in Britain and the Empire, and his pre-First World War total book sales, well over eight million, had outstripped all other living writers. His books continued to be popular after his death in 1919, with reissues of his novels right through the period, sometimes in syndicated episodic form in the regional press. In 1920, for example, *The Man from Newmarket*, about 'life behind the scenes on the Turf', was serialised.[79] His stories appealed to both women and men, and adopted a highly successful albeit relatively formulaic approach. The heroes of his books are often fairly wealthy, honourable, 'manly', self-made sportsmen, who own racehorses which are inevitably finally successful in a major race after some form of adverse experience. The hero often falls in love with and finally marries a society beauty, after solving some mystery committed by a stock villain often described in racist and class-biased ways. The settings are dominated by country estates, Ascot, Newmarket and Australia.

In *The Roarer*, for example, the hero, wealthy millionaire Wilton West, inherits his Sherwood estates after the unsolved murder of his father, a marked knife having been found nearby. He takes two of his horses to Australia with the intention of running them in the Melbourne Cup, and is accompanied by friends, including the mildly scandalous but attractive widow Lady Florence Evershed, who provides the sexual and romantic subplot. One of his horses, Viking, turns roarer, and is thought to have little chance of winning. The murderer of West's father is revealed as an Australian bookmaker, Baptiste Leon, the stock description of whom fulfils almost all the British racial, physiological and social prejudices of the early twentieth century. He is a 'bad lot', whose family were 'Spaniards of the lower class', with 'dark snake-like eyes' and dark, swarthy complexions. He owns the murder knife. Leon takes West's bets and is broken when Viking wins the Melbourne Cup. He attempts to default and escape, but is killed in a knife fight with a former accomplice Corti, who has learned the error of his ways. West returns to England, marries Lady Florence and wins the Ascot Gold Cup with Viking.

Book sales remained buoyant during the interwar years. At the upper end of the cultural continuum the sales of racing paintings also continued to find a market, although with more emphasis on steeplechasing than before the First World War, reflecting its increasing respectability and popularity amongst many of the *nouveaux riches*. Eric Fraser's *Derby Day* (1926) or Cermansky's *Frith's Derby Day Modernised* (1931) showed the continued popularity of racing realism in painting, and followed the earlier traditions of representing race-meetings found in nineteenth-century magazines like the *Illustrated London News*, while Sir John Lavery's *The Jockeys' Dressing Room at Ascot* (1923) shows a more 'modern', intimate, inside view of the sport. By contrast demand for racing prints diminished, perhaps with the decline in wealth of the land-owning group that had been major patrons of the genre.[80]

Conclusion

Despite the complex variety of regional and local experience, racing had become increasingly respectable by 1939, with its best-known races well integrated into cultural life and accorded high status. The BBC had 'brought the racecourse into every home'.[81] The varied representations of racing demonstrate that racing provided high levels of indirect employment opportunities. The number of those employed in the mass media to produce such material, at all levels from journalists and editors, directors and tea boys, to cameramen and commentators, must have been considerable.

More importantly this chapter provides an alternative insight into the fundamental character of British society between the wars by revealing that racing and betting images had become all-pervasive throughout Britain, part of a cohesive common culture, a shared frame of reference characterised by social inclusiveness and accessibility. Racing's representation in the national and sporting press, the BBC, the cinema, fiction and non-fiction, and other forms of mass media, together provided a cumulative cultural validation of the sport in British society.

The commonality of racing culture portrayed in the mass media helped both to define the collective identity of the British and to shift their interests more towards frank enjoyment of leisure. The period saw a substantive move towards the affluent consumption of sporting experience and betting, a view which the BBC was slow to embrace. This shared interest united individuals of otherwise widely divergent tastes in an increasingly diverse and complex culture. To individuals from all social classes and regions, the culture of the period was more likely to be reflected in films like *Come on George*, the racing tips and results in the press, or the wireless commentary on the National, than it was in the poems of W. H. Auden or the novels of Virginia Woolf.

At the same time however the picture of racing these cultural artefacts presented was ambiguous. Some images of racing were positive: honest owners or bookmakers, lucky punters, successful trainers and owners, exciting races. Others painted a more negative picture: of criminality, dishonesty or addiction to betting. It was the latter upon which the anti-gamblers fixed. The following chapter explores their beliefs, work and anti-gambling activities.

Notes

1   For an analysis of the importance of the notion of 'cultural citizenship' in linking the public and the private, consumers and producers, subjectivity and objectivity, pleasure and politics, see J. Hermes, 'Gender and media studies: no woman, no cry', in John Corner, Philip Schlesinger and Roger Silverstone (eds), *International handbook of media research* (London: Routledge, 1997), p. 88.

2   See David Morley, *Television, audiences and cultural studies* (London: Routledge, 1992).

3 J. B. Booth, *Sporting Times: the Pink Un world* (London: Werner Laurie, 1938), p. 238.

4 For the broader theoretical background to this field see David Rowe, *Sport, culture and the media* (Buckingham: Open University Press, 1999).

5 A useful source is Arthur J. Sarl, *Horses, jockeys and crooks: reminiscences of thirty years' racing* (London: Hutchinson, 1935), ch. 32, 'Gentlemen of the press'. See also Norman Pegg, *Focus on racing* (London: Robert Hale, 1963), and Eric Rickman, *On and off the racecourse* (London: Routledge, 1937).

6 *Sporting Life*, 23.2.1924.

7 Pegg, *Focus on racing*, p. 10.

8 Quintin Gilbey, *Fun was my living* (London: Hutchinson, 1970), p. 200.

9 Meyrick Good, *The lure of the turf* (London: Odhams Press, 1957), p. 207.

10 Foreword to George Hamlyn, *My sixty years in the ring: a racing and gambling autobiography* (Hungerford: Sporting Garland Press, 1994).

11 Eric Rickman, *Come racing with me* (London: Chatto and Windus, 1951), pp. 4, 9; Noel Fairfax-Blakeborough (ed.), *J. F.-B: the memoirs of Jack Fairfax-Blakeborough* (London: J. A. Allen, 1978), p. 71; Sarl, *Horses, jockeys and crooks*, p. 274, and ch. 32, *passim*.

12 M. Gilbert, *Winston S. Churchill, Vol. V, 1922–1939* (London: Heinemann, 1976), p. 731, quoted by David Dixon, *From prohibition to regulation: bookmaking, anti-gambling and the law* (Oxford: Clarendon Press, 1991), p. 285.

13 Peter O'Sullevan, *Calling the horses: a racing autobiography* (London: Hodder and Stoughton, 1994), p. 13.

14 Leonard Jayne, *Pony racing, including the story of Northolt Park* (London: Hutchinson, n.d.), p. 17.

15 Competition between the three leading racing papers, the *Sportsman*, the *Sporting Life*, and the *Sporting Chronicle,* to return 'official starting prices' was only resolved in the 1920s. See J. M. Scott, *Extel 100: The centenary history of the Exchange Telegraph Company* (London: Ernest Benn, 1972), p. 72.

16 1923 Select Committee on Betting Duty, Minutes of Evidence QQ6233–39 (Gulland).

17 Memorative biography, *Bloodstock breeders' review*, 1931, p. 116.

18 Gordon Richards's foreword to Quintin Gilbey, *Champions all: Steve to Lester* (London: Hutchinson, 1971).

19 D. L. LeMahieu, *A culture for democracy: mass communication and the cultivated mind in Britain between the wars* (Oxford: Clarendon Press, 1988), pp. 56–79.

20 The demand for racing material was such that a number of tipsters were also able to publish books. 'The Scout' (Cyril Luckman), *The Scout's guide to racing 1937* (London: Daily Express, 1937), for example, provided 512 pages of reference material for racing fans.

21 1923 Select Committee, QQ6380–6 (Gulland).

22 For more detailed discussion of the influence of tipsters on betting behaviour see James R. Hall, 'The racing media in Britain from Prince Charlie to Zafonic: some neglected perspectives', MA diss., University of Lancaster, 1993, ch. 3.

23 Michael Seth-Smith and Roger Mortimer, *Derby 200: the official story of the Blue Riband of the turf* (Enfield: Guiness Superlatives, 1979), p. 48.

24 *Yorkshire Evening Press*, 22–25.8.1932.

25 M. Seth-Smith *et al.*, *The history of steeplechasing* (London: Joseph, 1966), p. 126.

26 *The Times*, 3.6.1922; *ibid.*, 20.6.1919.

27 *Yorkshire Herald*, 28.8.1937; *Liverpool Echo*, 24.3.1938.

28 Although Fairfax-Blakeborough was a prolific writer between the 1930s and the 1960s, he often recycled the same stories. Good examples of his approach are Jack Fairfax-Blakeborough, *Paddock personalities: being thirty years of turf memories* (London: Hutchinson and Co., 1935), and Jack Fairfax-Blakeborough, *The analysis of the turf* (London: Philip Allan, 1927).

29 See Noel Fairfax-Blakeborough (ed.), *J. F.-B: the memoirs of Jack Fairfax-Blakeborough* (London: J. A. Allen, 1978).

30 See Richard Marsh, *A trainer to two kings* (London: Cassell, 1925); John Porter, *John Porter of Kingsclere* (London: Grant Richards, 1919); E. M. Humphris, *The life of Mathew Dawson* (London: Witherby, 1928); George Lambton, *Men and horses I have known* (London: Thornton Butterworth, 1924); Alfred E. T. Watson, *A great year: Lord Glanley's horses* (London: Longmans Green, 1921); R. C. Lyle, *Brown Jack* (London: Putnam, 1934).

31 For example, B. R. M. Darwin, *John Gully and his Times* (London: Cassell, 1935); E. M. Humphris, *The life of Fred Archer* (London: Hutchinson, 1923); E. M. Humphris, *The life of Matthew Dawson* (London: Witherby, 1930); T. H. Bird, *Admiral Rous and the English turf 1795–1877* (London: Putnam, 1939), or E. E. Dorling, *Epsom and the Dorlings* (London: Stanley Paul, 1939).

32 For example, D. H. Munroe, *The Grand National, 1839–1931* (London: Heinemann, 1931); T. H. Bird, *A hundred Grand Nationals* (London: Country Life, 1937); A. Macey, *The romance of the Derby stakes* (London: Hutchinson, 1930); J. S. Fletcher, *The history of the St. Leger stakes, 1776–1926* (London: Hutchinson, 1927).

33 For example C. M. Prior, *The history of the Racing Calendar and Stud Book from their inception in the eighteenth century* (London: Sporting Life, 1926); T. H. Browne, *History of the English turf 1904–1930* (London: Virtue, 1931).

34 *The Times*, 1.6.1922.

35 Sian Nicholas, 'All the news that's fit to broadcast: the popular press versus the BBC, 1922–45', in Peter Catterall *et al.* (eds), *Northcliffe's legacy: aspects of the British popular press 1896–1996* (Basingstoke: Macmillan, 2000), p. 127.

36 The following paragraphs are based largely on R. Glendenning, 'Race broadcasting', in Ernest Bland (ed.), *Flat racing since 1900* (London: Andrew Dakers, 1950), pp. 224–30.

37 For Allison see Dave Russell, *Football and the English* (Preston: Cicerone Press, 1997), pp. 106–7. Good, *The lure of the turf* gives details of Good's racing experiences. Another popular commentator was R. C. Lyle, the *Times* racing correspondent.

38 O'Sullevan, *Calling the horses*, p. 9. Good was paid 100 guineas for the commentary.

39 *The Times*, 30.5.1933.

40 Gilbey, *Fun was my living*, p. 160.

41 *The Times*, 26.3.1938.

42 Michael Seth-Smith, *Steve: the life and times of Steve Donoghue* (London: Faber and Faber, 1974), pp. 225–6.

43 *Bloodstock breeders' review,* (1931), p. 26.

44 *Daily Telegraph*, 3.6.1931.

45 *The Times*, 27.1.1938.

46 Jayne, *Pony racing*, p. 88.

47 *The Times*, 2.6.1938.

48 Rachael Low, *Films of comment and persuasion in the 1930s* (London: Allan and Unwin, 1979), pp. 53–6.

49 Edward Abelson and John Tyrrel, *The Breedon book of horseracing records* (Derby: Breedon Books, 1993), p. 245.

50 *Strand Magazine* (1896) quoted in Seth-Smith and Mortimer, *Derby 200,* p. 38.

51 *The Times*, 2.6.1921.

52 *The Times*, 29.3.1938.

53 Quoted in Low, *Films of comment,* p. 16.

54 *Liverpool Daily Post*, 30.3.1935.

55 *Liverpool Echo*, 21–24.3.1922.

56 *Yorkshire Herald*, 25.8.1938.

57 Seabiscuit supposedly got more column inches in 1938 in the USA than any other news figure. See Laura Hillenbrand, *Seabiscuit: three men and a racehorse* (London: Fourth Estate, 2002), p. xi.

58 *Liverpool Echo*, 22.3.1938.

59 1932/3 Royal Commission on Lotteries and Betting, para. 218.

60 Sporting Chronicle, *Racing up-to-date: a complete record of flat racing* (Manchester: Sporting Chronicle, 1938), p. 172.

61 S. Theodore Felstead, *Racing romance* (London: Werner Laurie, 1949), pp. 79–80.

62 *Hartlepool Daily Mail*, 30.7.1936.

63 Reviewed in the *Cleveland Standard*, 5.8.1939.

64 Stephen C. Shafer, *British popular films 1929–1939: the cinema of reassurance* (London: Routledge, 1997), pp. 1–2. See also Marcia Landy, *British genres: cinema and society 1930–1960* (Princeton, NJ: Princeton University Press, 1991) and Jeffrey Richards (ed.), *The unknown 1930s: an alternative history of the British cinema 1929–1939* (London: B. Tauris, 1998).

65 Ross McKibbin, *Classes and cultures: England 1918–1951* (Oxford: Oxford University Press, 1998), p. 456.

66 John Sedgwick, 'Cinema-going preferences in Britain in the 1930s', in Richards (ed.), *Unknown 1930s*.

67 Dennis Gifford, *The British film catalogue, 1875–1970: a guide to entertainment films* (Newton Abbott: David and Charles, 1973); John Walker, *Halliwell's film and video guide* (London: HarperCollins, 1998). The following sections on film draw partly on the summaries of films given here.

68 Several films, including *Lancashire Luck* (1937), were based round the potential problems a football pools win could cause. *The Last Coupon* (1932) and *Penny Paradise* (1938) both show how a family was adversely affected by an expected win before finding the coupon had not been posted.

69 Jeffrey Richards and D. Sheridan (eds), *Mass observation at the movies* (London: 1987), p. 34.

70 See for example Gary Cross (ed.), *Worktowners at Blackpool* (London: Routledge, 1990).

71 Shafer, *British popular films*, p. 23.

72 For the notion of 'active audiences' see John Fiske, *Television culture* (London: Methuen, 1987), and John Fiske, *Reading the popular* (London: Unwin Hyman, 1990).

73 *Film Weekly*, 3.4.1937; quoted in Shafer, *British popular films*, p. 44.

74 For his popularity see Jeffrey Richards, *Age of the dream palace: cinema and society in Britain 1930–1939* (London: Routledge, 1984), p. 160; McKibbin, *Classes and cultures*, p. 437.

75 Annual Report of the British Board of Film Censors, 1933, quoted in Shafer, *British popular films*.

76 It was later filmed as *The Lambeth Walk*.

77 Fairfax-Blakeborough issued his first six racing romances in 1933. See 'Some Good racing novels', *Bloodstock breeders' review*, 1933, pp. 160–1.

78 His first major work was Nat Gould, *On and off the turf in Australia* (London: Routledge, 1895).

79 *Cleveland Standard*, 21.8.1920.

80 Charles Lane, *British racing prints 1700–1940* (London: Sportsman's Press, 1990), p. 61.

81 C. R. Acton, *Silk and spur* (London: Richards, 1935), p. x.

3

Off-course betting, bookmaking and the British

In 1923 an assistant mistress of a London County Council boys' school reported that betting was fairly general in her class. While she and the head took this seriously, the boys treated it as nothing wrong, and her remonstrations as a joke. They were actually 'encouraged by their parents'. She felt helpless. She could not go to the police because 'in a poor neighbourhood it is a very dangerous thing to excite the animosity of the parents'.[1] The popularity of betting in that particular culture was clear. His Majesty's Inspectors of Schools felt in 1924 that such reports were exaggerated.[2] HMI were in no position to know. Pupils were unlikely to boast to an unknown, middle-class visiting school inspector of their involvement in illegal gambling.

Betting was probably exceeded only by cinema-going as the leading leisure spending activity during the interwar years.[3] The 1853 Betting Houses Act and 1906 Street Betting Act had both assumed that the perceived 'problem' of working-class cash betting could be substantially reduced by prohibition and police action. They were wrong. Enforcement was erratic, courts were unwilling to imprison offenders, and bookmakers evaded the law. By contrast both on-course cash betting and credit betting remained legal. So credit bookmakers in most towns catered for middle- and upper-class off-course horserace betting.

Despite betting's popularity we still know less than we should about its social and cultural meanings. The two state-initiated reports on betting, those of the Select Committee on Betting Duty of 1923 and the Royal Commission on Lotteries and Betting of 1933, were concerned almost entirely with the supposedly adverse consequences of working-class betting, mediating the views of punters through the eyes and ears of anti-gamblers, police, bookmakers, the Jockey Club, or similar interest groups. A pathological view of betting, and the ethical, moral, social and economic arguments surrounding its consequences, dominated. The real meanings of betting for ordinary people were neglected.

Recent academic research has also largely focused on working-class, 'popular' betting, reflecting contemporary state and press concerns, and interest in the economic difficulties of the interwar years.[4] This has been deleterious to more nuanced analysis. The neglect of upper- and middle-class betting has unbalanced research findings. Credit betting was different from working-class cash betting. British betting cultures were highly complex in other ways too. Firstly there were clear national and regional variations in betting's nature and volume. Second, as Stevenson has pointed out, attitudes within different social strata, personality and temperament also played a part.[5] We should further add age, gender, the nature of work or non-work, religion and ethnicity. The roles of police, publicans, punters and bookmakers were also different. The following sections begin to draw out British betting culture in more detail.

Betting's interwar growth and regional variation

Between the wars the cultural significance of betting was almost certainly at its twentieth-century peak. In Liverpool in the 1930s, the Pilgrim Trust found that the 'all pervading atmosphere of football pools, greyhounds and horses … has become such an important environmental factor that … it is an effort to develop interests unconnected with them'.[6] The period 1919 to 1939 was important in terms of gambling growth.[7] Alongside the rise in real wages the estimated amount spent on all forms of legal gambling rose from £63 million in 1920 to £221 million in 1938, ahead of other expenditure. Although these figures included football pools, gaming and greyhound racing as well as horseracing, the latter was the major betting medium. Figures on overall gambling expenditure as a proportion of total consumer expenditure rose consistently from 1.3 per cent in 1920 to 2.5 per cent in 1925, and rose again from 3.7 per cent in 1930 to 4.1 per cent in 1935. By 1938 gambling expenditure had reached an estimated 5 per cent of a much higher total consumer expenditure.[8]

Much of this was gambling on the horses, although greyhound racing expanded rapidly from the late 1920s, and pools expenditure rose from £10 million in 1934 to over £40 million by 1938. The actual amount spent by punters on racing each year aroused keen contemporary debate, marred by problems of evidence and definition. Those who wanted to demonstrate a high level of betting often used gross betting turnover, but bookies often hedged bets with other bookmakers to reduce potential liability. Betting money was always circulating from losers to winners. Someone betting at the races might start with £1, win £2 on two winning bets, and lose £2 on four others, and end up with the original pound, despite the £4 turnover. After considering widely differing views the 1923 Committee suggested an annual turnover of £200 million, and the estimate of the Racecourse Betting Control Board for 1929–30 was £230 million. The actual amount actually finally transferred by the end of each year to and from punters and bookmakers must have been much less. Bookies could always lose, and small bookies, who lacked economies of scale, went broke each year.

Such figures exclude the illegal and unrecorded street betting and sweepstakes, which probably substantially increased consumer expenditure figures, and the betting industry was certainly amongst the largest industries of the period. Even Seebohm Rowntree, no friend of betting, admitted that in York at least half the men bet, many of them each day during the flat-racing season.[9] A cautious judgement by a leading economic historian of gambling is that off-course betting was 'probably increasing' at this time.[10] Almost all of the witnesses to the 1923 Parliamentary Committee accepted that after a First World War lull betting almost immediately rose above pre-war figures. In most areas, prosecutions also rose, although at different rates: in Liverpool, for example, from 113 prosecutions in 1912–13 to 570 in 1921–22, in the Metropolitan Police District from 205 cases in 1912 to 269 prosecutions in 1922. The controller of the Central Telegraph Office believed that 7 per cent of general public telegraphic traffic was connected with racing. This was 'considerably in excess of before the war'. The number of convictions for street betting in the Metropolitan Police area rose from 2,520 in 1920 to 3,274 in 1922. In 1919–20 a total of 1,074 (mainly credit) bookmakers and turf commission agents were assessed for Income Tax Schedule D on the basis of £425,265 in assessed profits. By 1922–23 numbers had risen to 1,918, paying £1,040,232 in assessed profits. As a result of considering such evidence the draft report concluded that betting had 'an appalling hold' on 'the large majority of the community'.[11]

What were the reasons for this? Some contemporaries argued that gambling had increased because of the higher wages enjoyed by war workers. It is possible, indeed likely, that men in military camps, barracks or hospitals during the war filled their time in betting, and brought the habit home on demobilisation. Some felt that with the father away, children had been brought up with less discipline, and their 'natural instinct for self-gratification' had not been checked.[12] It was suggested that an influx of demobilised soldiers and officers increased bookmaking numbers.[13] Others, like Liverpool's chief constable, believed that after the war, 'the world has not settled down to the old humdrum experience', and the war had created 'a craving for excitement' which had led to a widespread change of attitude about betting.[14] This had supposedly been exacerbated by the increased publicity given by the press to betting news.

Others linked this more generally to changes in urban social and working conditions. Drab living conditions and the increased mechanisation and specialisation of industrial work meant few opportunities to exercise skill, and betting enlivened a monotonous and unfulfilling working life.[15] Some observers suggested that those who were struggling financially turned to betting for the chance of an occasional coup. Paradoxically, it was also suggested that betting was increasing because those with more money and more free time had increased opportunities to bet. Some portrayed it as a sickness, an 'infectious' vice, with tempted 'victims' trying to recoup losses or repeat the initial success. They also blamed a post-war increase in leisure time, the absence of more 'rational' amusements, and a lack of moral tone and guidance.

The size of any increase is difficult to determine. Formerly understaffed police forces could simply have put more of their resources into controlling betting on their return to peacetime duties, raising prosecution figures. One surrogate indication of the longer-term expansion of betting over the interwar years is a comparison of the census figures for bookmakers for 1921 and 1931, although these will have omitted most illegal cash bookmakers, and part-time workers like agents who collected bets on their behalf ('bookies' runners', 'takers' or 'lifters') or lookouts ('police-watchers'). In 1921 the census recorded 2,824 male bookmakers and 73 females. Of these some 326 men were employers, 1,040 were employees and 1,458 worked on their own account. By 1931 there were 9,330 male and 425 female bookmakers. This was a very impressive three-fold increase.

It is also clear that there was significant variation between regions, and different regional trajectories of change. Both the 1923 Committee and the 1932 Commission believed that betting was more prevalent in industrial towns and semi-rural industrial districts like Staffordshire or Durham. The number of bookmakers in different regions in 1921 and 1931 in census figures (Table 3.1) partially confirms this view. Regional variation was fairly consistent between the two censuses except in the case of the Birmingham district, which experienced rapid growth.

This was unsurprising since Birmingham was relatively prosperous between the wars. South Wales, which had the highest percentage of unemployment, showed the least growth.[16] The North-east, with the highest unemployment rate of any English region, shows the second lowest percentage growth. So rates of growth were probably linked to regional prosperity. More detailed evidence

Table 3.1 Bookmakers in industrial areas of England and Wales, 1921–31

	1921 census	1931 census
Greater London	452	1053
Lancashire and parts of Cheshire and Derbyshire	211	414
Yorkshire West Riding and City of York	135	277
North-east	79	148
Birmingham and district	48	187
South Wales	69	77

Source: Census

from the registrar general presented to the 1923 Select Committee supports such variation, although it conflated bookmakers, clerks and 'agents'. In London alone in 1921 there were 739 male and 12 female bookmakers, clerks and agents. Middlesex had 135 males and 7 females, Surrey 120 male and 8 females; Essex 83 males and 1 female, and Kent 36 males and 1 female. By contrast the Yorkshire West Riding had 271 males and 4 females, the East Riding 50 males, the North Riding 34 males, and Lancashire 375 males and 7 females.[17]

In figures of bookmaker prosecutions Liverpool and Manchester were always at the top of betting prosecutions in the north of England, well ahead of Leeds, Newcastle and other large northern towns in proportion to their population, and other evidence appears to bear out the popularity of betting there.[18] There were 1,034 convictions in Manchester in 1932 for a population of three-quarters of a million; Salford had 414 convictions in 1934 with a population of c.220,000, and Liverpool had 322 convictions in 1932 for a population of c.750,000.[19] However, Salford had a vociferous anti-gambling lobby, and had regular purges supported by local magistrates and the Watch Committee. A year later in similar-sized Cardiff there were only 77 arrests, and in Leeds, which was twice the size, there were only 28.[20]

We know less about rural interest in racing. Northern England mining villages were generally accepted as hotbeds of betting. One anti-betting campaigner believed that in the north of England there was 'less gambling in purely rural agricultural districts', but larger facilities in the mining districts *of course* [my italics]'.[21] But experience varied. While the Scottish street bookmaker James Croll claimed that he had 'not seen any village that did not have a bookmaker', his compatriot James McLean felt that in the Highlands there were 'any amount of towns and villages where there is no bookmaker', and large parts where there was 'no betting at all'.[22] Even in 1932/3 it was felt that the purely agricultural districts were 'without facilities for ready money betting'.[23] Rural punters may have lacked bookmakers but village publicans took bets, and the telephone or post could also be used.[24] In rural areas like North Yorkshire or the North Downs, where horses were bred or trained, there was significant interest in their later successes.[25]

Betting in working-class communities

Some British working-class betting was certainly careful, considered and calculated. Judgements were based on a study of the sporting press, form and other factors, although not all punters should be romantically assumed to be potential Albert Einsteins.[26] Betting could become a pleasurable hobby affording local status and some success. Some cultural theorists have portrayed the working-class pleasures of cultural consumption as involving a rejection of the mental, embodied in 'cultural forms, activities, symbols, interaction and routinized attitude'.[27] By contrast for at least some men betting was more like the public world of work, with its production and rationality. Late-morning penny editions of sporting papers provided full racing programmes, a summary of other newspapers' tipster forecasts, latest course news, form of expected runners and other useful betting information. In working-class betting overt intellectualism, and the development of systems, even if not necessarily successful, were both socially permissible and actively encouraged. Betting provided an important topic of conversation, and betting theorists see it as a response to budgetary constraints, the irregularity of income through lay-offs, accidents at work or illness, and difficulties of saving.[28] Even a small amount of surplus income allowed an occasional bet. Betting with small stakes, on a weekly basis, might provide a windfall to spend on a gramophone, a wireless set, an item for the household or a holiday.[29] Many British believed that betting in moderation was 'a pardonable habit and one that can fairly be reckoned among his amusements'.[30] For some workers, perhaps a majority, betting was often on doubles and trebles which offered much greater odds against success, but which increased the amount won and provided a cheap physical, psychological and pleasurable excitement.

Most bet only what they could afford, although for those on the margin of poverty the effects of betting could be adverse. For a few it became addictive. Clapson provides cases where betting to excess created financial hardship, poor diet and 'lives made miserable by bad-tempered husbands or wives'; Walton notes 'genuinely widespread secondary poverty on Merseyside' as a result of gambling, while Chinn makes clear its potential ill-effects.[31] Even the unemployed would bet. McKibbin argues that it was a culturally-sanctioned leisure activity.[32] As one man told one of Rowntree's investigators in the 1930s, he would rather 'have six penn'orth of hope than six penn'orth of electricity'.[33] The 1923 Select Committee concluded, 'there is considerable evidence to show that men in receipt of unemployment insurance benefit are using it for the purpose of betting'; the Welsh unemployed bet, while unemployed in Sheffield simply made smaller bets.[34] In 1932/3 several witnesses took the view that people receiving public assistance money, the bare minimum necessary for subsistence, were betting.[35] For the unemployed, a bet provided pleasurable planning, prospects of happiness and potential community status. The Pilgrim Trust argued cogently that their betting was a rare non-discriminatory area giving them as good a chance as anyone.[36] Their plentiful time could be profitably used for discussion, analysis and decision. In Greenwich, a visiting American sociologist saw betting as a characteristic British interest of the unemployed. Until the first edition of the evening paper came out, some time before noon, they would discuss the chances of horses they might back, then they would return home for dinner. In the afternoon they would go back to keep track of each other's winners, go home to tea, and in the evening boast about or excuse their luck. By forgoing a regular shilling's worth of comfort, the occasional win allowed them a brief climb out of poverty: 'It's your only chance to get out of a 26/- rut. It doesn't happen very often, but think of it when it does'; 'It gets dull living on 30/- with two kids to support … one of those thirty bob might bring you in a tidy sum'.[37] Gambling provided a temporary alleviation of their lacklustre lot.

For women too, betting forged mutual solidarity and community links, and was woven inextricably into their social and cultural environment.[38] Although women bet less regularly and for smaller amounts than men, both interwar government enquiries accepted that women bet to a large and steadily increasing extent. Canon Green believed that betting was very common amongst northern women, both mill workers and 'women in business', some of them even reading the *Sporting Chronicle* for betting information.[39] In the mid-1920s in one poor district of Liverpool over 50 per cent of women supposedly had the 'betting habit'.[40] The profound gendering and implicit masculine bias of much cultural analysis has often located women's leisures and pleasures in a private, gossiping, emotive world.[41] An analyis of their betting challenges such a view. Oral evidence from the St Helens, Leigh and Wigan areas indicated that women there regularly gambled. Gambling was not seen in the local community as a social and moral threat like drinking or sexual misbehaviour.[42] Women sometimes organised illegal betting shops in each other's households, which if well organised provided extra income. Here they could enjoy solidarity and excitement without fear of male reproaches. In one York factory, a female worker who took bets from the girls did 'a big business'.[43] More generally there was a 'considerable increase' in betting amongst women, especially in the mining villages, and in depressed regions like South Wales or the North-east, where, paradoxically, chapel was also a big influence.[44] Female domestic servants bet in large numbers, and in poorer working-class residential areas bookmakers even sometimes canvassed women's homes.

Many children too were acquainted with following form and placing bets, learning such cultural competences in the familiar settings of the home and street, which continued to be an active public space for recreation.[45] Children acted as messengers, bringing slips for parents or older siblings.[46] Glasgow concerns led to the passage in 1928 of an act prohibiting the use of Scottish youngsters taking betting messages.[47] Children also bet on their own account. The London schoolmistress above found that her pupils, mostly between 11 and 15 years, commonly bet on big races. Four bet more regularly, and one every day. They were aided by shopkeepers, one of whom took penny bets.[48] A. P. Herbert alleged that this made them 'grow up masters of subterfuge and devoted gamblers'.[49] Some bookmakers clearly employed children as 'runners' and other such spies, although the term 'children' was ill-defined, and probably meant different ages to different observers. Betting was common amongst older working teenagers, whose lack of responsibilities and spare money provided a betting invitation.

How much did people bet and how many were betting? Evidence to the 1932–3 Royal Commission suggested that most betting was small in scale and regular, with stake money varying from $1d$ or $2d$ up to $2s$ $6d$ for wealthier working-class punters. Outsiders, brought up on anti-gambling propaganda, found such low figures surprising. When the chief constable of Manchester tried to explain to the Commission that in his view an average of between $6d$ and $2s$ a week was bet, the chairman told him, 'it seems an extremely low figure and totally against anything I have ever heard of'.[50] Joseph Marshall, secretary of the National Sporting League, estimated that about three and three-quarter to four million people engaged in betting in 1923, and the average working man did not lose more than a shilling a week.[51] The latter may be special pleading, but the former is almost certainly an under-estimate. The anti-betting campaigner Perkins estimated in 1927 that about 80 per cent of the working class bet more or less regularly, and McKibbin and Chinn agree on a figure around eight million for this period.[52]

The working classes did not bet with each other. They placed their bets with bookmakers who illegally took cash starting-price bets. Various myths and cultural stereotypes grew up around bookmakers. Reformers demonised them as enemies of the poor, and created and constantly rehearsed dominant negative images. They were caricatured, criminalised and feared as exploitative parasites or social pariahs feeding on the weaknesses and gullibility of working-class communities. Interwar literature provided a famous fictional example in the person of back-yard bookie Sam Grundy in Walter Greenwood's *Love on the Dole*. The 1923 draft report saw them as a type of infestation, concluding that 'it is intolerable that the streets should be infested with bookmakers and their agents'.[53] They could also be presented as 'leeches' or 'vampires'. In the *Club and Institute Union Handbook* club committees were urged to refuse them admission, so that clubs did 'not become the happy hunting ground of the blood-sucking fraternity who prey upon foolish members in search of phantom fortunes'.[54] They were portrayed negatively in appearance and personality: corpulent, ring-bedecked, cigar-smoking, loud-voiced and check-suited, balding and flamboyant characters, who were variously callous and uncaring, seedy and unsavoury, miserly and miserable, villainous and violent, and despicable and rascally.[55]

Recent historical revisionism has challenged such myths, and portrayed bookmakers as small businessmen, popular local figures, far more benefactors than exploiters, giving to charities, and enjoying communal support, central to the informal leisure culture and economic life of working-class communities.[56] Appearances often belied the stereotype. One Welsh bookie of the 1920s was described as 'lean and tall', with 'long narrow face, small alert eyes', 'long thin legs' and 'soft and engaging voice'.[57] Bookies sometimes helped people in financial trouble, and most were reliable, honest and generally well-respected, providing what many perceived as an essential community service. They depended on the collaboration of the local community for shelter from the police. The community depended on them to pay up on winning bets, and cheating was commercial suicide. The 1923 Select Committee findings lent some support, arguing that 'the nature of the business requires that it must be carried out with scrupulous honesty'.[58] Several police witnesses claimed that they had 'never heard a complaint of dishonesty', and that bookies were 'exceedingly honest', or at the least 'fairly honourable' to clients.[59] Wealthier bookmakers were leading community figures, fulfilling a wide variety of social engagements and expected to buy drinks in the pub. In 1932 the chief constable of Manchester accepted that bookmakers 'were rather good to some of the poorer about them', and cited examples of them paying rents or doctors' bills, or giving banners to churches.[60] Some such comments were in danger of creating a new romanticised myth, of the bookmaker's total innocence.

To punters the local bookmaker was also the opposition, someone to be defeated. If bookmakers were generally honest, it was more than could be said of some punters, and the press reported a variety of punter scams to defraud the bookie.[61] Bookmakers occupied an ambiguous position in British society, simultaneously looked down on and looked up to, a tension indicated by the 1951 census which located them simultaneously as middling Social Class III, Socio-economic Group Ten (skilled manual workers), and Wage-earner Group B (equating with professional staff).

Actual numbers of 'street' bookmakers are unclear. Estimates from 1923 Select Committee and 1932/3 Royal Commission witnesses, the sporting press and elsewhere varied widely. The 1923 Select Committee was offered estimates of bookmakers ranging from 1,500 to 25,000, including credit and street bookmakers, onlookers and 'runners', yet 14,625 bookmakers actually purchased a licence in 1926, when street bookmaking was still illegal, and street bookmakers had no need of a license. In 1932/3 the number of street bookmakers in London was conservatively estimated as over 750, and in Manchester between 150 and 180, excluding agents or runners.[62] Religious minorities often went into bookmaking in higher proportions than their numbers might suggest. In Salford many of the leading back-yard bookies were Catholics, and in Glasgow many were Irish Catholics, damned through both religion and ethnicity by anti-gambling Protestants. There were also large numbers of Jewish bookmakers, on the racecourse circuit, in the East End of London, in Birmingham and Edinburgh and probably elsewhere.

Most bookies operated on a relatively small-scale basis, some as family businesses, others with a few workers. Punters brought cash stakes wrapped in scraps of paper carrying details of the race, the horse, stake and *nom de plume* so that they could remain anonymous. Evidence from 1923 suggests that street bookies took an average of £20 a day in the summer months, varying with the pitch.[63] Almost all paid out on starting prices. To avoid paying out too much, many bookies imposed a limit on both the odds and the payouts offered. This ensured that most bets were small.

Bookmaking could be precarious. Some failed. Contemporary estimates of bookmakers' gross profit varied between 10 and 15 per cent, but street book-makers often had significant overheads.[64] Many had to pay for runners, col-lecting bets on a commission basis, generally ranging between 5 and 7.5 per cent although a new bookmaker might, with some risk, go as high as 10 per cent. Some runners were 'travellers', collecting bets door-to-door or on a round of shops, pubs and works. Milkmen or window-cleaners were suited to the former role. Other runners would have a small block of houses, or small area where everyone knew them. Most large manufacturing industries, shops, ship-yards and mines had runners, in fact the 1923 Select Committee quoted figures suggesting any business with over twenty men could support one. The 1932/3 Royal Commission concluded that in many cases employers turned a blind eye to betting on their premises, provided it did not directly affect the work of the factory.[65] Even ill-educated runners needed to be reliable, and not all were effi-cient, while some attempted to defraud the bookie. It was possible to take an accomplice's bet after the race and pretend it had been received earlier, and to stop this clock bags were sometimes used, which had to be closed before the race, with the time then recorded on a register. Many bookies also employed lookouts to keep watch for the police. When warned before a police raid, book-makers often paid people to be arrested on their behalf. They either had to pay fines or bribe police to leave them alone. In some communities like the East End they had to pay protection money. Then again most street bookmakers had days when they lost overall. As a result of such cumulative costs net profit margins were probably quite low, although one bookie's assessment of around 2.5 per cent gross was almost certainly special pleading.[66]

Bookmakers employing runners usually had some sort of base, an unofficial 'office', where winnings could be paid out as paying out was *not* illegal. A few 'house' bookies used their own homes; most rented a room elsewhere, a pow-erful incentive for poor families. Paying out was sometimes at well-recognised 'pitches', street areas which they saw as their own territory, although these were by now more commonly used by runners. As public phones became more widely available, trusted runners could clock-bag the bets, phone bookmakers directly to get the results and runners, and pay out after each race on the basis of carbonised copies. In Glasgow, this method, called 'shovel' betting, was com-monplace by the 1930s.

Most working-class communities, especially in poorer urban areas, had street bookmakers or runners. There were also occasional public betting grounds, like the Market Place in Chesterfield or the 'Wag Back' in Blackburn.

Establishing and defending one's 'pitch' was difficult. Pitches could be back lanes, as in Tyneside or Wearside, street corners as in much of London or Liverpool, or courts and passages, yards and alley-ways. New 'bookies' bought an existing territory, took over a vacant pitch or set up a new one on fresh territory. Territorial battles, where a bookmaker infringed someone else's pitch, or took custom from longer-established businesses, were rarely conducted amicably, although they were sometimes sorted by the police to maintain order. Green gave one instance where an existing bookmaker complained to the police, who started arresting the new man's runners, telling him, 'We don't mean to have you cutting in on Pete's ground'.[67] Chinn admits that most bookies were 'hard' men.[68] Defending territory, and dealing with difficult punters, they needed to be.

Differences in location depended both on local custom and police attitudes to enforcement of the betting laws. Many bookmakers used public houses, since if a bookmaker used premises without the knowledge and consent of the licensee or staff he could not be convicted. This forced police to observe for longer, making policing more costly and offences more difficult to prove. In 1923 a superintendent detective of police estimated that between 100 and 150 public houses were used for betting in the City of London alone.[69] The pub exploited the key relationship between betting and sociability, since big winners often stood a round of drinks. In Bolton betting and sport accounted for 29 per cent of all conversations observed by Mass Observation. Betting and booze, camaraderie and conversation interacted well. One leading Bolton pub bookie, who employed about 170 runners, went round the public houses where his agents were employed, buying drinks. As a prestigious local celebrity he was expected to contribute to annual picnics or bowling handicaps, while his agents facilitated money lending. As one local landlord admitted freely, 'a good bookie is a great asset to a pub'.[70] In the North-west of England, Yorkshire and Wales working men's clubs were another common locus of betting activity throughout the period, as were Conservative clubs and billiard halls.[71] In Oldham in 1923, some fourteen clubs were supposedly used by a majority of betters.[72] Pubs and clubs of many kinds were havens of resistance to anti-betting views, just as churches were havens of support.

Clubs were alert to betting custom in other ways too, and a credit totalisator, a machine pooling all bets, was being used in London by June 1923.[73] By the early 1930s commercial 'Tote clubs' were proliferating in towns and cities throughout Britain, often on a cash basis after a favourable House of Lords judgment making betting facilities available all day. About a quarter also sold alcohol, and up to 2,000 people thronged a single Baker Street Tote Club. Membership fees varied from 5s to a penny. By December 1932, there were approximately 250 clubs in England and Wales, and they were increasingly creating a moral panic. Reversing the judgment in the spring of 1933 allowed widespread prosecutions of clubs in London, Birmingham and Manchester. They were made explicitly illegal by the 1934 Betting and Lotteries Act.[74]

Illegal bookmakers were found everywhere, even at the heart of the London establishment. In 1921 a War Office clerk and an Admiralty electrician were prosecuted for running a book in the Household Cavalry Brigade canteen. They had 108 slips in their possession.[75] Small shopkeepers, such as barbers, tobacconists, confectioners, greengrocers, butchers or newspaper sellers, generated increased profitability by taking cash bets. This may well have drawn in more female bookmakers. At Middlesbrough, for example, the Normanby general dealer Annie Round was prosecuted for taking some sixteen bets in her shop between 12 noon and 2 p.m.; Rosie Pickering, a popular Birmingham bookie, owned a fish and chip shop.[76]

In those areas where street betting was common, the law's perceived inequality produced resentment. Although there were working-class people who objected to betting, bookmakers were usually sustained and supported. Police witnesses unanimously told the 1923 Select Committee that 'the sympathy and active assistance of the general public in the neighbourhood is with the bettor, whether bookmaker or backer, and against the police'.[77] This eroded police–public relations in working-class communities. The evidence to the 1928/9 Royal Commission on Police Powers and Procedures made very clear that the laws were 'out of harmony with public opinion'. The betting laws were regarded as 'class legislation', and enforcing them created 'a distinct worsening of relations between the police and the public'.[78] In fact, as Dixon points out, working-class community attitudes were hostile to the law more generally, and he argues that this period was one 'in which class-discriminatory prohibition was at its zenith'.[79] For working-class punters bookmakers were the opposition, but they were part of the local community and once the police were involved perceptions shifted.

Senior police attitudes were ambiguous. Most felt, with Trevor Bigham, the assistant commissioner of the Metropolitan Police Force, that the law was 'inadequate, obscure, illogical, and ineffective'.[80] It placed heavy demands on police time and budgets. In 1923, Liverpool alone employed twenty-eight full-time anti-betting officers, costing far more than the fines they raised.[81] Some policemen wanted more severe punishments, and condemned betting. Others felt that even prison sentences would have little effect. Superintendent Denton felt, with pardonable hyperbole, that 'it has such a hold on the people today. Even if they made it a penalty of two years it would have little effect'.[82] Officers complained that bookmakers organised lookouts and escape routes, and observed, corrupted and bribed policemen. They complained too of very varying attitudes by magistrates.[83] Police disenchantment with the prohibition strategy increased through the 1920s. It was exacerbated by the ill-fated attempt at the imposition of betting duty in 1926. By 1932 the police concluded that at best their actions merely restricted the volume of betting and acted as some deterrent.[84]

Even high levels of prosecutions had little impact. They were costly, and harmed consensual policing. Consequently, many forces tackled street betting irregularly, usually following press or written complaints or on a ritual annual level. Alternatively, betting was moved from place to place, a form of social zoning. In Blackburn, police prosecuted street betting but left club betting alone.[85] Elsewhere illegal betting shops or street betting in areas well off the main streets would be allowed. By 1932/3 the Committee of Chief Constables would have preferred to see legalised betting shops and licensed bookmakers to aid control.[86] Betting in shops, pubs or other premises was much more accepted by the police in Scotland, the North of England and Northern Ireland than in the Midlands and the South. Enforcement became a matter of practicalities. When, where and how the 'offence' was being committed and by whom determined whether it was to be overlooked, suppressed or harassed. The activity was often connived at by the police in order to maintain control, with informal arrangements widespread, and betting regulated by payoffs and ritualistic set-up arrests. The arrival or departure of a keen anti-betting superior officer, or eager officers seeking promotion, and varying levels of complaints, all affected prosecution levels. In York prosecutions dropped from 165 in 1936 to only 5 in 1937.[87] In racing Newmarket it was claimed that the police 'turned a blind eye as much as they could', and 'the magistrates were lenient'.[88]

Widespread allegations of corruption challenged the powerful myth of the police as having a special relationship with the public based on shared values and assent to British law. Some complaints were probably unfounded, others were attempts by bookmakers to get rid of over-zealous anti-betting officers. Some were true. Street betting offered a serious temptation to the police, not least because many policemen bet. Dixon suggests that 'until 1960 police–bookmaker relations of varying degrees of impropriety were normal practice'.[89] Both sides gained. The bookmaker avoided dislocation of business, or getting key staff arrested, by putting up well-paid stooges. The police either increased their untaxed income, or arranged arrests with full confidence of convictions, improving their prosecution record. Senior officers thus faced adverse press publicity from righteous anti-gamblers about police corruption, and had to claim that it was rare or infrequent. With public opinion divided, the police could never win. If they tried to enforce the laws they damaged police–public relations. If they did not they were accused of laxity, corruption or both.

Betting and the middle classes

Modern historians and the interwar establishment both presented the middle classes as having rarely bet on sport.[90] The Report of the 1932–33 Royal Commission stated that betting among the 'more well-to-do classes' had been decreasing, a decrease earlier claimed in evidence given to the Select Committees of 1902 and 1923.[91] Such perennial 'decreases', based on police and credit bookmaking evidence, helped to maintain the myth of middle-class respectability. The police knew little of middle-class betting because of its credit legality. Credit bookmakers only knew their own business. In the early 1930s, following the world-wide depression and drop in disposable income, credit bookmakers claimed a considerable decrease in custom, suggesting that in some cases turnover was 'only half of what it was a few years ago'.[92] Much of this, however, was probably a reduction in the size of individual bets rather than the number of people betting, although Ladbrokes found it somewhat more difficult to obtain new clients in the 1930s than they had in the 1920s.[93]

In reality there was a significant middle-class betting market. The 1923 Select Committee on Betting Duty concluded that 'practically every class bet'. The more detailed evidence supports this view. The chief constable of Liverpool claimed that betting was widespread 'amongst all classes in the community'. Even Canon Green believed that there had been an increase in betting 'among the middle-class people', citing one better-class office where each betting worker was 'either a public school man or a 'varsity man'. Street bookies were found in the West End as well as the East End, according to the assistant commissioner of the London Metropolitan Police District. Commercial travellers placed bets with 'boots' in hotels. Most of the clients of credit bookmakers were drawn from the upper and middle classes. Evidence suggested that 'the majority of people of standing, business people especially, prefer to open an account', and credit firms usually expected bank details or other forms of 'sporting' references.

Further direct evidence of middle-class betting surfaces in court cases, newspaper reports and oral testimony, even though the patterns of middle-class social communication concealed it more easily, with bets placed by phone or managed through the post. We learn of middle-class betting accidentally, as when a particularly big winning bet became known locally. An article fondly reviewing the life of the seaside theatrical entrepreneur Billy Scarrow, for example, listed some of his experiences and then said that 'better still will his good fortune in backing "King of Clubs" when it won the Lincoln at 100–1 be remembered'.[94] Such references are almost certainly a large under-estimation. The prospects of the Derby or Grand National were a major topic of conversation in social contexts such as gentlemen's clubs, the Stock Exchange or even the barber's shop. One 1937 cartoon illustrates this latter point well. A barber is being dismissed from what is clearly a high-class establishment, with another of the staff saying confidentially, 'The Guv'nor just HAD to sack the fellow. He hadn't a tip for the Derby'.[95] Clerks also found betting appealing, sometimes using runners or street bookmakers. Many of those using the betting pubs in the City of London were clerks.[96]

The clients of credit bookmakers also surface in oral testimony. One woman credit bookmaker, advertising herself as 'London's only lady bookmaker', had clients who were accountants and actresses, mayors and manufacturers, publicans, stockbrokers, tradespeople, shopkeepers, company directors and insurance agents, and her daughter claimed that 'even neighbouring bank managers, whose terms of employment were supposed to veto any form of gambling, would ring up on big race days'.[97] Sometimes, too, betting was an apparent contributory factor to newspaper-reported middle-class crimes such as fraud, where bank clerks or other middle-class employees used funds in attempts to recoup betting debts. Such cases undoubtedly contributed to betting being perceived as unrespectable amongst some middle-class groups.

Middle-class betting could be found both inside the racing world itself and amongst the wider betting public. For some betting began at grammar school or public school.[98] Inside racing many owners and trainers backed their own horses when they fancied they had a chance, while there were also a few plungers, betting £10,000 or £20,000 in a day on the course, although most racing commentators felt that the number of heavy gamblers was in rapid decline, and increasingly few bookmakers would lay the odds to such amounts.[99] Information about horses' progress provided by the press limited opportunities for betting coups. Bookmakers were also far more careful not to bet excessive odds, and larger bets immediately reduced them. Plungers inevitably failed, and the MP Horatio Bottomley may well have lost £1 million over his horses. Those middle-class gamblers who did get into debt were targeted by carefully-phrased advertisements for private loans: 'Sportsmen deal with sportsmen. How humiliating to be refused by a pal or your bank. We are here to obviate that. A chat, a smoke, a drink (if you like) and an open cheque'.[100]

Most 'professional backers' were middle-class either by origin or by previous occupation. The former racing correspondent Archie Falcon, who was friendly with betting owners such as Bob Sievier and trainers like the Newmarket trainer John Watson, was very successful in the early 1920s, and reputedly 'worth a quarter of a million' in 1923, although some major losses thereafter, failure of his stud, and a bad Stock Exchange run, reduced his capital to some £20,000 when he retired.[101] Another middle-class backer, Charles Beaty (d.1931) left £189,000. Geoff Harbord, the son of a clergyman, formerly in the Horse Guards, was also highly successful.[102] Middle-class social skills developed good contacts to supplement observation of form. Although the 1923 Select Committee felt the professional backer group had 'grown up in recent years' this was an ahistoric view. They had existed throughout the nineteenth century. Given the increased volume of racing information, the speed of communication and the well-organised bookmaking system, their task was actually becoming more difficult. Alfred Heathorn, a Piccadilly bookmaker, conceded that a professional backer could hold his own, if he had good knowledge and judgement of form.[103] To have any chance of success they needed large amounts of capital, since they were certain to have losses as well as wins. One professional backer at Ascot supposedly placed bets amounting to £60,000 during the day but only won or lost £100.[104]

Although the *proportion* of betters amongst the middle classes may have been lower than that amongst the working classes, the actual *numbers* involved in the wider middle-class betting public must still have been quite significant. Credit firm numbers provide a useful surrogate indication of middle-class involvement, especially since, as even Green conceded, there was 'very little credit bookmaking amongst the working class'.[105] Credit betting was available right across Britain's larger towns. In South Wales alone, for example, as early as 1921, the Turf Guardian Society listed credit bookmakers in Abertillery (1), Bargoed (2), Cardiff (15), Chepstow (1), Llanelly (1), Neath (2), Newport (7), Pontypridd (1) and Swansea (6).[106] In 1923 the assistant commissioner of the Metropolitan Police estimated that there were about 800 credit bookmakers in London. In Liverpool the chief constable estimated that there were over 250 legal offices, 'exceeding strict' in the way they carried out their business, and 'well-conducted'.

How many clients were there? Walter Randall, a wealthy credit bookmaker, and secretary of the Turf Guardian Society, formed in 1918, which had both layers' and backers' sections, estimated that there were about 2,000 credit book-makers in Britain. If this is correct, middle-class punter numbers can be esti-mated from figures offered to the 1923 Select Committee by the secretary of the National Sporting League. On his calculations, based on systematic enquiry, each credit bookmaker required an average of 250 clients to make a living, thus suggesting 500,000 clients. But some clients will have had accounts with more than one bookmaker. A proportion of clients would have been upper-class, and a few others artisans, who could sometimes get accounts if they could prove that they were given credit by coal merchants or shopkeepers.[107] Some credit offices also laundered a substantial amount of cash betting. Even so this suggests a sub-stantial upper- and middle-class betting public, rendered credit-worthy through wealth, income and status, who could bet by letter, phone or visit.

More positive middle-class attitudes to betting are also to be seen in the ways some magistrates dealt with betting prosecutions. Some bet themselves. The *Church Times* expressed the view that 'the magistrate who imposes a fine in his court for street betting, may ... as likely as not, have his own credit account run-ning with a firm of bookmakers'.[108] Many court proceedings were fairly ritual-istic, and betting offences were clearly not looked upon by most magistrates as real crimes. Many magistrates were very reluctant to give a conviction at all. Where bookmakers had been arrested three times, thus qualifying for a large fine or imprisonment, many magistrates avoided using imprisonment as pun-ishment or deterrent. The 1923 Select Committee was told that in Liverpool, men were 'never' imprisoned for a third offence; a Glasgow bookmaker felt imprisonment was 'very rare'.[109]

Off-course credit bookmaking firms were often large enterprises. McLeans, one of the largest starting-price bookmakers in Scotland, in 1923 had a staff of sixty, rented thirty telephone lines, and took an average of three hundred telegrams and £5,000 in bets a day.[110] The 'Douglas Stuart' firm employed over a hundred, with twenty answering the phones (in pairs to prevent fraud) and decoding telegrams, twenty checking telegrams and phone slips against results, ten opening letters, five people in accounts, and fifteen typists, as well as filing, printing and other workers. It sifted its clients carefully and had few bad debts.[111] Most big bookmakers advertised for clients through the racing press. David Cope Ltd, for example, regularly requested clients to 'send your name and address, in confidence, if you would be interested to receive particulars of our service. Every class of bet is catered for, at Ante-Post or Starting Price, or at Totalisator Odds if desired. All transactions are treated with the privacy that attaches to banking. Daily or Weekly Credit Accounts are opened'.[112]

Many credit firms were long-standing, in business from well before 1914. Like the street bookmakers, they were generally highly honest, though there were occasional examples of swindlers who set up a bogus betting office, took bets, then failed to pay.[113] The London region clearly dominated, with Lancashire the leading provincial region. Larger firms increasingly had several branches. Scotlands, for example, claimed by 1938 to be 'the largest bookmakers in the world', with '106 branches throughout the country'.[114] The wording of advertisements gave a clear insight into the factors appealing to customers. Such factors included reputation for honesty, fair dealing and integrity in meeting obligations and dealing with clients, the length of time established, their high status and tone, and whether or not they had limits on the amounts bet. Positive press comments were also quoted. Smaller firms could be started up with relatively small capital. A dispute between two bookmakers carrying on a phone credit business at a London flat showed they had each put in £200 and were making an average £20 weekly profit.[115]

Some office bookmakers, including Littlewoods with its football pools betting, acted as credit bookmakers and also sometimes illegally took money in advance by post for horseraces. This was more common in Scotland, where firms specialising in ready-money postal betting had long been established in Glasgow and Edinburgh. They took bets from throughout Great Britain. Up to 1925 a High Court judgment had not allowed sealed letters to be opened if a bookmaker's office was raided, but this then changed. In Edinburgh bookmakers' offices were raided annually by the police, and fines of £100 were levied. This was a symbolic act, since their activities were very well known. Any reader of the sporting papers would know what their advertisements really meant. Some firms invited 'letters'. Others had an 'industrial branch' in Scotland. Yet others gave an English address for credit, 'otherwise' a Scottish one. Some offered very limited credit, where clients paid a deposit and got credit of up to twice the amount sent in. As evidence to the 1932/3 Royal Commission indicated, the Post Office had to have special vans for deliveries of postal bets because of the volume of the Scottish bookmakers' business.[116]

Anti-betting groups firmly believed that bookmakers made excessive profits, but credit bookmakers often had bad debts. Small credit bookmakers with limited capital were most at risk. Frederick Stringer, for example, a successful street bookmaker through the 1920s, turned to credit bookmaking in 1934 but found himself bankrupt by 1935, 'a considerable number of bad debts being incurred'.[117] Ladbroke and Co., one of the largest firms, employing forty or fifty clerks on Fridays just to balance and send out accounts, estimated in the 1920s that about 12.5 per cent of credits were bad debts. They had a very large number of 1*s* and 2*s* bets, but other bets could be substantial.[118] In 1932/3 one witness saw bad debts as 15 per cent of the turnover.[119] So overall gross profits were not excessive. The 1923 Select Committee estimated that net profits on turnover, while varying with the type of business, were about 3 per cent overall. Munting sees this as an under-estimate, but one 'not too far off the mark', citing similar figures from later in the century.[120]

To improve profits bookmakers often tried to increase turnover by offering commission for bets passed on to them by smaller firms or individuals, although quoted rates vary widely, from 1.25 to 10 per cent, and bookmakers may not have been prepared to give away such confidential business information.[121] These small 'commission agents' sometimes started by taking bets from friends, local business men or acquaintances and passing them on, profiting from the commission. Some of these themselves then set up in business, installed telephones and opened accounts with a number of credit firms.

Top bookmakers could accumulate substantial wealth, though the number of such earners was few. Usually their high earnings reflected a smaller but often very wealthy clientele, an increased risk, and sufficient capital to lay and sometimes lose large amounts. When Joe Pickersgill, the Leeds bookmaker, died in 1920, his will was proved at £746,459, while George Herring (d.1915) left £1,371,000. Another London bookie, William Howett, died in 1924 worth £102,737.[122] Some bookmakers started as backers, or as street bookmakers, others as bookmakers' clerks. Harry Slowburn, initially a clerk, set up on his own in the early twentieth century and was friendly with all the leading owners and trainers. He left more than £100,000 on his death in the 1940s.[123] At the other end of the scale, while the odds were in favour of the bookie in the long term because of the way odds were calculated, in the short term a combination of several bad debts and a run of punter successes could mean bankruptcy.

Bookmakers were usually well organised, managing disputes, dealing with defaulters, or increasingly lobbying Parliament. The Rules Governing Betting were controlled by Tattersalls' Committee, which had dominated the settlement of betting disputes nationally since its incorporation of the Newmarket Rooms Committee in 1899. Bigger bookmakers increasingly had their own organisations, including the Bookmakers' Protection Association (BPA). First founded in 1921 in the South of England, largely in response to the course 'protection' and extortion gangs of the period, this became the National BPA in 1932, with its own publication, *Banyan*, circulated privately.[124] Other organisations with significant bookmaker membership included the Victoria Club, the National Sporting League and the Turf Guardian Society. The Victoria Club in London was the centre of the ante-post betting market, the first odds offered well before major races, with quick-fire transactions done by word of mouth across a billiard table, with horses backed to win £250,000 or more. It provided the first press-published odds. Here, and in other homo-social sporting clubs such as the Beaufort Club, such betting was seen as 'enormous'.[125] The National Sporting League was more political, arguing for the legalisation of betting and putting pressure on politicians to support the racing industry. The Turf Guardian Society was dominated by larger bookmakers, who wanted bookmakers to play the key role in looking after turf interests.[126]

Sweepstakes, luck and British culture

Working-class betting rationality was usually partial. To bet rationally a better really needed information about the likely starting price. Unfortunately even in 1931 only a minority of the daily regional and national press published forecasts of future odds. Major circulation evening papers like the *Evening Standard* or the *Manchester Evening News* did not carry them. Equally the jockey was important, but papers only rarely provided lists of probable riders. Only the specialist racing press provided the full details of previous form punters required. To that extent punters were betting blind. The various so-called systems, such as following a leading jockey, or backing favourites or second favourites, all lost money in the longer term if followed consistently, as the sporting press regularly demonstrated.[127] Some attempts to cash in on the vogue for systems, such as *The System-Workers' Gazette: Organ of the System Workers' Association: A Monthly Review Devoted to Systematic Turf Investment*, published in Bournemouth in 1922, lasted only a few months, but the *Racing Library* in Manchester specialised in reprints of famous betting systems and continued through the 1920s.

Some more impulsive betters made their selections according to luck and chance, although there is no means of identifying the proportion, and the rational and irrational merged together in the several books published between the wars with titles that suggesting astronomy/astrology could help pick a winner.[128] In one further betting form, the sweepstakes, reliance on chance was even clearer. While a successful long-odds winning double simply provided a temporary windfall and pleasure, winning a huge prize sweepstake, with far longer odds stacked against it, could be a life-changing experience, something both the working- and middle-class family could usually only dream about, a subject of radio, pub, film and family fantasy. Cultural analysis of pleasure has identified fantasy as a key driving source of motivation, ideologically enabling people to symbolically or potentially gratify specific needs not met in real life. Others have seen it as a form of resistance to economic and social pressures, entailing a playful and enjoyable way of transcending reality.[129] Both arguments applied to social life between the wars, and the grand fantasy of a large sum for a small one was a powerful motivator. Sweeps were an irrational form of betting. Tickets could cost 10*s* or £1, and winning was reliant on chance since only a very few purchasers drew runners, and the big prizes went to those who drew the winner and placed horses. But as the lucky city workman who drew the favourite in a Liverpool sweep explained, 'it was a bit of a push raising ten shillings, but I felt my luck would come off'.[130]

Sweeps were technically illegal, but, like the football pools, they were a hugely popular cultural form between the wars, thanks at least in part to economic uncertainty and the coverage the daily press gave to their large prizes. Even the unemployed could buy an annual sweepstake ticket. Sharing in the widely held social dream of having a large sum of money, changing one's life and perhaps moving up in status was highly attractive. The 1923 Select Committee referred to the 'extra-ordinary recent growth of sweepstakes' in its report, and while it provided no quantifiable evidence to support this view, the commonality of references to sweepstakes seems to confirm it.[131]

Racing sweeps operated right across the spectrum of class, and could be organised by high-status groups, trade unions, popular charities or publicans. Some sweeps were organised abroad. Just after the war the Calcutta Turf Club had the leading sweep with three prizes of £75,000, £35,000 and £15,000 for the top three Derby horses. The Dublin bookmaker Richard Duggan regularly ran a £25,000 Derby sweep in the early 1920s 'in aid of the Meath Hospital, Dublin', depositing the prize money with the editor of the *Sporting Life*, and the Sporting Club of Monte Carlo had a first prize of 222,592 fr. for its Grand National sweep.[132]

The involvement of the British financial world and clear evidence of middle-class approval can be seen in the high prizes offered by the supposedly private but widely available London Stock Exchange Members' Mutual Subscription Fund (£25,000 first prize) and the Baltic Exchange Sweep (£10,000). As the subscriptions for the Stock Exchange Sweep rose ever higher, reaching £1 million in 1929, there were increased anti-gambling complaints. In the 1920s Liverpool had a Liverpool Exchange Newsroom Sweepstakes open to the public, and a separate private one involving 'well over £2,000' for the Cotton Association and their friends.[133] By 1930 the Cotton Exchange Mutual Subscription Fund offered a first prize of £16,000 for the owner of the ticket with the winning horse for the Grand National; second and third got £2,500 and £1,000 respectively, all finishers got £200 and other horses starting £100. Over 70,000 10s tickets were sold. Organisers of sweeps covered the political and social spectrum. In 1924 such diverse organisations as the Actors' Association in Liverpool, Bootle Trades Council and Labour Party, Caversham Constitutional Club, Kingswynford Divisional Labour Party and Otley Conservative Club were prosecuted. The racing establishment organised sweeps at the H. B. Club, or the Derby dinners.[134] Works, public houses and even families often organised their own. The Otley Bowling Club in Yorkshire ran a large, very successful 10s Derby sweep despite regular police prosecutions in the 1920s, before winding up in 1932.

Prices and organisational involvement both show that sweeps were attractive to the middle classes. A *Daily Mirror* cartoon, entitled 'You can't keep out of sweepstakes', shows two men, clearly contextualised as middle-class by clothing and room furniture, such as office stool and bureau, discussing sweeps. One intent on selling yet another sweepstake ticket opens by asking the other if he is in many sweeps this year. The other complains that he has been in 'at least ten each year for thirty years and never drawn a horse'. The other extends his sympathy over the next three frames, telling him he is 'right to keep out of them', is 'very strong-minded', and that 'this sweepstakes business is abominably overdone', before getting to the sales pitch, telling him he 'mustn't miss this one – quite a small affair – you're bound to draw a horse'.[135] That *The Times* always printed the names of lucky drawers assumes reader interest. Buying a ticket was part of the ritual preceding leading racing events, although different race sweeps had a somewhat different regional distribution. St Leger sweeps, for example, were particularly popular in Yorkshire.[136]

Sweeps fulfilled a variety of social needs. Many who otherwise never bet took part. Sweep promoters generally acknowledged that as many women as men bought tickets. Purchasers came from all walks of life. Purchase was often a highly social joint activity, sharing the investment, the risk and the excited anticipation, and was deeply rooted in associational forms like the public house, the workplace or the family. The Derby Irish Hospital Sweepstake of 1933 had *inter alia* 'thirty engine fitters', 'the four doms', 'fourteen villains', 'ten good pals', 'four old pals', 'ten wise crackers', 'five hard-ups', 'the tennis workers club' and 'weneedit'.[137] A contemporary described how 'newsboys dash frantically though the streets, selling their papers giving alphabetical lists of owners. Their supply is immediately exhausted, as men, women and children leave their jobs, whatever they may be, buy papers and eagerly scan their lists'.[138]

The police had real difficulty in responding. Stopping sweeps alienated the public and caused paperwork. Law enforcement appeared anti-social, or even, considering the popularity of sweepstakes for Britain's big races among British expatriates and colonial administrators, anti-Empire. Generally forces only acted if a complaint was lodged, or questions were asked in the press or Parliament. Then the promoter would be told to abandon the scheme, thus avoiding police-work. Quite often however the promoter would continue. Magistrates' attitudes depended very much on circumstances and personal attitudes. Fines for organisers of charity sweeps were usually only between £5 and £15, and could be non-existent.[139] In Greenwich, police prosecuted the Printing and Kindred Trades Blind Aid Committee, run by men 'held in highest esteem', who had a sweep on the Manchester Handicap. It had raised £25,000 for blind institutions over five years, and the 1932 sweep raised £4,700 gross, with clerical expenses of £200. Prizes were of £380. The rest went to the charity. Here the magistrate said the lottery was illegal, but dismissed the summons on costs.[140]

Government concerns about money in Britain being invested in large foreign sweepstakes first resulted in police warnings in 1921, when the Post Office returned illegal remittances to their senders.[141] Parliamentary irritation strengthened in 1930 with the introduction of the Irish Hospitals' Trust (IHT) sweeps, again promoted by Richard Duggan, partly for the benefit of Dublin hospitals, but overtly supported by the Free State government.[142] These were successful in Ireland, but more successful still in England, even with 10s tickets. They were attractive to ticket sellers because the IHT promoters paid a sellers' commission of about £1 on every £6 of tickets sold, and gave sellers' prizes too. Money flooded out of Britain to benefit the recently created Irish Free State. At its peak it was a regular flutter for around five million people in Britain alone, with a further two million in the Irish Free State, the USA and Commonwealth, buying tickets in bookmakers' offices, pubs, clubs and shops. The 1930 draw was on the Manchester November Handicap, with a first prize of £100,000. Later the three draws each year focused on the Grand National, the Derby and Cesarewitch. In total, the first eight sweepstakes generated about £27,000,000 in subscriptions, with about £18,500,000 coming from Great Britain. Of those who drew a horse, about 60 per cent usually had English addresses.[143] The success of the IHT sweeps adversely affected British sweeps. The April 1931 Stock

Exchange prizes dropped to £15,000, £6,500 and £1,400 and 100 runners-up prizes of £150. It had become a quasi-private sweep once again, supported by Stock Exchange employees and their friends.

The British government saw the sweeps as a fiscal drain, benefiting the Irish Republic.[144] They attempted to prevent the entry of advertisements and tickets and the sending of money, and prosecuted English agents, strategies which they were already applying to other foreign lotteries, but agents received only nominal penalties in the courts. In 1933 the prime minister reacted to news of a slight fall in receipts by saying, 'I am glad of that. I hope that the next one will produce nothing at all'.[145] The measures the government could take also alienated public opinion. A Strube cartoon pointed out that a man could bet at greyhound races, phone a credit bookie, back horses on the Tote, invest on the Stock Market, or play for money in his home, 'BUT when he buys a sweepstake ticket for the good of the hospitals, THEN THE LAW STEPS IN - Which is absurd'.[146] What seemed equally absurd was that an attempt, supported by the Duke of Atholl, to launch a British equivalent in aid of British hospitals, with nine million tickets, and large prizes, was quickly stopped.[147] As we saw earlier, a large part of the 1932/3 Royal Commission was devoted to gathering evidence on the operation of the lotteries, especially the IHT sweeps, and the 1934 Lotteries and Gaming Act made greater legal provision for charity and sporting club sweeps, while prohibiting the advertising of foreign lotteries, the sending of tickets through the post, and buying such tickets. IHT sales dropped thereafter.

Conclusion

Gambling is a powerful theme in social and cultural history. Racing and betting went together in terms of their wider cultural significance, and this chapter has focused on the extraordinary popularity and resilience of betting not just in working-class culture, but also, albeit in different forms, across the other classes. The extent of credit betting challenges the view that middle-class betting was negligible, while the sweeps were a further form of middle-class participation in the betting world. One hitherto singularly under-explored theme in broader historiography is the extent to which the middle classes found cultural contexts in which to be naughty was nice, and in which the excitements, anticipations and pleasures of activities like betting could be safely enjoyed.

Within the working classes, the government prohibition of cash betting, and police efforts to curtail its spread, were defied, skirted round or ignored by the betting population, who could be found across the boundaries of age and sex. Its powerful prevalence in the face of a pervasive climate of disapproval and repression in the churches and other respectable contexts showed betting's strong resilience. Even the unemployed bet. This chapter has shown how for the vast majority of punters, gambling was simply a pleasurable recreation characterised by self-regulation, a reasonably rational approach and a measure of self-assertion. Many bet regularly, but modestly, and a very limited proportion of the personal or family income was involved. Such general moderation undermined all attempts to marginalise gambling. This chapter has also stressed the important extent to which betting was a social activity, enjoyed communally, and found in both work and leisure contexts, with bets placed in private houses and shops, the pub and Tote clubs.

It has also shown the extent to which bookmaking was a formal and highly commercial activity. Numbers involved were unquantifiable, although an estimate in the *Economist* in 1936 of 66,000 people directly dependent on bookmaking, plus many other part-time agents, is regarded by Chinn as 'plausible'.[148] Different perceptions of the role of street bookmaker in working-class society have been explored here in order to illustrate the complex roles they played. Previous work has tended to underplay the importance of credit bookmakers in sustaining middle- and upper-class betting. McKibbin, for example, ignores it, while over-stressing more rational approaches to betting. This chapter has balanced such views with a renewed emphasis on the importance of chance *as well as* rationality, most encapsulated in the fantasy of the life-changing win on the big sweepstakes. Between the wars, at a time of economic uncertainty and widespread distress, the sweeps played an important part in maintaining a mood of optimism and hope. A big win offered the prospect of escape from all difficulties, a prospect which the more rational, small-scale betting and the temporary alleviation of a small win could never achieve.

Notes

1 1923 House of Commons Select Committee on Betting Duty, minutes of evidence QQ8722–59.

2 Roger Munting, *An economic and social history of gambling in Britain and the USA* (Manchester: Manchester University Press: 1996), p. 198.

3 *Ibid.*, p. 171; David Dixon, *From prohibition to regulation: bookmaking, anti-gambling and the law* (Oxford: Clarendon Press, 1991), pp. 187–8.

4 Mark Clapson, *A bit of a flutter: popular gambling and English society c.1823–1961* (Manchester: Manchester University Press, 1992); Munting, *History of gambling*,

George Harris, 'Street betting in the twentieth century: its social significance in the working-class Community', Unpub. MA diss., University of Lancaster, 1978.

5 John Stevenson, *British society 1914–45* (Harmondsworth: Penguin, 1984), p. 386.

6 The Pilgrim Trust, *Men without work* (Cambridge: Cambridge University Press, 1938), pp. 98–100.

7 Munting, *History of gambling*, pp. 172–3.

8 R. Stone and D. Roe, *Measurement of consumer expenditure and behaviour in the UK 1920–1938* (Cambridge: Cambridge University Press, 1954), pp. 91–2.

9 B. Seebohm Rowntree, *Poverty and progress: a second social survey of York* (London: Longman Green and Co.; 1941), p. 403.

10 Munting, *History of gambling*, p. 94.

11 1923 Select Committee, QQ7401–11, 7417 (J. Lee); Appendix IIIA Metropolitan Police Convictions; p. 593, Evidence of Inland Revenue; QQ813–19 (Caldwell); Q1335 (Bigham); Q7152 (Green). Draft report para. 26.

12 1923 Select Committee, Q7354 (Lyttleton).

13 Carl Chinn, *Better betting with a decent feller: bookmaking, betting and the British working class, 1750–1990* (Hemel Hempstead: Harvester, 1991), p. 165; 1923 Select Committee, Q4118 (Randall).

14 1923 Select Committee, QQ1153–4. Dixon, *From prohibition to regulation*, p. 187.

15 1923 Select Committee, Q7357 (Lyttleton); Report p. 41. 1932/3 Royal Commission on Lotteries and Betting, report para. 204.

16 See Stevenson, *British society 1914–45*, p. 272.

17 1923 Select Committee, Q2377 (Hamilton).

18 For the extent of betting in Liverpool despite the economic difficulties of the period see Liverpool Council of Voluntary Aid, *Report on betting in Liverpool* (Liverpool: LCVA, 1926).

19 Mark Clapson, 'Playing the system: the world of organised street betting in Manchester, Salford and Bolton c.1880-1939', in Andrew Davies and Steven Fielding, *Workers' worlds: cultures and communities in Manchester and Salford 1880-1939* (Manchester: Manchester University Press, 1992), p. 157.

20 See Chinn, *Better betting*, pp. 270–1.

21 1923 Select Committee, Q6206 (Gulland).

22 1923 Select Committee, Q4778 (Croll); QQ5039–41 (McLean).

23 1932/3 Royal Commission on Lotteries and Betting, report para. 131.

24 Chinn, *Better betting*, pp. 127–8

25 1923 Select Committee QQ4514–21 (Tyler).

26 More recent empirical research suggested that in the 1970s those who claimed to use skill, usually male, were far more likely to read both racing pages and the specialist racing press. See D. M. Downes, B. P. Davies, M. E. David and P. Stone, *Gambling, work and leisure: a study across three areas* (London: Routledge and Kegan Paul, 1976), p. 136.

27 Philip Corrigan and Paul Willis, 'Cultural forms and class mediations', *Media, culture and society,* 2:3 (1980), 306.

28 See Downes *et al.*, *Gambling, work and leisure*, p. 24.

29 Ross McKibbin, *Classes and cultures: England 1918–1951* (Oxford: Oxford University Press, 1998), p. 375.

30 1932/3 Royal Commission, report para. 188.

31 Clapson, *A bit of a flutter*, p. 47; John K. Walton, *Lancashire: A social history 1558–1939* (Manchester: Manchester University Press, 1987), p. 343; Chinn, *Better betting*, pp. 174–5.

32 Ross McKibbin, *The ideologies of class* (Oxford: Oxford University Press, 1990), p. 244.

33 Rowntree, *Poverty and progress*, p. 403.

34 1932–/ Royal Commission, report para. 216. Minutes of evidence, QQ5312–25 (Evans); QQ8826–8 (Denton).

35 1923 Select Committee, draft report para. 31.

36 The Pilgrim Trust, *Men without work*.

37 E. Wight Bakke, *The unemployed man: a social study* (London: Nisbet and Co., 1935), pp. 189–90, 199.

38 A point emphasised by Stephen Jones, *Workers at play* (London: Routledge, 1986), p. 92.

39 1923 Select Committee, Q6759 (Green).

40 Liverpool Council of Voluntary Aid, *Report on betting in Liverpool* (Liverpool: LCVA, 1926).

41 See Seyla Benhabib, *Situating the self: gender, community and post-modernism in contemporary ethics* (London: Routledge, 1992), for a critique of such positions.

42 Alethea Melling, 'Wicked women from Wigan and other tales: licentious leisure and the social control of working-class women in Wigan and St Helens, 1914–1930', *North-west labour history*, 24 (1999/2000), 39.

43 Rowntree, *Poverty and progress,* p. 400.

44 1923 Select Committee, Q763ff.(Caldwell); Q4095 (Randall); Q5122–6 (Evans).

45 1923 Select Committee, Q5133 (Evans).

46 Chinn, *Better betting*, p. 170.

47 The Betting (Juvenile Messengers) (Scotland) Act, 1928.

48 1923 Select Committee, Q1369 (Bigham). Chinn, *Better betting*, p. 170 provides further examples.

49 *Daily Telegraph*, 6.2.1926.

50 1932–3 Royal Commission, minutes of evidence Q809.

51 1923 Select Committee, QQ8470, 8494–5 (Marshall).

52 Chinn, *Better betting*, p. 168.

53 1923 Select Committee, para. 35.

54 Rowntree, *Poverty and progress*, p. 402.

55 Chinn, *Better betting*, pp. xii, xiii. This continued the dominant picture of earlier anti-gambling writers. See M. J. Huggins, 'The first generation of street bookmakers in Victorian England: demonic fiends or decent fellers?', *Northern history*, 36: 1 (2000), 133.

56 Chinn, *Better betting*, pp. 232–6 and *passim.*
57 Walter Haydn Davies, *Blithe ones* (Bridgend: Bridgend Printing, 1979), p. 97.
58 1923 Select Committee, report, p. xiii.
59 1923 Select Committee, Q1366 (Bigham); Q780 (Caldwell); Q9048 (Denton).
60 1932–3 Royal Commission, minutes of evidence Q736. See also Clapson, *A bit of a flutter,* pp. 58–9.
61 For example, *The Times*, 25.8.1937; *ibid.*, 19.2.1938.
62 1923 Select Committee, draft report, p. xxxvi; 1932/3 Royal Commission, report para. 130.
63 1923 Select Committee, Q8298 (Yates).
64 Chinn, *Better betting*, pp. 187–8.
65 1932/3 Royal Commission, report para. 126.
66 1923 Select Committee, Q4798 (Croll).
67 Rev. Peter Green, *Betting and gambling* (London: Student Christian Movement, 1934), pp. 54–63.
68 Chinn, *Better betting*, p. 168. Some nineteenth-century bookmakers were involved in a hard-drinking, fighting, more criminal subculture. See Huggins, 'The first generation of street bookmakers', pp. 130–45.
69 1923 Select Committee, Q290 (Thompson).
70 Mass Observation, *The pub and the people* (London: Cresset, 1987), pp. 178, 187, 262–5.
71 Chinn, *Better betting*, p. 127.
72 1932–3 Royal Commission, Q8603 (Marshall).
73 1923 Select Committee, Q3056–7 (Grieve).
74 See *The Times*, 28.6.1933; *ibid.*, 10.1.1934; Clapson, *A bit of a flutter,* pp. 125–6.
75 *Northern Daily Mail*, 16.7.1921.
76 *North-Eastern Daily Gazette*, 21.5.1920; Chinn, *Better betting*, p. 123.
77 1923 Select Committee, report p. xiii.
78 1929 Royal Commission on Police Powers and Procedure, report paras 196–9, 280.
79 Dixon, *Prohibition to regulation*, pp. 262–6.
80 1923 Select Committee, Q1641 (Bigham).
81 1923 Select Committee, Q851–5.
82 1923 Select Committee, Q9045 (Denton).
83 1923 Select Committee, Appendix of District Conference of Chief Constables, District No 1. See also Dixon, *From prohibition to regulation*, pp. 219–56.
84 1932/3 Royal Commission, report para. 133.
85 1932 Select Committee, Q8610 (Marshall).
86 See R. Munting, 'Social opposition to gambling in Britain', *International journal of the history of sport*, 10:3 (Dec. 1993), 306.
87 Rowntree, *Poverty and progress,* p. 401.
88 Phil Welsh, *Stable rat: life in the racing stables* (London: Eyre Methuen, 1979), p. 32.
89 Dixon, *From prohibition to regulation*, p. 223.

90 McKibbin, *Classes and cultures*, p. 371.
91 1932/3 Royal Commission, report paras 199–200.
92 1932/3 Royal Commission, para. 117.
93 Richard Kaye, *The Ladbroke's story* (London: Pelham Books, 1969), p. 66.
94 *Cleveland Standard*, 23.6.1934.
95 *London Evening News*, 21.5.1937. See also another cartoon: 'Usefulness of opinions of barbers', *Daily Mirror*, 26.5.1935.
96 1923 Select Committee, Q554.
97 Elizabeth Dawson, *Mother made a book* (London: Geoffrey Bles, 1962), pp. 21, 27, 35.
98 For example, Gregory Blaxland, *Golden Miller* (London: Constable, 1972), p. xi.
99 Noel Fairfax-Blakeborough (ed.), *J. F.-B: the memoirs of Jack Fairfax-Blakeborough* (London: J. A. Allen, 1978), p. 182.
100 *Sporting Life*, 19.5.1924.
101 Theodore Felstead, *Racing romance* (London: Werner Laurie, 1949), pp. 100–2.
102 John Hislop, *Far from a gentleman* (London: Michael Joseph, 1960), p. 177.
103 1923 Select Committee, QQ7957–67 (Heathorn). W. Bebbington, *Rogues go racing* (London: Good and Betts, 1947), pp. 120–1 took the same view.
104 1923 Select Committee, Q2244 (Hamilton).
105 1923 Select Committee, report p. 41; Q749 (Caldwell); Q1368 (Bigham); QQ6781, 6782 (Green); Q4543 (Tyler); Q6856 (Green).
106 Turf Guardian Society, *Directory of turf accountants and commission agents* (London: TGS, 1921).
107 1923 Select Committee, Appendix 3 and QQ745–9 (Caldwell); Q8277 (Randall); QQ4049, 8473, 8524 (Marshall). See *The Times*, 24.4.1923 for the anti-duty conference the Turf Guardian Society organised.
108 Quoted in *The Times*, 21.4.1923.
109 1923 Select Committee, Q1257; Q4751–4 (Croll).
110 1923 Select Committee, QQ4890, 4893, 4898, 4900 (McLean).
111 C. R. Acton, *Silk and spur* (London: Richards, 1935), p. 209. Norman Pegg, *Focus on racing* (London: Robert Hale, 1963), pp. 94–5.
112 *Ruff's guide to the turf*, 1933, p. viii.
113 1923 Select Committee QQ3356–62 (Randall).
114 Sporting Chronicle, *Flat racing up to date: yearly part 1938* (Manchester: Sporting Chronicle, 1938), frontispiece.
115 *Sporting Life*, 22.2.1924.
116 1932–3 Royal Commission, paras 120–1.
117 *Sporting Chronicle*, 27.3.1935.
118 1923 Select Committee, QQ3665, 3758, 3804, 3911 (Crump). See also Munting, 'Social opposition to gambling', p. 306; and Kaye, *The Ladbroke's story*.
119 1932/3 Royal Commission, report para. 117.
120 Munting, *History of gambling*, p. 102.
121 Charles Sidney, *The art of legging* (London: Maxline International, 1976), pp. 74–5. 1923 Select Committee, Q8211 (Heathorn).

122 Jack Fairfax-Blakeborough, *The analysis of the turf* (London: Philip Allan, 1927), p. 265.
123 Felstead, *Racing romance*, p. 127.
124 Chinn, *Better betting*, p. 193.
125 1923 Select Committee, Q2851 (Hawkins).
126 See Clapson, *A bit of a flutter*, pp. 31, 122.
127 The *Sporting Chronicle* began analysing the effects of such systems, and the relative success of different sporting tipsters, in the 1920s.
128 See Clapson, *A bit of a flutter*, p. 62.
129 See Barbara O'Connor and Elisabeth Klaus, 'Pleasure and meaningful discourse: an overview of research issues', *International journal of cultural studies,* 3:3 (2000), 369–87.
130 *Liverpool Echo*, 20.3.1930.
131 1923 Select Committee, report p. 42.
132 Duggan was regularly prosecuted in Britain. See *The Times*, 29.6.1923 and 14.6.1924 for examples. He maintained a London office, e.g. *Sporting Life* 28.5.1924. For the Monte Carlo sweep see the *Sportsman*, 29.3.1924.
133 *Liverpool Post*, 27.3.1925.
134 Sidney Galtrey, *Memoirs of a racing journalist* (London: Hutchinson, 1934), pp. 263–6.
135 *Daily Mirror*, 25.5.1925.
136 See *The Times*, 21–23.6.1923.
137 *The Times*, 30.5.1933.
138 A. Edward Newton, *Derby day and other adventures* (Boston: Little, Brown and Co., 1934), p. 9.
139 *The Times*, 7.2.1933.
140 *The Times*, 7.2.1933.
141 *The Times*, 29.1.1920; *ibid.,* 16.2.1920.
142 The following section draws heavily on Clapson, *A bit of a flutter*, pp. 190–3.
143 C. L'Estrange Ewen, *Lotteries and sweepstakes* (London: Heath Cranton, 1932), p. 350.
144 In 1933, for example, of those who drew Derby horses for the £30,000 prizes, only one came from Ireland, one from Switzerland and three from North America; and fourteen were British.
145 *The Times*, 1.6.1933.
146 *Daily Express*, 11.11.1930.
147 *The Times*, 22.6.1933; *ibid.*, 24.6.1933.
148 'Britain's betting industry – II', *Economist*, 7.3.1936, p. 517; Chinn, *Better betting*, p. 228.

4

Declining opposition to betting on racing

When Mass Observation studied Bolton in 1938 it noticed a number of 'major oppositions' which cut across the life of the community, separating married couples and families – issues about which persons apparently alike with respect to income, age, appearance or knowledge might violently differ or feel resentment. One was the drinking of alcohol. Another was betting.[1] They were defined as part of dominant popular culture or as part of oppositional culture, depending on one's social identity. Betting was an intensely social activity, which avoided direct competition within families or communities by focusing interest on indirect competition between horses and jockeys. Even if people disagreed about a horse's chances, the only personal competition for the punter was between him and the bookmaker. Yet betting aroused powerful emotions and strong opposition in wider British society. To understand its place we need to examine the nature of the opposition to betting, and those who disliked it, found it irrelevant or disagreed with it, now we have examined those who enjoyed betting, accepted it or felt involved with it.

Over much of the nineteenth century there had been 'respectable' opposition to both racing and betting, but by the early part of the twentieth century there was less opposition to racing itself.[2] The practice of offering alternatives to the race meetings continued in the form of events like the Newcastle 'Hoppings' or in the common arrangements made by Sunday schools to take their pupils away during the races. The Middlesbrough Sunday School Union, for example, organised extra excursions each year during Stockton Race Week, and 13,000 travelled by their trains in 1921.[3] But people could take an excursion trip one day, and attend the races another. Even arguments against the cruelty to horses had less impact, although Aintree in particular continued to attract RSPCA proposals for change, and letters of complaint to the press.[4]

Declining opposition was due partly to the decreased visibility of racing's noisy crowds, since courses had increasingly moved away from town centres. For example, in 1882 Leicester's meeting had moved out to Oadby, and Newcastle's to Gosforth Park, while Nottingham's went to Colwick Park in 1892. In part too the increasing enclosure of courses and the creation of more sub-enclosures within them had made behaviour easier to control, while upper- and middle-class support for approved courses was more overt. Another reason was the great increase in the volume of working-class off-course betting, although from the 1890s this attracted vociferous campaigns of opposition. Although such opposition spread to other forms of popular gambling, its application to racehorse betting is the main focus here.

Anti-gamblers' arguments

Between the wars gambling was growing in popularity, while anti-gambling and anti-betting feeling was losing some of its power. The peak in negative feeling amongst a vociferous section of middle-class and respectable working-class society was the later nineteenth century. The keynote of their anti-gambling strategy was the state prohibition of working-class cash betting via the 1853 Betting Houses Act and the Street Betting Act of 1906, alongside the preservation of legal on-course betting and bookmakers in the interests of horseracing and upper-class gamblers.[5] This class-discriminatory policy had at best only slowed down the increase in gambling, but the anti-gambling movement still had the support of many Liberal, Labour and Nonconformist church leaders and members, and opposition to betting clearly crossed class boundaries.

This meant that punters were always conscious of the 'anti-gamblers', that powerful minority of the population who supported state action against gambling. Those about whom we know most, those who opposed betting more publicly, were strong in their certainty. They cared about the issue. They spoke with passion. Many, though not all, were Christians, with a faith that transcended the material world. Their dominant rhetoric reflected a long-standing and powerful Protestant tradition. Although they were in a minority, they often held power within local communities. They were leaders in politics, on the magistrates' bench, press editors or local businessmen. What they said could not be ignored. Punters saw the displayed notices banning betting in public houses, the notices about the consequences of betting outside churches, or came across reports of anti-betting sermons in church, and perhaps felt guilty. Religious rituals spoke of the sacred, betting rituals of sin.

Protestantism rather than class was the major determinant of attitudes. Protestantism stressed prudence, rationality and thrift. To the Nonconformist, work, merit and reward went hand in hand. Gambling was based on chance and thus undermined 'proper' ethical approaches to life. It violated the legitimate ethical, economic and social system. It attacked modern economic life. It was a competing and thus highly dangerous subculture. Yet Nonconformist industrial success was based on similar values to those exhibited by gamblers, including competitiveness, boldness, innovation and risk-taking, although these were carefully rationalised by industrialists and their biographers. Luck was not supposed to play a part in their lives, so they were portrayed as models of ability and diligence, prudence and perseverance, even if their rewards were extreme due to high-risk investments. There were always hidden elements of tension, ambivalence and guilt about the anti-betting position, and the relationship between cash and culture was always ambiguous. The cultural theorist Dyer has pointed out that popular entertainments like betting provided apparent alternatives to capitalism in a capitalist form.[6] To cope with this, anti-gambling groups tried hard to culturally locate betting in spheres of activity which could be presented as segregated, differentiated and illegitimate, so its norms did not challenge the 'legitimate' economy. Most of their efforts were directed towards permissible and desirable attacks on illegal aspects of betting, such as sweepstakes or cash betting. Gambling functioned as their scapegoat, a target for potentially disruptive ambivalences, a useful symbol for guilt projection.[7] Self-made Nonconformist industrialists were admirable folk heroes; grasping, greedy, gambling bookmakers were folk villains, targets of righteous indignation. Such dualisms strengthened anti-gambling opposition.

The anti-gamblers' genuine feelings were also stirred by direct experience of what they saw as the immorality and ruinous social consequences of gambling. Their experience, like that of the gamblers, was social, mutually reinforcing and self-confirming. They preached about it, talked about it and shared their observations. Being an 'anti-gambler' was part of their self-identity. They met with and wrote to others. As the Salford-based Canon Peter Green explained, his 'best source of information' on gambling was drawn from his 'wide circle of friends' of all classes. These friends were:

> godly policemen, devout soldiers, earnest foremen and forewomen – Sunday School teachers in their spare time, at some church or chapel, and horrified at what they see going on all round them – newly confirmed boys and girls trying to stand for Christ in the workshops, big employers of labour, magistrates of both sexes amazed at the revelations that come to them on the bench, doctors and other professional men.[8]

Green wanted others to learn gambling's evil. He validated his views by pointing them to the evidence. Anti-gamblers constantly found the evidence for which they constantly searched. This mutually-shared experience of selected aspects of the social pathology of gambling structured and shaped their understandings, so it was unsurprising that their evidence was uniform in its condemnation of betting's role. Their dominant model of the punter was a dupe on an inevitable road to disaster. So they did not question average, unproblematical punters, who remained shadowy figures.

In the self-validating circles in which most anti-gamblers moved, betting was unrespectable. So they often lacked any real understanding that betting was widely perceived as a rational act. Anti-gamblers tended to present themselves as of higher status, as intellectually, morally and ethically superior. Green contemptuously dismissed all betters as intellectually dull, claiming they showed no 'symptoms of intelligence'.[9] His arguments focused on the physical, social, moral and economic effects of excessive betting, which he then applied to most betters. The anti-gamblers studied these effects as a social problem, but divorced betting from its cultural context. There is never any impression that any had ever placed a bet themselves.

Because so many anti-gamblers held strong Christian beliefs, they talked about betting in religious, ethical and medical language. Gambling seemed to pose a direct challenge to their faith. The Christian Social Council in 1932 stated firmly that 'gambling challenges that view of life which the Christian Church exists to uphold and defend'.[10] Betting was a 'sin' to those in the Nonconformist churches, but publicly they rarely used the word. It was probably deliberately avoided when giving evidence about gambling in secular public contexts. In part this was because the question of whether it was a sin was an area of debate amidst Christian moral theologians, and this potentially weakened anti-gambling arguments. The Roman Catholic Church accepted betting fairly easily, as it did the drinking of alcohol, unless it was excessive, and Catholic moral theologians argued that gambling was not essentially sinful.[11] The Church of England was divided. On the one hand, an article in the *Church Times* in 1923 argued that 'a very strong case can, as our readers are aware, be made to show that under certain conditions the practice is not morally blameworthy'.[12] On the other, Church of England anti-gamblers argued that this was 'a sin against God'. Combating it was part of one's duty; part of the doctrine of good stewardship. Increasingly the latter view gained strength in the early 1930s, as those then moving into senior posts were opposed to gambling. William Temple, a future archbishop of Canterbury, collaborated on a book on gambling and ethics.[13] Anti-gambling became Protestant orthodoxy.

The distribution of strong religious opposition to gambling in the 1920s was illustrated by resolutions sent in to the 1923 Select Committee on Betting Duty. Almost all of these came from Nonconformity, and were the result of an active campaign waged within their convocations to encourage the forwarding of resolutions. The Wesleyans, who had an active membership of 470,000, and claimed over a million and a half worshippers, organised resolutions against the imposition of betting duty in all thirty-three synods in England, Scotland and Wales. Ministers made up 25 per cent of synod membership and the real extent of lay support remained unclear. Other senders of resolutions included the Sunday School Union, which claimed a membership of three million, and the Evangelical Free Churches, who claimed a membership of two million. If *all* members of these churches were strong in their anti-gambling beliefs therefore, this was indeed powerful opposition. Yet reports of

Table 4.1 Resolutions sent in to the Select Committee on Betting Duty, 1923

Organisation	No. of resolutions received
Free Church Council	85
Sunday School Union	61
Brotherhood Movement	279
Primitive Methodist Church	365
Wesleyan Methodist Church	311
United Methodist Church	35
Calvinistic Methodist Church	16
Independent Methodist Church	3
Baptist Church	147
Congregational Church	122
Society of Friends	3
United Free Church of Scotland	8
Free Presbyterian Church of Scotland	2
Reformed Presbyterian Church of Scotland	1
Presbyterian Church of England	1
Presbyterian Church of Wales	1
Moravian Church	1
Miscellaneous	92

Source: 1923 Select Committee on Betting Duty, minutes of evidence

local meetings occasionally provide a more mixed picture. At a South Caernarvonshire Congregational Association meeting, for example, when the chair moved a resolution deploring gambling, and others spoke in favour, there were three dissenting voices, arguing that this was hypocritical since the church had raffles, while 'church deacons and even women members were said to be amongst those addicted'.[14]

Christians who gave anti-gambling evidence to the 1923 Select Committee on Betting Duty included the Rev. Benson Perkins, assistant secretary of social welfare for the Wesleyans; Rev. Robert Gillie, an ex-president of the Sunday School Union and of the National Council for Evangelical Free Churches; Rev. Hon. E. Lyttleton, a former head of Eton; Dr Welldon the Dean of Durham; and Canon Peter Green, whose unscientific generalisations had a particular impact on the Committee's report. To avoid the potential problems of discussing gambling as a sin in a secular context, the word they much more regularly applied to gambling was 'evil'. In religious terms fighting against gambling was part of the eternal struggle, and so the term 'evil', preceded by adjectives like 'gigantic', 'inherently' or 'national', was the main noun applied to gambling, permeating the anti-gambling evidence given. Gambling was described as the greatest evil in the country, a 'habit that cannot be cured' except by moral and spiritual means.[15] In 1925 the Society for the Propagation of Christian Knowledge published a thirty-one-page pamphlet explaining *A Christian View of Gambling,* making it clear that betting was an 'evil' sin. Later organisations and individuals maintained this choice of words. In his 1930 book *Gambling and Christian Ideals,* for example, Cecil Rose described it as 'one of the greatest social evils of our times'.[16]

For these more religious anti-gamblers, moral arguments had priority. In earlier attacks on betting, it had been seen as wrong largely because of its effects.[17] The campaigns of the interwar years had a more strongly moralistic tone running alongside restatements of the earlier arguments. A tax on betting would be morally disastrous, a serious condemnation from the view of Christian citizenship. Betting was a weakness which reduced moral qualities, not just those of the individual, but in a much wider sense. Green summed up such arguments in terms of Christian duty. To combat it was part of one's duty to God. It was also part of one's duty to oneself, since gambling was unquestionably injurious to character. It did not help the gambler to 'say his prayers and to worship God … or be zealous in good works to his neighbour or keen on matters touching public welfare'. Betting was a 'sin against one's own soul'. Anti-gambling was part of the duty to one's neighbour because getting money out of someone else could 'do financial harm to them and set a bad moral example'. It was anti-social and selfish. It was also a sin against 'all men, a sin against society', which wasted wealth, ruined the innocent and made homes miserable.[18] It had a further moral cost to the nation, in taking men from the Church, night school and education. More betting would 'weaken the moral strength of the nation and therefore lessen the moral influence of Great Britain in the thought and life of the world'.[19]

Betting was also seen as irrational, appealing to chance and rejecting reason. Lotteries allowed huge amounts of money to be won by sheer luck, a denial of the Protestant virtues of thrift and hard work. As the archbishop of York explained, introducing the evidence of the churches to the 1932/3 Royal Commission, 'as a social factor its essence is the distribution of wealth on the basis of chance ... that is plainly indefensible'.[20] It encouraged superstitious beliefs and a preoccupation with luck, and fostered laziness, irresponsibility and fatalism. It encouraged workers to be spendthrift and hedonistic, wasting time and money.

While for Christian anti-gamblers the main arguments were ethical and moral, some Christians did not share their views, and in an increasingly secular society religious arguments alone were losing their power to persuade. Secular arguments about the effects of gambling had always been a commonplace of the anti-gambling position, and the ever-growing variety of popular gambling forms caused alarm to a range of other, more secular interest groups. By the time of the 1932/3 Royal Commission on Lotteries and Betting, the constituency giving anti-gambling evidence included groups such as social workers, probation officers and charity organisations, and had proportionately fewer overt Christian anti-gamblers such as the archbishop of York and the bishop of Manchester.[21]

Opposition to betting and gambling therefore also covered a range of arguments concerned with the economic, physical and social damage they caused. Firstly anti-gamblers argued that attempts to legalise betting were 'condemned by experience'. They appealed to the weight of history, arguing that repeated judgments against the legalisation of betting over the last century years were 'presumptive evidence' of the principle.[22] The allegedly pernicious effects of the lotteries in the early nineteenth century, the betting houses of the early 1850s, or the street betting of the late nineteenth century were regularly cited as reasons not to make any retrograde move. Any weakening of laws against betting, such as introduction of a betting duty, would be a state sanction of a national evil. State dependence on gambling revenue would implicitly endorse betting, and would lead to increased levels of betting activity, and thus increased social problems.

The experience of other countries was also cited as an argument against making betting easier, although examples were selected which favoured the anti-gambling cause. It was claimed that in New Zealand the state sanction and support provided by the betting tax on bookmakers and the introduction of the Totalisator had added enormously to the volume of betting. Softening of the law would therefore be counter-productive. Countries such as Canada were praised for introducing new laws to ban the advertising of betting facilities.

Other arguments were located in the economic and social spheres. Betting was seen as being based on unsound economic principles. Betting was an 'illegitimate form of exchange' – to be contrasted with the Protestant ethic of legitimate forms.[23] It was an unproductive occupation and an illegitimate form of profit- or loss-making activity. No service was provided, the anti-gamblers argued, and betting weakened the sense of value, so hard work was impossible, and people stopped trying to save. Any gain in state revenue by taxation would be outweighed by the weakening of the economic foundations of society. In their eyes there were only three legitimate forms of exchange – value, labour and benevolence – and in their eyes betting satisfied none of these. It depreciated the sense of values which people ought to possess, and encouraged unhealthy speculation. In part such arguments were also about the right use of money. Whilst some argued that money could be spent on betting without appreciably affecting income, the anti-gamblers argued that such money could be spent to much better purpose. They also took the view that money easily won was generally spent recklessly.

Some saw the issue in wider economic terms and linked arguments to more structural economic features such as concerns over competition with USA and Germany. To Arthur Shadwell, betting had 'an injurious influence on industrial efficiency'.[24] In this view obsession with betting hindered production. The Accrington chief constable felt that betting in mills and factories tended to 'draw the attention of workers from their work'.[25] Work was stopped and damaged by the amount of time given to discussion and thought about betting. Canon Green claimed to have gathered supporting qualitative evidence from workshops, mills, warehouses, offices, mines, builders' yards and railways, and argued that while owners supported him and gave him information, they would not provide statistics which put them competitively in a bad light. He was certain that gambling affected production, and that this was made worse because some overlookers, supervisors and foremen actually coerced people to bet.

People even read betting papers in the toilet. He estimated that betting created a 20 per cent national loss of production due to wasted time, wasted material and the internal friction that betting created. There were also safety issues, a point he illustrated with one anecdote describing a railway signal operator using his safety phone to get racing results, and then leaving his signal box to walk down the track to pass on the results to nearby pub bowls players.[26] To a more limited extent gambling was putatively linked to the rise of socialism, and what the 1923 Select Committee chair called the 'something for nothing' arguments about society. [27]

Any betting gains were at the expense of another's losses, so all gamblers, and most especially bookmakers, could be demonised as predatory. The demonisation of bookmakers was associated with the belief that 'without bookmakers there would be no betting'.[28] There was therefore real concern that licensing and hence legalising large numbers of cash bookmakers would create a new 'vested interest', a new national institution. In fact it was in large part the opposition to gambling that had forced bookmakers to become an increasingly powerful political lobby in the first place. The National Sporting League had first been founded around 1900 for political reasons to defend racing and betting. Its membership was varied, but it had a large number of small-bookmaker members. They raised funds used at election times to back candidates who supported racing or to oppose those who did not. Indeed in 1929 they put pressure on the Conservative government to abandon betting taxation by lending their support to the Labour Party at the North Lanarkshire by-election, even though Labour opposed betting.

While moral arguments had only very limited effect outside the movement, and the economic arguments were finely balanced, the evidence that excessive betting could have profound social effects was much more influential in wider society. By 1932 it was this aspect which most concerned the Royal Commission on Lotteries and Betting. The Commission recognised that there were no available social statistics, and so was anxious to talk to experienced witnesses with first-hand knowledge. Its 1932/3 Final Report had a special section on the 'social effects of betting at the present time', which covered 'Gambling and Impoverishment', 'Gambling and Crime', and 'Effects on Character'.

Most people recognised that excessive gambling could lead to poverty, and that if gamblers gambled more than they could afford this could have social costs. Families were ruined thanks to betting, and it was argued to be a cause of working-class poverty. F. B. Meyer wrote in 1922 that he could 'recite story after story of men whose lives, homes and prospects have been destroyed by the insidious ravages of the betting craze'.[29] Anti-gambling evidence in 1932/3 claimed that a significant proportion of poverty was caused by gambling, while unemployed men, receiving dole money, were wasting their meagre resources on betting. There were 'a considerable number of cases' where gambling and not drunkenness was the main cause of household distress and family destitution.[30] The Royal Commission took the view that impoverishment due to gambling was not uncommon, and that 'in very many cases sums are being spent on gambling which on any reasonable view ought to be devoted to the proper support of the home'.[31]

Gambling was also presented as a frequent cause of crime. The earlier 1906 Street Betting Acts had been passed because of concerns about betting as a contributory factor to working-class poverty and crime. The results of gambling supposedly placed a heavy economic burden on the trading community, including losses because of theft, possible bankruptcy and consequent out-relief. Such concerns resurfaced powerfully in the anti-gambling evidence given to both the 1923 Select Committee and the 1932 Royal Commission.[32] Fraud and embezzlement were perhaps the two most common middle-class major crimes, and in anti-gambling rhetoric such crimes were often seen as having a direct link to betting. According to the leading anti-gambling organisation, the National Anti-Gambling League (henceforth NAGL) in May 1919 'more crime and misery are attributable to it than any other national evil, not excluding intemperance', and this was a generally-held view.[33] Betting was supposedly a strong temptation for clerks and others handling large sums of money for their employers.[34] Whilst no statistical evidence for this was provided, it was claimed to be a matter of common experience that betting encouraged employees to steal from employers to feed their habit. Discovery and ruin was the final result. Green cited many individual examples, and in 1923 estimated that betting was responsible annually for 100,000 suicides, thefts and bankruptcies.[35] The 1923 Committee was less convinced, suggesting that the few available statistics did not show any increase in the last years, rather the reverse. The anti-gamblers had explanations. It was due to the increasing leniency of magistrates, or perhaps firms didn't go to court to avoid bad publicity, but simply sacked offenders and refused to provide a reference. Anti-gamblers and police who gave evidence to the 1932/3 Commission generally avoided statistics, but argued that there were 'many' or 'numbers of cases', and that it was 'a very large factor' and played 'a very prominent part'. The chief constable of the West Riding claimed that of the 457 embezzlement and fraudulent conversion claims of the last 5 years, gambling had been a factor in 58 cases. Such evidence led the Commission to conclude that 'the weight of evidence shows that gambling is responsible for a considerable proportion' of such cases.[36]

Gambling was also linked to violent crime. The anti-gamblers noted the evidence of racecourse criminality. They saw betting as a means whereby violent criminals were recruited. The violent outrages of the London and Birmingham race gangs, the outbreaks of violence on small courses, the blackmail and extortion practised upon bookmakers, were all seen as further evidence of its potential dangers.[37] Also linked to criminality was the recognition that betting caused demoralisation and corruption amongst the police, and that many apparent convictions were bogus. Green claimed that in Salford there was an almost universal and unshakeable belief amongst workers that the plain-clothes men of the detective department were hand in glove with the bookmakers and were bribed by them.[38]

Evidence to the 1923 Select Committee and the 1932/3 Commission emphasised betting's negative effects on character, especially in young people. Social workers claimed that 'the whole outlook of young men and boys becomes changed' and were 'only too well aware of the deterioration of character that follows upon the gambling habit'. Commissioner Lamb referred to its effects on children. The secretary of a Mile End club for young men said that it made them 'disgruntled', and 'loungers'.[39] 'Youth' were seen as particularly attracted to it. Children after the war were being 'brought up with less discipline' and now had 'a natural instinct for self-gratification'.[40] Opponents of a betting tax argued that it was the duty of the state to safeguard child development by eliminating or restricting such temptations to gamble.

Betting was presented as a 'menace to wholesome social life'.[41] Sexual roles were threatened by gambling and many of the anti-gamblers argued in lectures, especially when addressing more male audiences, that gambling by women would affect male roles, female health and family prosperity. It would break up homes, children would be underfed, and rent would be in arrears. Any evidence that betting led some women into financial difficulties was seized on with alacrity. Women's betting was argued to destroy family life.[42] While this had once been a common argument, however, the extension of the suffrage brought fresh challenges to such views. The secretary of the International Women's Suffrage Alliance, for example, writing in 1924, was quick to point out that money spent by the wife on amusement and personal desires was no greater loss to the family income than money similarly spent by the husband.[43]

Ways in which opposition was mounted

Opposition to gambling took a number of forms, each with its own chronology. There were peaks and troughs in its efforts, and shifts of focus as new forms of gambling emerged. In 1922 the threat that betting duty was being considered by the government led to much more organisation and reporting of anti-gambling activity in efforts to influence the Select Committee. The new greyhound racing tracks of the late 1920s, with their regular meetings, the development of racecourse totalisators from 1929, the Irish Hospital Sweepstakes, and the 'increasing evil' of the urban Tote clubs around 1930 all generated anti-gambling activity hoping to sway the 1932/3 Royal Commission, and much of the anti-gamblers' attention was diverted away from racing towards these new betting forms. In 1934 and 1935, following the Royal Commission's report, anti-betting activity was at a low ebb judging by the lack of coverage in the press, and the focus shifted to football pools betting. This was run by 'financial interests which were entirely lacking in conscience and were exploiting the community for their own ill-gotten gains', while in the industrial areas people were 'frequently' spending 5s a week on football pools.[44]

Although the shifting arguments against betting and gaming are important in understanding the range of motivations and attitudes behind the anti-gambling campaign, the movement did far more than merely offer argument. To have any chance of influencing wider public opinion the anti-gambling groups had to engage in effective action. So what forms did anti-gambling opposition take?

There was clearly strength in numbers, and several organisations provided support. In the period at the beginning of the twentieth century the major reform pressure group had been the NAGL, a secular body, although with much Church support.[45] Before the war it had offices at Westminster, Manchester and York, each publishing anti-gambling material, but it became far less influential after the First World War, and lost much of its former force. Leading figures of the pre-1914 period retired. Their efforts to counter gambling had apparently had little effect. The League had always argued that social, moral, economic and physical damage was caused by betting, and wanted not softening of the law, but further prohibition, including the banning of off-course credit betting and the publication of betting materials. For the League, betting was a national menace, and members were particularly shocked at evidence of women and children gambling.[46] At a time when its membership was increasingly Church-based, the decline of the Liberal Party and the move to secularisation in broader society eroded its appeal. As its membership and committee aged in the 1920s it became weaker.

The leading historian of the NAGL, David Dixon, sees it as becoming 'progressively less coherent and influential, as it slumped from crisis to crisis'.[47] Although it tried to create a broader base of support it was increasingly becoming an organisation of and for the churches. As a secular organisation it had previously avoided this. A first attempt was made to relaunch it by John Gulland at the beginning of the 1920s. This focused on structural changes, constitutional rationalisation, a merger of the London and provincial organisations, and new officials, though the wealthy industrialist and social researcher Seebohm Rowntree remained treasurer. The changes had little impact on membership, or financial and political support, which was eroding. In 1923 most of the NAGL were still opposed to the suggestions that prohibition should be substituted by regulation of cash bookmakers. A betting duty would not reduce betting, and would make it more difficult to deal with bookmakers, while making it appear that the State approved of betting. Although at least two of the League's members gave evidence to the Select Committee, it was otherwise largely inactive in the 1920s, with membership dropping and no money to support more active involvement. When gambling on greyhounds and on football grew too, the NAGL was not flexible enough or resourceful enough to respond.

Membership continued to fall in the early 1930s. The League was in financial difficulties and receiving an ever more sceptical reception. The executive committee was increasingly old and inactive. One key illustration of this was the failure to make any public response to the publication of the 1933 Final Report of the Royal Commission on Lotteries and Betting. The NAGL was increasingly dominated by the 'Nonconformist conscience'. Two-thirds of its vice-presidents were Church representatives by 1933, and NAGL speakers mostly spoke at Church conferences. Little material was now being produced. Attempts at another reorganisation in 1934 had little effect, although John Gulland produced policy statements on the report and related legislation, and made a public appeal for funds. Seebohm Rowntree lacked the skills to be a popular leader.[48] He was propping up the organisation financially and was obsessive in his opposition to gambling, but it clouded his judgement. The new committee of the NAGL was as ineffective as the old one.

As secular interest in anti-gambling declined, however, concern in the Protestant churches about gambling grew, partly as a result of the new commercial forms of gambling like greyhound racing, and because they were constantly being called upon to give a lead in responding and contributing to debates about betting duty and gambling. A Nonconformist of whatever class was most likely to oppose betting. Strict anti-gambling beliefs had become Protestant orthodoxy. Church figures became vociferous opponents, while the Christian Social Council also contributed to the debate. In working-class areas, missions and Nonconformist chapels were the main places were such views were propagated through meetings, leaflets and lads' clubs. The churches became the custodians of traditional morality, reflecting a Christian outlook 'no longer shared by the majority' of the population.[49] New cross-church organisations such as the Scottish National League against Betting and Gambling maintained an influence greater than that of the NAGL.[50] Mirroring the national joint organisations were more local groups like the Anti-gambling Committee of Manchester or the Salford Council of Christian Congregations.

Wider Church support was generated as betting became a regular topic at annual convocations, assemblies and meetings of particular church groups. In the spring of 1923, for example, when the report of the Select Committee on Betting Duty was being compiled, a number of religious bodies, including the Baptist Union, the Congregational Union and the Presbyterian Church of Scotland, all passed anti-gambling resolutions, and the York Convocation also discussed it. In the summer and autumn, further resolutions came from groups like the Christian Fellowship, the Wesleyan Methodist Conference and the National Free Church Council. In a rare spirit of ecumenicalism the various religious groups also managed to work together. A Council of Action of Religious and Social Reform Organisations was set up in May 1923, and a more powerful body, the Conference of Christian Politics, Economics and Citizenship, was set up in Birmingham in April 1924, initially focusing largely on betting.[51]

Like some modern psychologists of gambling, such groups felt that excessive gambling was due to irrational thinking, so better education should achieve a conversion. Preaching, writing and other forms of communication would help people understand the irrationality of betting, and would change attitudes. Some hoped that the government would 'institute a publicity campaign against betting' in the interests of 'national efficiency and the general well-being of the people', or perhaps even provide 'a syllabus of instruction on the moral and economic evils of betting, exposing in particular its anti-social character' for the day schools.[52]

They felt that control over knowledge was power. Some wanted to cut off the public from knowledge about racing results, betting odds and tipster advertisements, and supported the introduction of legislation to do this. Betting had been supposedly banned in public libraries since the Library Offences Act of 1898, and public libraries in a minority of local authorities helped by cutting or blocking out racing information from newspapers, although this slowly became less common. It was, for example, discontinued in West Ham in 1928, although Wolverhampton continued through the interwar period.[53] More positively, anti-gamblers produced articles, pamphlets and books to inform and influence opinion, although the volume of such propagandist literature was heavily outweighed by the books of guidance for bookmakers or punters. Before the Great War the NAGL had played a leading role with an annual *Bulletin* and leaflets from its branches helping to put forward anti-gambling arguments. After the war the NAGL's attempts keep its *Bulletin* going were unsuccessful. It abandoned it by late 1921, although it continued to publish annual reports addressing particular gambling issues.[54] Thereafter it was left to individuals to publicise the cause. Benson Perkins, drawing greatly on his experience in a working-class area of Sheffield, was a leading social reformer who played a major role in anti-gambling activities between the war, gave evidence to the two government enquiries, and was on the committees of the various inter-denominational anti-gambling organisations. He wrote many books and articles, arguing that all commercialised bookmaking should be banned.[55] John Gulland was another major figure, active in the NAGL from the beginning of the twentieth century, and later a highly efficient and hard-working secretary and organiser. He produced a whole range of anti-gambling leaflets, pamphlets and books on behalf of the NAGL and gave evidence to both enquiries.[56] Canon Green was a leading national critic of gambling from the late Edwardian years to the 1930s. He addressed public meetings and wrote booklets, tracts, books and articles in the *Manchester Guardian*, the leading anti-gambling daily paper of the time.[57]

Preaching in churches and chapels was another way of promoting the cause and sermons against all forms of gambling seem to have been a commonplace in interwar churches. Mass Observation noted that gambling and drink were by far the two commonest 'social evils' attacked in the five hundred sermons it observed in Bolton.[58] This may well have been effective in shaping the attitudes of at least some church congregations, but as Rev. Gillie admitted in evidence to the 1923 Select Committee, there was no attempt to go outside the Church to persuade.[59] Effort was probably wasted in constant preaching to the possibly already converted. As another anti-gambler pointed out, 'you may preach all the sermons you like, the bookmakers are not there to hear them'.[60]

Yet few noted that many Christians and other religious believers were involved in racing and betting. In racing towns the Church of England always had large numbers of racing followers in its congregations. In London there were numbers of Jewish bookmakers, and in the North of England many Catholic bookmakers. In these areas where congregations were more supportive of racing and betting, there was much less anti-gambling preaching, and what little there was, was carefully focused. A Liverpool pulpit critic of Aintree, for example, attacked only the use of 'National mascots' to bring betting luck.[61] Here, as elsewhere, local religious leaders kept themselves attuned to pro-racing local opinion. In more strongly anti-gambling churches, punters kept quiet.

Anti-gamblers rarely attempted the challenging task of preaching to the massed unconverted. Canon Green was exceptional in taking on the difficult, arduous and time-consuming work of anti-gambling preaching to workshops, mills and factories during the dinner hour. Through the years he lived in central Salford, Green claimed to have delivered 'scores, I might almost say hundreds of addresses in workshops and factories, in halls and in churches on gambling'.[62] The earlier practice of giving out tracts at the racecourse still occasionally occurred, although often subject to jeers, insults and abuse, and evangelical religious groups sometimes demonstrated inside or outside racecourses. Their placards concentrated on the punishment the racegoer would experience in the afterlife. One photograph of the road leading up to the Epsom grandstand in 1922, for example, shows a group holding large posters telling racegoers 'After Death the Judgement', 'Prepare to Meet thy Doom' or 'The Wages of Sin is Death', a phrase sometimes also projected through a megaphone just after the 'off' for maximum impact.[63]

If the anti-gamblers really wanted to change attitudes, then changing government policy was likely to have more fruitful results, and so the anti-gambling groups were strongly represented both on the membership of and amongst those giving evidence to the 1923 Select Committee of the House of Commons on Betting Duty, although here they now faced a somewhat more hostile reception than in previous years. Such publicly-reported political contexts were a rare and therefore important opportunity to influence public and political opinion. The texts of the exchanges demonstrate, for example, how carefully-weighted leading questions by Committee members were used in the hope of getting witnesses to agree to some extent with their cause. They show, too, the extent to which the thinking of the anti-gamblers reflected their culture, identity and social-class experience. Some of the difficulties the police faced in attempting to give their views in evidence to the Committee are also made clear.

During the hearings there was a short exchange between one of the anti-betting Welsh MPs on the Committee, Dai Grenfell, and Superintendent Evans of Glamorganshire, after Evans had presented evidence of betting in South Wales. It neatly encapsulates reference to two of the themes of this chapter: the arguments used by anti-gamblers, and the ways their opposition was mounted.

Grenfell was a former miners' agent who was elected MP for Gower in 1922 and was a staunch Nonconformist, part of a culture rooted in respectability, temperance and anti-betting. This culture was increasingly out of step with the values of South Wales mining communities, and Grenfell may well have been sensitive and defensive about that.[64] He began by trying to get Evans to agree that the 'whole of the public expression of opinion' in South Wales was anti-gambling, referring him to the resolutions and joint expressions from anti-gambling groups. Evans however was equivocal, saying that there 'certainly is a great opposition to betting but there is a great number otherwise'. Grenfell also suggested to him that 'useful citizens', those who have an 'interest in public life' and 'public morality', did not 'resort to gambling'. Evans suggested that 'people will bet because it is an attribute of the Britisher to bet'. This complacent myth, if held more widely, would have promoted disbelief in the effectiveness of anti-gambling legislation. Grenfell, his Welsh pride perhaps stung, seemed not to believe that 'there was a marked tendency among the Welsh people' to gamble, and asked whether it could really be a thing 'essentially Welsh', making Welshness synonymous with Britishness. This was not unusual in the rhetoric of the period. Evans avoided the question, responding that they would call it not gambling but 'a little sport'.

Grenfell's next remark, asking whether 'I do not know my own country', could be variously interpreted as new humility, scandalised dismay or sarcasm. Evans, who again avoided a direct answer, told him that 'down in Swansea where you are ... they gamble very freely'. Grenfell then challenged the notion that it was British to bet, arguing from a position of supposed racial superiority, asking if it was 'not generally well known that it is the inferior races of the world who gamble and not the superior races', placing those who bet as occupying a lower position on the evolutionary ladder. Grenfell also appealed to his own expertise, experience and political position, saying 'I represent the men and have lived with them all my life', only to be told by Evans, 'Well, they do not tell you all, you see'.[65] In Wales secular activities and attitudes were eroding the hold of the chapels, and the dangers of losing touch with the community from which he came must have been an issue here.

Limited anti-gambling success

Even in 1939 there were still strong social and economic objections to betting, but they were in process of decreasing. Betting was now simply a small part of the wider problem of the 'right' use of leisure, and of the slowly changing patterns of class relationships. What Dixon has described as the earlier 'authoritarian paternalism whose tool was prohibitory legislation' was in process of being undermined by a more democratic social philosophy.[66]

As a result the anti-gambling movement lacked any real unity. It was generally agreed that some restrictions needed to be placed upon organised facilities for betting and gambling, and that restrictions should certainly be imposed to help maintain public order. But thereafter there were divergent views about what should and could be done. At one end of the spectrum were more radical anti-gambling opponents who felt that not just street betting but all forms of bookmaking should be made illegal, and wanted to go further along the prohibition path to abolish credit and racecourse bookmaking. John Gulland, for example, really wanted to 'prohibit the betting trade but not private betting', yet recognised the difficulties.[67] Green thought all betting was wrong. The most extreme body of all, the Scottish National League against Betting and Gambling, saw betting as a 'social and moral calamity to the state' which should not be recognised in any of its forms.[68] The elimination of inducements to bet by the reduction of existing betting facilities was often proposed, though with no support from governments. Much anti-gambling evidence to the Royal Commission of 1932 urged that any amendment of the law should be in the direction of banning use of the telephone, telegraph or the post for betting purposes, along with publication of betting odds and news, or advertising of bookmaker and tipster services. They were also keen to restrict the Tote betting on racecourses to cash bets, and not allow its various credit manifestations.[69]

Moderates believed that the 1906 Act was enough, but needed better enforcement and more willingness from magistrates to imprison regular bookmaker offenders. Rev. Gillie, for example, pragmatically felt that it would not be possible to prohibit betting altogether, admitting that 'in legislation you have to consider what you can achieve'.[70] The Rev. Hon. E. Lyttleton, a former chairman of the NAGL, also recognised that to make betting absolutely illegal was impractical. So did the dean of Durham, who felt betting was not immoral in itself: it was a question of degree. Those who took the fundamentalist view that all betting was wrong actually estranged 'the great body of moderate Christian opinion', and ended up as enemies of reform.[71] Moderates took the view that legislation banning betting would not help, and that betting was excusable if carried on in moderation. It was only a source of national demoralisation if carried to excess. That was not to say that they would not ban betting if they thought it was a practical option, and they would support anything that would reduce its level.

The NAGL was therefore disunited. Some radicals wanted more stringent action, further regulation and prohibitions. Others were prepared to accept regulation if it would tackle gambling, and some would accept betting duty as a form of regulation. A minority had come to accept that the earlier Street Betting Act prohibiting cash betting was simply not effective. The failure of liquor prohibition in the USA increased their interest in more practical and effective alternatives.

The British Civil Service was pragmatic about betting, but different departments of state had different views. Departments like the Post Office or the Exchequer were less concerned with ethics than with revenue-raising. The anti-gamblers had most success with the Home Office, which had to ensure the practical working of government anti-gambling legislation and so over time increasingly shared in the opposition to gambling and bookmakers, adopting a moralistic, authoritarian and paternalistic approach. Its senior officials continued this conservative approach through the interwar years, and took an uncompromising stand against any legislative changes, which they felt would be ill-informed and unworkable.

In part this was due to the way the social evils its data provided seemed to confirm that a majority of the country would oppose change. The powerful permanent under-secretary at the Home Office, Sir John Anderson, was a strong defender of gambling laws. In his evidence to the Select Committee in 1923 the legal assistant under-secretary, Blackwell, felt that changes would be bitterly opposed, not only by the Nonconformist conscience on grounds of principle, but by 'a very large section of the population'.[72] The department believed that legalisation would mean more betting and increase its socially harmful effects. It strongly supported the status quo of apparent containment. Blackwell feared that otherwise the 'considerable proportion of the weekly employment dole' devoted to betting would increase still further. He felt that there was overwhelming evidence to support the view that crimes like embezzlement and larceny, and bankruptcies of firms, were mainly due to 'excessive betting'.[73] But when pressed by the 1923 Commission he was unable to provide firm statistical support for his views, and fell back on departmental 'common sense'.

In Parliament the Conservative Party, with a few exceptions, had a relatively positive attitude to betting. Up to 1914 the Parliamentary Liberal Party had been more opposed, and after 1918 many Labour MPs took a similar view, despite their constituents' more positive attitude. There was a widely held New Liberal and Fabian Society view, shared by some Labour and Liberal MPs, that while it would be impossible to stop betting totally, all professional book-making activity, of whatever sort, should be banned. The Labour shadow chancellor in 1923 saw gambling as 'the second greatest curse of the country'.[74] Although the impact of Labour opposition on the 1923 findings was fairly limited, Isaac Foot, a member of both the 1923 Select Committee and the NAGL, but inexpert in his knowledge, prepared an alternative minority draft report. Much of the work on this was actually done by Benson Perkins, who briefed him before each hearing, and worked hard to ensure that the Committee would not recommend that betting duty was desirable. The Labour MP the Rev. James Barr opposed the Tote's introduction as another part of the 'public iniquity' of betting, and wanted to do away with all forms of betting.[75] Even in 1929 Prime Minister Ramsay McDonald was quoted as seeing betting as 'leading to the demoralisation of our people', while Snowden, the chancellor, who held very strict Puritan views, regarded betting as 'the ruination of innumerable promising careers', and had the reputation within racing as always taking up 'an antagonistic attitude' to turf speculation.[76] Yet the Labour Party as a whole showed little willingness to politicise the issue. Working-class betting long preceded its formation, and though Labour origins were rooted in respectability, rational recreation and Nonconformism it also had a libertarian socialist tradition, while some activists actively enjoyed betting. Unwilling to lose electoral support,[77] it took little part in either sponsoring or encouraging any form of sporting activity, least of all racing, with its traditional, elitist, upper-class governing bodies, or in supporting class-based betting legislation.

Recent revisionist views arguing that the process of secularisation only really began in the 1960s get little support from this work.[78] Even by 1923 the evidence seems to suggest that anti-betting arguments were in decline. The comments and draft report of the 1923 Select Committee met the argument that betting was immoral by moving to a secularist approach, one where morality was constructed by the individual and society. They argued that the millions who bet, and many others, regarded betting in no sense as either moral or sinful. They dismissed the argument that if the state recognised and controlled betting this would lower moral standards by citing those other countries which had done so, suggesting that there was no evidence that moral standards there were lower than in Britain. The churches and education had exercised any supposed moral force unavailingly over the previous twenty-five years. The arguments that betting caused poverty were seen as grossly exaggerated. In response to the claim that betting was the prime cause of dishonesty, the Committee cited the Home Office Returns of larceny, embezzlement and other frauds from 1906 to 1920, pointing out that there had been a decline in links with crime over the period. The argument that betting was unproductive, and should be banned on economic grounds because it provided no goods in exchange for the punter's money, also failed to appeal. The Committee pointed out that people paid for concerts, the theatre and other leisure activities that provided no goods. Betting was part of leisure, and the person betting got pleasure and excitement in exchange. As a luxury it was therefore fit for taxation.

But to an extent the 1923 Committee still accepted some of the anti-gamblers' arguments, and reflected the concerns of previous decades. It felt that there were evils associated with betting, that excess betting was a great social ill, leading to demoralisation and suffering, and wanted to see the extinction of the street bookmaker, whom it saw as contributing to the growth in betting. The Select Committee accepted that breaking of the law by millions had a demoralising effect on character and weakened respect for law. As part of the male establishment it was especially shocked by the canvassing of women, particularly 'in the absence of their husbands', a clear indication of the Committee's assumptions about the male/female roles of the 1920s. The high level of street betting in the industrial regions was 'morally undesirable', especially since clandestine. Although the report was never finally completed due to the election, the subsequent return to power of the Conservatives saw the introduction of betting duty by the chancellor, Winston Churchill, in 1926, and the Racecourse Betting Act which introduced the Totalisator in 1928, although the puritan, anti-gambling home secretary W. Joynson Hicks ensured that the criminal laws against betting would not be changed.

By the time of the 1932/3 Royal Commission the concerns about betting on horseracing had been overtaken by the complex betting issues surrounding the Tote, pools, dog racing and sweepstakes, although the traditional arguments were still being reiterated and concerns to do nothing to increase gambling still dominated. The policy was now to prohibit or restrict only such facilities as had serious social consequences, and it was increasingly clear that there was a widening gap between the ideals of anti-gamblers and those in wider secular society. An exchange between the secretary of the Scottish National League against Betting and Gambling, F. Watson, and one of the commissioners, W. L. Hitchen, illustrated this well. Hitchen had suggested that betting laws had enjoyed public support. Watson dismissed this, explaining that 'The point is that we do not take our ethic from the man in the street', only to be told impatiently that 'The man in the street does not take his ethics from you'.[79]

The Commission also accepted the argument that attacks on ready-money but not credit betting were simply 'class legislation'.[80] They recognised that police action was largely ineffective. The major debate was whether cash betting offices should be allowed. But while the police and bookmakers both supported this, the opposing evidence of the churches, representatives of social organisations, the Association of Municipal Boroughs and the Convention of Royal Boroughs led the Commission to decide against it on the ground that it would encourage more betting. It went some way towards this by recommending that cash betting by post should be made legal and they were prepared to allow betting offices open both for credit betting and ready-money betting by letter or deposits left in collecting slots. This was a majority proposal, and had a number of practical weaknesses, while the Commission still failed to exhibit sufficient social understanding of betting contexts. As a result its proposals were rejected by the government. The possibility that any legislation would be divisive, and would stir up anti-gamblers, bookmakers, the press, the Church and the betting electorate, was too great.

In that sense, as a potential powder keg of dissension, the anti-gambling opposition should not be under-estimated. They were still the custodians of traditional morality, and were able to exert a powerful influence, not for change, but for inertia, for the maintenance of the status quo. Christianity continued to influence many aspects of civic society and social behaviour, and Christian attitudes to betting thus helped to shape the character of Britain between the wars.[81]

This Christian outlook was no longer shared by the majority of the population. Britain was an increasingly secular society. In relation to leisure its character was changing. So despite their continued political and cultural influence, in terms of public perceptions the anti-gamblers were increasingly portrayed as out of touch, single-issue fanatics. They were becoming subject to ridicule. British cultural forms almost all reflected a pro-gambling approach. A 1928 David Low cartoon shows a deputation approaching Winston Churchill. In the background a large, lively and excited crowd are queuing for a dog-racing stadium. A newspaper boy is selling the *Daily Gambler* with its racing selections. A series of wall posters advertise 'Toy Gamble', 'Monte Carlo Cigarettes – Free Roulettes' and other gambling services. The deputation of 'Right-Thinking Persons' addresses Churchill, asking him politely, 'Sir, is not this appalling increase of the gambling spirit among us threatening the fabric of our social system and sapping that thrift which is the foundation of our national greatness?' Churchill replies in vox pop mode, 'I'll bet yer it isn't'.[82]

The anti-gamblers between the wars built on earlier traditions, when they had enjoyed a measure of success in promoting betting legislation. But they failed to respond sufficiently strongly to the economic, social and political changes of the 1920s and 1930s. The anti-gamblers represented an old form of cultural dissent, often derived from their Christian faith and a view of work and rational recreation rooted in the Protestant ethic. They made little attempt to adapt or update the programme in the light of the changing secularisation of society, the increased 'social problem' of leisure, or the changing forms of commercial culture and the betting market. A cultural dynamic in which puritanism was increasingly vying with alternative views was reshaping British society, and the central imperatives of anti-gambling were becoming increasingly threatened by inner contradictions.[83]

Those opposed to gambling failed to make use of the new forms of mass media – the cinema, the popular press or the radio – in ways which might have challenged the dominant pro-betting rhetoric. Indeed they sneered at and showed little knowledge of such media. They continued to use traditional forms of communication which were increasingly less heard or read. The detachment of many, though not all, from the realities of contemporary life meant that their reform agenda failed to galvanise the general population, and their ageing arguments were continually reiterated in the face of public apathy.

Notes

1 Mass Observation, *The pub and the people* [1943] (London: Cresset Library, 1987), p. 44.

2 See Mike Huggins, *Flat racing and British society 1790–1914* (London: Frank Cass, 2000), pp. 204–11.

3 *North-Eastern Daily Express*, 18.8.1922.

4 For example, *The Times*, 30.3.1922; *ibid.*, 1.6.1922.

5 Huggins, *Flat racing*, ch. 8, *passim*; David Dixon, *From prohibition to regulation: bookmaking, anti-gambling and the law* (Oxford: Clarendon Press, 1991), ch. 2 .

6 Richard Dyer, 'Entertainment and Utopia', in Rick Altman (ed.), *Genre, the musical: a reader* (London: Routledge, 1981), pp. 177–89.

7 See Edward Devereux, *Gambling and the social structure* (New York: Arno Press, 1980,) pp. 919–20, 937–8.

8 Peter Green, *Betting and gambling* (London: Student Christian Movement, 1934), p. 11.

9 1923 Select Committee on Betting Duty, report with minutes of evidence, Q7085 (Green).

10 1932–3 Royal Commission on Lotteries and Betting, Appendices, Christian Social Council statement, p. 260.

11 Michael B. Walker, *The psychology of gambling* (Oxford: Pergamon Press, 1992), p. 132.

12 Quoted in *The Times*, 21.4.1923.

13 W. Temple and E. B. Perkins, *Gambling and ethics* (London: Pilgrim Press, n.d.).

14 *Liverpool Post*, 24.3.1925.

15 1923 Select Committee on Betting Duty, QQ5578, 5632 (Perkins); QQ6898, 6993 (Green); Q7347 (Lyttelton).

16 Cecil H. Rose, *Gambling and Christian ideals* (London: Epworth Press, 1930), p. 1.

17 see Huggins, *Flat racing*, pp. 204–28.

18 Green, *Betting and gambling*, pp. 69–3.

19 1923 Select Committee, Appendix IV, 'Can We Support the Betting Tax?', United Council of Action.

20 1932–3 Royal Commission, ch. IV, para. 186.

21 1923 Select Committee, Appendix IV, 'Can We Support the Betting Tax?', archbishop of York.

22 1923 Select Committee, Q5569 (Perkins).

23 1923 Select Committee Q5616 (Perkins).

24 Arthur Shadwell, *Industrial efficiency: a comparative study of industrial life in England, Germany and America* (London: Longmans, Green and Co., 1920), p. 509.

25 Report of District Conference of Chief Constables, District no. 1, Blackburn, 4.5.1923.

26 1923 Select Committee, QQ6768, 6789, 6804–5 (Green). Green, *Betting and gambling*, pp. 34-7.

27 Dixon, *From prohibition to regulation*, p. 204.

28 Rev. Dr John Clifford in speech to the Baptist Union, reported in *The Times*, 24.4.1923.

29 *The Times*, 20.4.1923.

30 1932/3 Royal Commission, report paras 215–16; Astbury statement, p. 379 para. 4; Burgess, Q2215.

31 1932/3 Royal Commission, report para. 216.

32 See Dixon, *From prohibition to regulation*, pp. 321–9.

33 *Bulletin* 6:74 (May 1919), 109, quoted by Dixon, *From prohibition to regulation*, pp. 298–9.

34 Headlines frequently called attention to these, although they often formed a persuasive part of a plea. See for example 'Bank Clerk's Bets. Tempted to steal money to get straight – a plea for leniency', *Liverpool Echo*, 13.1.1922.

35 1923 Select Committee, QQ6766, 6826 (Green).

36 1932/3 Royal Commission, report paras 211–13; Bigham, QQ550–2, Knight statement, p. 220 para. 17; Biron, Q3080; Burgess statement, p. 145 para. 2; Brook Statement, p. 64 para. 26.

37 See Green, *Betting and gambling*, p. 50.

38 *Ibid.*, p. 54.

39 1932/3 Royal Commission, Chamberlain statement, p. 300; Lamb statement, p. 176; Lockwood, QQ3609, 3649.

40 1923 Select Committee, Q7354 (Lyttleton).

41 1923 Select Committee Appendix IV, 'Can we Support the Betting Tax?', United Council of Action.

42 See Carl Chinn, *Better betting with a decent feller: bookmaking, betting and the British working class, 1750–1990* (Hemel Hempstead: Harvester, 1991), p. 172.

43 *The Times*, 11.1.1924.

44 *Ibid.*, 31.3.1938.

45 See Dixon, *From prohibition to regulation*, pp. 82–108, 149–85; Huggins, *Flat racing*, pp. 220–5.

46 Mark Clapson, *A bit of a flutter: popular gambling and English society c. 1823–1961* (Manchester: Manchester University Press, 1992.

47 Dixon, *From prohibition to regulation*, p. 299. The following two paragraphs are largely based on his work.

48 See A. Briggs, *Social thought and social action: a study of the work of Seebohm Rowntree 1871-1954* (London: Longmans, 1961).

49 John Stevenson, *British society 1914–1945* (Harmondsworth: Penguin, 1984), p. 370.

50 Roger Munting, *An economic and social history of gambling in Britain and the USA* (Manchester: Manchester University Press, 1996), p. 35.

51 COPEC, *A report of the meetings of the conference on Christian politics, economics and citizenship held in Birmingham, April 5–12, 1924* (London: Longmans, Green, 1924).

52 Rev. Hugh Jenkins, reported in *The Times*, 13.5.1924.

53 *The Times*, 28.11.1928; Chinn, *Better betting*, pp. 220–1, A. H. Thompson, *Censorship in public libraries in the twentieth century* (Epping: Bowker, 1975).

54 For example NAGL, *The great waste and the cure: 31st annual report* (London: NAGL, 1921); NAGL, *Gambling and the state: 43rd Annual report* (London: NAGL, 1933). Amongst other major anti-gambling works should be included Rose, *Gambling and Christian ideals*, and J. Bretherton, *Why gambling is wrong* (Manchester: Purpose Publications, 1936).

55 E. B. Perkins, *The problem of gambling* (London: Epworth Press, 1919), *Betting facts* (London: Wesleyan Methodist Church and SCM, 1925) and *Gambling and youth* (London: Sunday School Union, 1933).

56 Good examples of his work are John Gulland, *Gambling: the modern problem* (London: NAGL, 1932) and *Youth and gambling* (London: British Christian Endeavour Union, 1936).

57 See Peter Green, *Is gambling morally wrong?* (London: Friends Book Centre, 1926) and *Betting and gambling* (London: Student Christian Movement, 1924).

58 Mass Observation, *The pub and the people* (1987), p. 162.

59 1923 Select Committee, QQ6086–93 (Gillie).

60 1923 Select Committee, Q6709 (Welldon).

61 *Liverpool Echo*, 24.3.1938.

62 Green, *Betting and gambling*, p. 11.

63 'Coaching to Epsom', Central Press, 1922, in Michael Wynn Jones, *The Derby* (London: Croom Helm, 1979), p. 174. See also Jack Fairfax-Blakeborough, *The analysis of the turf* (London: Philip Allan, 1927), pp. 3–4.

64 See Kenneth O. Morgan, *Rebirth of a nation: Wales 1880–1989* (Oxford: Oxford University Press, 1982), p. 198.

65 1923 Select Committee Q5432–50.

66 Dixon, *prohibition to regulation*, p. 354.

67 1923 Select Committee, Q6280 (Gulliland).

68 1932 Royal Commission, Watson statement, p. 164.

69 1932 Royal Commission, Church of Scotland statement, p. 151; Christian Social Council statement p. 261; Gulland statement, pp. 185–7.

70 1923 Select Committee, Q5947 (Gillie).

71 1923 Select Committee, QQ6452, 6586 (Welldon).

72 Home Office Memorandum, 15.2.1923, quoted in Dixon, *From prohibition to regulation*, p. 191.

73 Blackwell memos and letters, quoted in Dixon, *From prohibition to regulation*, pp. 195–6.

74 Dixon, *From prohibition to regulation*, p. 189.

75 Quoted in Stephen Jones, *Workers at play: a social and economic history of leisure 1918–1939* (London: Routledge, 1986), p. 172.

76 *The Times*, 22.2.1929; *The Racing World and Newmarket Sportsman*, 5.7.1929.

77 See Stephen Jones, 'The British Labour movement and working class leisure 1918–1939', unpub. Ph.D., University of Manchester, 1983, pp. 208–25; Chinn, *Better betting*, pp. 190–1.

78 Callum Brown, *The decline of Christian Britain* (London: Routledge, 2000).

79 1933 Royal Commission, minutes of evidence, p. 171, QQ2537–8.

80 1933 Royal Commission, report para. 279.

81 Stevenson, *British society 1914–1945*, p. 370.

82 David Low, 'The Sporting life', *Evening Standard*, 21.1.1928.

83 The more theoretical work on gambling in American society before and after the Second World War, carried out by Goffman and Devereux, certainly seems to support such a view, and there are strong similarities with British society. See D. M. Downes, B. P. Davies, M. E. David and P. Stone, *Gambling, work and leisure: a study across three areas* (London: Routledge and Kegan Paul, 1976), p. 28.

5

Racing culture: the racecourse and racecourse life

While people could not avoid having views on racing only a minority actually attended race-meetings, and it is to the cultural and social life of the racegoing public that we now turn. The anticipatory thrill of travel was important, and a first section deals briefly with changes in travel over the period. A following more substantial section deals with social relationships, behaviour and attendance in relation to social class and gender. Changes and continuities in the comfort and facilities of the course, and in the ancillary activities such as sideshows, food and drink provision, tipsters or bookmakers are next explored, before the chapter concludes with an assessment of the 'moral panic' associated with the racecourse crime of the early 1920s.

Transport

Travel to the races was important to the racing experience. Changes in the dominant mode of transport, with their implications for conspicuous display, social interaction, and patterns of accommodation use in the racing towns, form a peripheral but important theme in the social history of racing. As a sport with its roots in rural horse-owning life, racing, and especially steeplechase and point-to-point meetings, still attracted rural dwellers travelling on horseback in the early 1920s, as entrance figures show, although motor enclosures were raising more than twice as much revenue by the later 1920s. Carriages became rare, although the larger four-in-hand coach was to be found occasionally at Epsom for the Derby, at Ascot, or at more prestigious point-to-points. Their continued appeal was partly sentimental. At Aintree in 1922 a colonel's coach party was seen as lending 'a picturesque touch to the traffic'.[1] Carriages were also excellent portable grandstands.

The railways still dominated travel to race meetings in 1914, but the delay and discomfort of the war years, and the artificially high rail fares of the post-war transition, saw the beginnings of their decline, although they continued to be central for core race attenders like the bookmakers, their assistants and others. They were a reliable source of income to rail companies, who often put on special trains between meetings. Race-day excursions were also potentially profitable. From York in the 1920s there were cheap race-day excursions to each of the most easily accessible northern courses. The top races attracted special trains from all over the country, supplementing usual services, although they could be slow, uncomfortable and overcrowded. In 1930, for example, Aintree had forty-three special trains on Grand National Day, including nine special trains from London, plus further trains from Manchester (four), Birmingham, Gloucester, Scotland and South Wales, Northumberland, East Anglia and the South. By 1935 it had over sixty long-distance specials. The journey, its fun and food were part of the experience, and catering on the £5 Pullmans was a major operation, with 2,500 lb. of fish alone.[2] At Doncaster, despite the growth of motor coach and car traffic, the railways alone still carried 100,000 to the St Leger meeting in 1929.[3] York's Ebor Stakes attracted 'specials' from Yorkshire, Lancashire, Cumbria, Newcastle and the North-east, Nottingham, Lincoln and Chesterfield, and Birmingham. Trains were still the main way racehorses got to meetings, although small trainers occasionally walked horses from training stables to meetings in the 1920s, as did others during the rail strikes. The London and North-Eastern Railway gained revenue through the provision of special trains, with two or three horseboxes per carriage, from Newmarket to and from all the major meetings, and was well known as being 'most obliging, patient and anxious to be of assistance'.[4]

The interwar rise in the status symbolism of car ownership, mostly but not entirely amongst the middle classes, saw major increases in petrol-driven traffic at meetings. Even by the mid-1920s the volume of traffic for the Derby had forced the police into using air balloons, patrol vehicles with wireless communication, motorcyclists, and traffic points linked by telephone. First the charabanc and then the coach became a mainstay of the more working-class attendance at more popular meetings, and a new form of racecourse revenue. Over two hundred buses were applying for parking facilities for the Epsom Derby in the early 1920s.[5] Although charges at some courses could be as low as 1s, York charged 2s 6d for cars and 6s for coaches for most of the period, and at Goodwood charges ranged from 2s to £1.[6] In the North of England working-men's clubs often organised race excursions, hiring a charabanc, and carrying cases of beer and sometimes parcels of food. Although statistical data are lacking, contemporary correspondents believed that road transport was growing. At York the local paper felt that in 1929 road traffic was 'of greater volume even than last year or any preceding year', and even in the depressed year of 1931 the volume was 'perhaps never greater'.[7] Some innovative trainers were using the motor horse van, based on the design of the railway box, to transport horses to meetings more comfortably and with less injury, by the early 1920s. These soon rapidly increased in numbers and popularity.[8]

For the even wealthier, Doncaster began planning a racecourse landing strip in 1928, since some owners possessed private planes, and a forty-two-seater aircraft carried racegoers paying £8 each from Croydon to Speke Airport near Aintree in 1930.[9] Air travel proved convenient for top jockeys and trainers, although the jockey Gordon Richards had a miraculous escape when an aeroplane taking trainers, jockeys and friends back to London from Doncaster in 1933 crashed, killing the pilot. In 1933 one trainer flew from Beckhampton to Chepstow, saddled the winner of the first race, and was at Lewes for the last race.[10] By 1935 there was a regular air service for the Newmarket meetings from London, and a landing ground was constructed at Goodwood in 1936. Even so, only five air taxis (from Heston, Bristol and Newcastle) landed at York municipal Aerodrome for the 1936 Ebor, while when less than a month later the Aga Khan's plane was one of some twenty planes arriving for Doncaster, it was his first flight.[11]

Social relationships, behaviour and attendance

While support for racing could be found at all levels of society, the nature of support varied with wealth, status and social class. The ardours and discomforts of the race-day journeys formed part of the occasion, and even before the races, the large crowds at a big meeting like Doncaster had plenty to entertain them, from the morning gallops or the tipsters in the marketplace, to the arrival of valuable horses at the railway station or the yearling sales. The crowds around town were also extremely peaceable. Indeed, so orderly were the crowds and traffic that owners had no hesitation in walking horses worth several thousand pounds through the main streets.[12]

The most visible form of racing support was actual attendance, and here the press constantly emphasised the socially-mixed nature of crowds. Racing functioned as a cross-class leisure activity, as *The Times* recognition of the way that at Ascot in 1925 'all sorts of people are happily behaving as if amusement were a legitimate human function' showed.[13] Many of the top races had 'a tremendous fascination for all classes of people', and were events where parties would come from nearby villages and towns, and noblemen would 'rub shoulders with workers enjoying the greatest sport of the Englishman'.[14]

The different social groups enjoyed the meeting in a complex mixture of similar and different ways. For the upper classes, horse-racing was a major element of sociability and leisure, exhibiting conspicuous consumption patterns, while allowing opportunities for exclusivity and the reinforcing of social superiority, more ambivalent social mixing, or for heavy, light or no gambling according to choice. Going to those elite races that were part of the London 'season' demonstrated display of wealth, while allowing sociability and the reinforcement of 'traditional' status and authority. The Royal Enclosure at Ascot, with entrance only by invitation, for example, was highly select. Even clothing signalled this, with the men in tailored dark suits, stiff-collared shirts and high top hats. Even more select was the Royal Box, a feature at other prestigious meetings. In the Enclosure one could see and be seen, and for favoured individuals the queen might sometimes send an equerry with a specially-worded invitation to join her. The Private Stand at Newmarket, where members of the Jockey Club had to sign and countersign guests, was also highly select.

The royal family stood at the apex of the upper class, sharing much of the landed aristocracy's tastes and lifestyle. King George V had a good knowledge of thoroughbred breeding and racing.[15] He enjoyed going to the races, especially at Newmarket, where he would stay at the Jockey Club rooms, and attended elite courses with the queen, prince of Wales, duke of York, Prince Henry and other members of the royal household. He regularly watched the Grand National, often from Lord Derby's private stand near the Canal Turn. With so many runners, members of the racing press sometimes 'accompanied the party to "read" the race'.[16] In 1921 the king also went to the Household Brigade Hunt Meeting to watch the prince of Wales riding. The latter registered his flat colours at the end of 1924, and his National Hunt colours in 1925. After George's death and Edward's abdication in 1936, George VI continued the Royal Stud and racing stable. In 1937 he and his wife attended Aintree as guests of Lord Derby, and also went to Epsom and to Ascot. In 1938 the king, queen, Queen Mary and the members of the royal family received a 'thunderous reception' at Epsom.[17]

The pageant, pomp and circumstance of royal arrival at the major meetings helped to confirm the established order. They strengthened the monarchy's cultural centrality through their effect on the crowd and on wider popular imagination through press and film portrayals. Such repackaging of regal splendour supports Cannadine's argument that there was a strong rearguard defence of hierarchy in the twentieth century.[18] Processions were public, colourful and glamorous. Royal arrival at Epsom was by train and open landau, or from the early 1920s, by motor car, but the royal procession at Ascot was an even more major occasion. For upper-class 'society' Ascot was the most fashionable meeting in the racing calendar. The metropolitan press, ever anxious to exploit and to be exploited by it, usually gave more column inches to it than to any other meeting except the Epsom Derby. To the public, the semi-state royal coach procession from Windsor which featured not just the dignified royal family but also postilions dressed in quaint costumes with jockey caps and grey-curled wigs, outriders in scarlet and gold uniforms and top hats, and equerries-in-waiting in sombre black, was an impressive, picturesque and popular feature of racing 'tradition', and a symbol of British pride, loyalty and national identity. The royal coach was continuously cheered as it drove up the course, suggesting that the ceremony helped to create a moral unity, an exercise bringing the classes temporarily together. When it was replaced for one day with a motor car procession in 1933 due to bad weather and royal ill-health it was not so well received. The support of royalty was important to racing and in turn the royal family received support from racing crowds. When at Epsom, for example, the royal standard was raised over the grandstand, one observer noted how one heard on all sides 'the King, the King' and occasionally some old man or woman would add, 'God bless him'.[19] When Princess Mary and Viscount Lascelles visited Stockton it aroused 'keen interest' and 'an unusually large proportion of the fair sex'.[20]

The aristocracy may have suffered some decline in constitutional terms, but their territorial influence was still strong in racing. Some regional meetings, such as Goodwood, Salisbury or York, performed similar functions for fashionable county society as Ascot performed for the monarchy. Such meetings could be easily identified. The descriptions of York's Ebor meeting, for example, often used the adjectives 'fashionable' or 'social' for the gathering, or likened it to Ascot, as in 'the Ascot of the north'. Lists of royal and aristocratic attenders made its status still clearer.[21] Some courses had 'County' stands. Local magnates, during the summer months, often attended meetings in areas where they owned estates. The marquis of Zetland attended York, Stockton and Redcar meetings near his Aske estate during August.

Race-meetings brought together the older aristocracy and the new members of the peerage, wealthy industrialists, cabinet ministers, the judiciary, military leaders, and bankers, helping to integrate old and new money and power. House parties were another long-standing tradition for the races, offering excitement, intrigue, betting and select sociability, alongside ostentatious display. While this was at its peak for Royal Ascot it could be found in the provinces too. Despite the growing impact of death duties, and reduced income, the Aintree meeting still attracted the north-western upper classes in large numbers. In 1930 Lord Derby stayed at Knowlsey, Lord Sefton at nearby Croxteth, while the duke and duchess of Westminster had forty guests at Eaton Hall, laying on lavish entertainment, and chartering a special train for the races.[22] There were similar houseparties for York and Doncaster. Select meetings also began creating boxes for the wealthy which could be hired or purchased. At Doncaster in 1933 Lord Derby had two boxes 'knocked into one' to accommodate his large party.[23]

The upper classes provided financial support for meetings. They were sometimes shareholders in the urban grandstand or racecourse companies, which paid dividends of up to 10 per cent, although free admission seems to have been as great an attraction. In the nineteenth century, when most courses were unenclosed, upper- and middle-class groups had provided subscriptions to the race meetings. By the interwar period this practice had died out on flat courses, which were almost all enclosed and reliant on entrance money through the turnstiles. The traditional pattern continued, however, in the smaller National Hunt courses, where elite patronage allowed status positioning within the county community. Race committees here were usually dominated by members of the aristocracy and gentry, masters of foxhounds, and military men.[24] Shareholders often expected no dividend, and the pleasures of ownership, spectatorship and expected deference were key motives. Subscriptions were usually collected locally. At Melton Hunt steeplechases, for example, there were separate collections for the General Fund, the Ladies' Purse and the Town Purse. Of the eighty-nine subscribers to the general fund in 1921 or 1922, giving an average of over £7 each, 24 per cent were titled and 37 per cent held military rank.[25] Many of the others are identifiable as publicans, lawyers, businessmen, industrialists and shopkeepers. Here, as elsewhere, local MPs often contributed.

Such strong middle-class support provides further evidence that significant sections of the middle classes enjoyed racing. Their role as attenders, as well as shareholders in courses and stud farms, organisers and managers of racing enterprises, racehorse owners and betters was common even in the nineteenth century.[26] Despite an appreciable loss of real earnings by some sectors of this class after the First World War, most experienced a more or less continuous rise in real incomes from 1923 to 1938, and spent more on leisure. The middle classes were leading figures in course management. In 1923, for example, a local colliery proprietor and wine merchant were respectively director and secretary of Haydock Park.[27] At Epsom, Edward Dorling, who became general manager in 1920, was a clergyman and former headmaster of the Cathedral School, Salisbury. He was made a member of the Royal Commission on Historical Monuments in 1928, and was a majority shareholder in a local printing business. Charles Langlands, the clerk of the course (and Chairman of the Epsom Grand Stand Association from 1926), was an experienced surveyor.[28]

Large numbers of the middle classes were spectators, especially at the more prestigious events like Royal Ascot or the most popular races like the Derby, and autobiographies of racing enthusiasts from middle-class backgrounds show this clearly. John Hislop, for example, whose father was a soldier in the Indian Army, first went to Sandown as a preparatory school pupil with middle-class adults, and was bowled over: 'The excitement of the racing and the thrill and romance of the scene made a lasting impression on me'.[29] Seaside race meetings too were potentially attractive to middle-class holiday makers. The expensively produced 'Come to Sussex' 324-page tourist guide of 1934, for example, thought it worth pointing out that 'Brighton is a great centre for racing and at the end of July and beginning of August there is the famous racing "Sussex fortnight" when meetings are held at Goodwood, Brighton and Lewes. Brighton Racecourse also has racing in June. Other courses within easy travelling distance are at Gatwick and Lingfield Park'.[30]

High-status races benefited larger local hotels with their middle-class clientele. For Aintree, for example, the big hotels in Liverpool like the Adelphi, the North-Western Hotel or the Exchange would be booked up months before. At select Southport, the Prince of Wales, Royal, Palace and Victoria Hotels would also attract visitors, while Chester, Manchester and Cheshire hotels would take 'disappointed race enthusiasts' who failed to book early enough. Houses and cottages near Aintree were rented for the week.[31] For towns with less prestigious courses, however, the increased use of motor cars limited hotel use by spectators, who arrived just before the races began and left immediately they were over. Revenue came almost entirely from trainers, jockeys and other racing insiders.

The working classes composed the largest group interested in racing and betting, although the Scottish and Welsh had less interest in racegoing than the English. Within Scotland, there were far more days' racing in the West, around Glasgow, than in the East. That said, however, there were many towns throughout Britain whose race meeting was a key regional holiday period. In West Yorkshire workers took the week of the Doncaster St Leger meeting as a holiday equivalent to the Wakes Weeks in Lancashire. Stockton and York's August Meetings, the Chester Cup, or Newcastle's 'Pitman's Derby' were all popular 'traditional' festivals, which often closed down local industries for the week.[32] Absenteeism was common in industries which refused to shut down, such as the pits of the North-east or Nottinghamshire. Even in York, where the National Anti-Gambling League was relatively strong, factories regularly closed down for the popular August Ebor Meeting, and in some York factories anyone who wished to attend a race meeting could obtain unpaid leave of absence. York's races attracted thousands of racegoers from both industrial and rural Yorkshire.[33]

One reason for racing's popularity was that its relative infrequency in any one area made it affordable. Many people only went to their local meetings. In the Lancashire/Cheshire/Derbyshire region there were only about thirty days of racing annually, of which Liverpool had ten and Manchester nine days. Horse-racing was most popular in Greater London, which by 1938 sustained sixty-five days of flat racing a year, spread out over courses at Alexandra Park, Ascot, Gatwick, Hurst Park, Kempton Park, Lingfield, Sandown Park, Windsor and Epsom. Yorkshire sustained fifty days' racing spread over eight racecourses. In both Yorkshire and the South no single course had more than eight days' racing annually, partly due to Jockey Club restrictions, but also because few working men could afford to go racing more regularly, so further meetings would not have generated sufficient profit. While cinema-going became a weekly event, going to the races was still a special occasion.

In part this was because of the higher costs of admission, although not all courses were fully enclosed. Free areas could still be found at a few long-established high-status flat courses like Epsom or Newmarket in 1939. At Epsom too there was always Derby Sunday, when London working people, dressed up in their best clothes, took a day out to picnic on the Downs and join in the pre-week fun.[34] A similar event took place at Aintree. Courses increasingly became fully enclosed during this period. In 1935, for example, the *Sporting Chronicle* announced that 'Beverley racecourse has now been fully enclosed and a charge of one shilling was made for admission to the famous Westwood side that used to be free'.[35] Even a shilling was by no means cheap, and the more select the enclosure or meeting the higher the price. At the Ebor meeting prices remained steady for most of the period, from 25*s* for men (ladies only 17*s*) through £1 (ladies 12*s*) for enclosure and paddock, to covered stands at 6*s* and open enclosure 3*s* a day.[36] At Goodwood in 1937 the Tattersalls enclosure cost £2 a day. At National Hunt meetings the paddock and stand charges averaged around thirteen shillings, and ranged from around 18s to 10s at smaller courses like Wenlock. Most had a larger enclosure holding the bulk of paying spectators at about 2s each.

Racing attracted spectators of all social classes and ages despite its somewhat ambiguous moral status. Its equivocal nature allowed freedom from the constraints of respectability. Roles and personalities could be invented, assumed and experimented with, away from the expectations of neighbours or work. Racing maintained its own subcultural features. Codes of behaviour, etiquette, rituals and language were held partly in common, and were partly more specific to the area of the course they inhabited, but all in an atmosphere of solidarity, sociability and generally relaxed goodwill. Courses attracted higher numbers of women than most other sports and codes of dress and language were in part specific to the stewards' stand, grandstands, paddock or popular areas, showing little difference from those described in Kate Fox's recent anthropological analysis.[37] In members' enclosures there were often more women than men. Each male Club member was entitled to two ladies' badges and these were usually used. The racecourses were a liminal locus for sociality, dressing up in one's best clothes, drinking, betting, some gambling, a temporary relaxation of social inhibitions, and a high level of goodwill and social interaction.

Jeff Hill's work on the FA Cup Finals as festival is a reminder that the races too were far more than a betting outing.[38] The rituals of going to and watching the entertainment were equally important. The collective fun and excitement of the occasion also mattered. Owners had the pleasure of going to the paddock, meeting the trainer and jockey, and the anticipation of the race. The Aga Khan 'bubbled with excitement' as his horse Bahram went to the post for the Derby of 1935 and his biographer felt that he had 'never seen the Aga Khan happier than he was that day' when Bahram won.[39]

Kate Fox has also stressed strongly the 'unusual sociability' of the modern racing micro-climate, with amicable exchanges between strangers, a friendly, tolerant, welcoming spirit, and an absence of aggression even from drunks. The same was true of the interwar period, where the 'friendliness of the whole scene' was commonly stressed.[40] Racing had a carnival and festival spirit. Conventional behavioural norms were loosened. Even The *Times* golfing correspondent, Bernard Darwin, claiming to be 'entirely uninterested' in racing, accepted that 'he who has not been to the Derby ... has to confess that he has not fully lived' and that its 'spectacle of colour and movement' made up 'a composite attraction'.[41] People went to the races for a day out, to meet friends, to eat, drink and enjoy themselves. Racing was a site of pleasure and irrationality, characterised by a rose-tinted positive approach. In terms of social dynamics, reports make few distinctions of class, although motives for going to races were probably mixed. People across the social scale remarked positively upon attitudes and behaviour. The Aga Khan, for example, claimed that the crowd was 'amazingly orderly, and as far as the regular racegoers are concerned, honest and temperate. It is rare indeed to see a drunken man'.[42] The American Edward Newton described the 'good-natured and laughing crowd at Epsom'.[43] Most regular racegoers had a genuine interest in and love for racing, and would visit both major meetings and meetings at local courses. Some just loved watching the horses. Others would study the horses in the parade ring, look for the best odds with the bookmakers, watch the race in the stand, and see the winner into the winner's enclosure. Turfites could be seen as 'one big family', by the interwar years able to have a 'flutter of interest in results at races elsewhere' even at their local meeting.[44]

Many went to reinforce or establish social bonds, enjoying the social interaction rather than watching the horses or even the races themselves. Racing was a place for meeting potential partners, or for taking potential partners, providing sufficient distraction in its action but with plenty of room for chatting, flirting or seduction. At courses with open areas, or cheap silver rings, family groups were always well in evidence. At point-to-points, where there was no admission charge, although a charge for parking or racecards was made, attendances rose rapidly in the 1930s, aided by its grass-roots connections and an increase in the quality of racing, horses and riders. Its fun character attracted rural workers and their families in droves. Farmers were hospitably entertained by the hunt. The 'county set' went. So did artisans and tradesmen whose children had joined the pony club, while middle-class owners also participated.

Racing, like other sports, contributed to the social construction of local, regional and national loyalties. The distinctive regional differentiation in England was between North and South, a friendly rivalry encouraged particularly by the northern England press, who would boast when 'the north had a satisfactory share of the victories'.[45] Northerners often claimed too that the North was friendlier. The trainer John McGuigan, for example, argued that there was 'an intimate atmosphere about the North-country courses which seems to be lacking in the bigger meetings of the south'.[46] Locally-owned or trained winners were always popular amongst the punters. But so were royal successes. When the king's horse won a Maiden Plate at Beverley it got a thrilling and tremendous reception, with loud cheering and shouts of 'hats off for the King'.[47]

After 1919 societal changes in gender attitudes meant a growing acceptance of women's involvement in racing, as spectators, betters and owners. This was strongly reflected in the press, always anxious to improve circulation, which increasingly foregrounded women's attendance at meetings. Part of this was related to the assumed interest by women readers in current fashions and hence in women racegoers' clothing. Fashion features appeared during major meetings, some written by writers with upper-class-sounding pseudonyms like Marianne Mayfayre, who announced that at Ascot in 1933 'women racegoers cling to their furs'.[48]

Male anxieties and concerns about women at the races still surfaced in interwar cartoons, which provided an impressive, highly compressed, visual and verbal narrative of women's attendance, using experiences either directly familiar to audiences, or linked to their lives, in comic form. Women's ignorance (and infuriating luck) was a common theme. One cartoon, for example, showed a young girl getting her uncle to back a horse because of its colour, and then, having won, boasting that racing was 'fun, and dead easy', while a background crowd of racing experts 'fail to pick a winner'.[49] A second theme was the manipulative way women might get men to place their bet to avoid paying for losing bets. One example showed women pressuring a passive man to find a 'nice little winner' at a long price for them, and then complaining to him when their horse lost, 'It's robbery!' and 'It's lucky I didn't give you my sovereign that you've lost'.[50]

Traditional expectations held that women should know little about racing and horses so that their more informed menfolk would place bets on their behalf. Pre-1914, few self-respecting women entered betting enclosures, with their noise, pushing and commotion. But after the war some women began accompanying their escorts, and in 1925 the *Daily Sketch* thought it sufficiently noteworthy to provide a large 'shock-horror' headline on the day of the Epsom Oaks, traditionally also Ladies' Day, 'Unescorted Women among the Bookmakers'.[51] On the evidence of cartoons some women were now placing their own bets. An *Evening News* cartoon shows a woman in the betting ring telling a meek man, 'I'm afraid that's the housekeeping money gone Henry, but thank goodness you're quite fond of rissoles'.[52] Cartoons that accepted women's increasing knowledge of the sport also began to surface. One *Daily Mirror* cartoon portrayed 'the modern girl' at the Derby, who was not 'having any' of the passivity of the past but drove herself down 'in her two-seater', inspected the horses, talked to jockeys, bet with the bookies and got home again 'just in time to go out again to celebrate her winnings'.[53]

Racing was more popular between the wars than previously, peaking in the early 1920s and then declining significantly before rising again in the later 1930s. Yet there were many local fluctuations, due perhaps to economic vicissitudes, attendance or non-attendance by famous jockeys, the impact of dog races or vagaries of the weather. Bad weather always affected racing. In any one year between ten and twenty days' flat and National Hunt racing might actually be abandoned due to the weather, although it could be insured against, and bad weather always deterred the casual spectator. National Hunt races could be abandoned because of frost. Heavy rain usually caused cancellation, postponement or low attendances. The huge thunderstorm on the second day of the 1930 Ascot meeting led to the death of a bookmaker, killed by lightning, and less serious consequences included ruined clothing, bogged-down cars and the abandonment of five of the seven races. The Epsom Derby of 1935, in a year of better attendance nationally, had receipts which were £5,000 down on the previous year because the morning's heavy rain had 'a substantial effect'.[54]

The increased popularity of racegoing from 1919 onwards was not confined to the heartlands of racing, such as London, Yorkshire and Lancashire, but was more general. And some of this greater popularity was retained even in the difficult times that followed. Even in County Durham, an unemployment blackspot, though the number of employed mineworkers was shrinking, and attendances dropped in 1929 and 1930, most mining towns and villages still sent large numbers by train or charabanc to their regional meetings at major holidays like Whitsuntide. Such trips were saved up for in what were called 'pleasure party funds', and money saved was sometimes blown over the course of a single day.

Traditional racing towns valued their race meetings highly. They brought income. Chester Chamber of Trade estimated that the three-day meeting there was normally worth £70,000 in revenue to the town in the late 1930s.[55] Taking passengers between the station, hotels and course represented a good business opportunity for cab drivers, although at Newmarket, as elsewhere, there were complaints that fares coming back from the course during rain were 'pure robbery'.[56]

Attendances were highest at flat-racing meetings. Attendances from 1919 onwards were larger than in previous years at almost all of the urban enclosed courses which provided attendance figures. This was thanks to a rise of 11 per cent in average real wages between 1913 and 1920, and crowds who had been starved of racing for almost five years making it more of a family day out.[57] The peak years were 1920 and 1921. At Redcar Races, for example, the local paper in 1920 reported 'Redcar's Great Day, all previous records likely to be eclipsed'.[58] The same year Epsom had really 'stupendous' attendance, and at Ascot all records were broken. At both meetings the press reported the cosmopolitan and complex class, age and gender mix of the crowds, with many languages spoken in addition to English, turbaned cavalry officers from India, Australian soldiers, notable officers of army and navy like Lord Haig, the Church, the West End and East End rubbing shoulders, and 'top hats and bowler hats and straw hats and plush hats and thousands of men without hats', 'ladies in silks and satins', and 'old men and maidens'.[59]

Following a short period of post-war prosperity, however, industrial profits and average real earnings fell, and by 1922 crowds were fewer in the North of England, although still above pre-war levels. The largest national attendances for flat racing were at Epsom and Doncaster. Estimates of over half a million in the Derby crowd were fairly common, and at Doncaster crowds were usually around 200,000.[60] Large crowds also attended Aintree, where estimated numbers by the 1930s were between 200,000 and 300,000.[61] The Grand National increasingly appealed to American spectators, and by the 1920s it was becoming an event on the international tourist circuit. In 1925 the lure of the race attracted a New York man who said, 'last year my wife and I went to the Riviera but this year [we] mean to see the Grand National'.[62] In 1930 about two hundred Americans from New York, Boston, Washington and Chicago arrived in a single White Star liner to see the race while other liners brought spectators including Fred Astaire. A Canadian Pacific liner delayed sailing until well after the race to wait for passengers.[63]

Chester's single annual meeting provides a useful illustration of declining attendance at a more traditional course. The highest pre-1914 attendance had been 73,345 in 1907 but in 1919 and 1920 the interwar figures peaked at 137,763 and 150,497. In 1921 there was no meeting due to a national coal strike, supported by transport workers, and crowds thereafter declined. Total three-day attendances averaged round the 100,000 mark from 1923 to 1932, around 40% higher than pre-war levels. The highest attendance in the 1930s was 115,639 in 1936.[64]

At Leicester, a more modern but minor course putting on both flat and steeplechase events, a more fluctuating pattern was evident, although in 1928 and 1929 the balance sheet claimed that 'in consequence of trade depression, the serious effects of the betting tax, and inclement weather the attendance at meetings was much reduced'. Although some dividend was still paid there were losses on the revenue account in the years around 1930, before attendance revenue increased again later in the decade.[65]

Attendances rose slightly in the 1930s at some courses, in part probably linked to the national rise in real wages.[66] Brighton's receipts on the first day of its spring meeting in 1935 were £320 more than the previous year, although here facilities had also improved.[67] Even in the depressed North-east attendances began rising again in 1935/6. Redcar attracted large numbers of Durham miners, and attendances at its Whit Meeting in 1936 were the 'greatest' since 1929.[68] The rise in 1937/8 was most noticeable at National Hunt courses, with The *Times* correspondent claiming that 'it is many years since so much active interest has been taken in the sport'.[69] A good example was the Melton Hunt steeplechases, which had taken £1,713 gate money in 1920, but subsequently fell fairly consistently to a nadir of £623 in 1936 before 1938 saw its highest ever interwar profit.[70] Attendances at National Hunt courses are difficult to assess, given their part-free nature. Melton had a crowd calculated at 11,450 that year, but only 1,450 paid to enter the paddock/main stand or the cheaper stand rather than just the free course.[71] Tote figures based on those who actually paid are distorting, but show National Hunt paying crowds in 1939 averaging around five thousand, with as many as eight to ten thousand at Torquay, the Shirley and Quorn Hunt meetings, and less than two thousand at Melton or Wenlock.

To an extent, however, crowd numbers were depressed by the unwillingness (and financial inability) of many course executives to modernise. The sport was not run on sound financial principles. Stakes never covered the costs of racing for owners since prize money was only about a third of the cost of maintaining a horse in training, the betting industry made no real contribution to racing, and there was little or no investment in improved facilities. The amenities for the paying spectator were inadequate at some racecourses, and a few were primitive until improvements stimulated by Tote revenue between 1936 and 1938.[72] Even then most courses still had shabby facilities and were in a state of general disrepair, as the Ilchester Committee, set up in 1943, would later reveal. As McKibbin succinctly points out, 'lower stakes and low investment made race-going uncompetitive'.[73]

Facilities, comfort and ancillary entertainments

Despite being used only rarely for racing, courses were large and expensive to develop and maintain. Rent, rates, taxes and insurance, repairs, upkeep, improvements and additions were always by far the largest major expenditure items on balance sheets. After 1907 all flat-racing courses were inspected by a racecourse inspector appointed by the Jockey Club, while from 1910 the NHC had three regional course inspectors to examine the obstacles and course conditions. Rising running costs forced course managements to prioritise their spending and this focused on owners, trainers and horses, not the casual spectator. Between the wars there was growing press concern about poorer accommodation for the general public than for racing insiders. Most informed commentators believed that the Jockey Club and racecourse companies cared little for spectators. The standard of public accommodation and comfort was far worse than in most other countries.[74]

The wealthier and highest-paying spectators got the bulk of facilities. Ascot, which was the most elite meeting of all, reflected this even in its annual redecoration. Its only three floral focal points were the Royal Box with its array of hydrangeas, the rhododendrons in the Royal Enclosure, and the rambler rose beds. Its Club tents were also decorated with masses of flowers and shrubs, like the tents at the Chelsea Flower Show. Elsewhere red and white paint was annually renewed on posts and fittings.

Any new building was most likely to be new grandstands or dining facilities for the elite. The new Epsom Grand Stand, which cost £250,000, had three sections, including the East Stand and the Club Stand, which housed the Royal Suite.[75] York was always well decorated. For its elite customers it extended the grandstand to make a 240-seater luncheon room in 1925, and erected a champagne tent beside the unsaddling enclosure.[76] The 1930s began to see more improvements. Kempton's new £100,000 members' stand was built only because fire destroyed the previous one, but Lingfield got a new grandstand in 1933. In 1934/5 Brighton got a new judge's box and stand improvements, including an imposing members' stand, built on the cantilever principle, with an uninterrupted view of the racing.[77] When northern attendances increased, Beverley got an additional meeting in 1938 and a new grandstand in 1939.[78]

Most park courses perpetuated the club membership system under which only better-off males joined, getting admission to the members' stand and free admission for two female guests. When in January 1935 Lingfield Park challenged tradition and took the startling step of allowing ladies to be members in their own right there were headlines in the press.[79] Members' fees varied with the status of meetings, highest at elite courses like Sandown, much lower at Hurst Park.

At Newmarket, two new stands were built in 1925 and 1935, but facilities were generally still poor in the 1930, and sight lines were poor too. Only half the Cesarewitch course, for example, could be seen from the stands. The most expensive development was the reconstruction of the Jockey Club premises in Newmarket itself. Many courses became increasingly out of date in terms of their accommodation for spectators. The cost of going racing was out of all proportion to the amenities provided, and high in comparison with leisure competitors such as the cinema, greyhound racing or the seaside holiday.

By the end of the 1920s most major courses had built stabling and accommodation for stable lads. Gatwick was offering free stabling as an extra inducement for travelling entries in 1921. At Doncaster, most of the extensive improvements, additions and extensions between 1913 and 1939 were for the benefit of jockeys, trainers, owners and officials, although the catering for the general public was also improved. When Thirsk racecourse was rebuilt in 1924 it supposedly offered the most up-to-date stands and appurtenances. But in fact Thirsk's facilities for ordinary race-goers were relatively basic. Although a portion of the grandstand was railed off for ladies, the ordinary roofless stand had twenty-six cemented steps, and part of Tattersalls' sloping enclosure was cemented, and the remainder newly turfed. Far more attention was paid to comfort of its racing insiders, and the facilities for owners, trainers, press and telegraphists were described as 'excellent'.[80] Thirsk had fifty new horseboxes, with saddlery, forage store, drying room and caretakers' quarters.

The difficulties of raising revenue with so few meetings meant flat race-meetings were reluctant to invest in facilities, and most steeplechase courses spent even less. It was pony racing, and Northolt Park course in particular, which led racing innovation. Its stands, cloakrooms, restaurants, bars and track facilities were the best-appointed in Britain, and all enclosures could see the entire course, a rarity in British racing.[81] It was the first British course to introduce floodlighting, in 1934, and the first to have photo-electric timing. It was also the first, in April 1936, to have loud-peaker commentary on each race in full detail provided by an expert race reader in all its enclosures, a facility which increased the enjoyment of the crowd, and something not provided on Jockey Club courses until 1952.[82]

Ordinary race-goers were there to enjoy themselves. There were core racing regulars whose function was to supply them with a variety of further facilities and entertainment, and who provided a large measure of continuity over time. In 1919, for example, the ancillary activities at the more open courses showed little change from 1914, and *The Times*, reporting 'Unchanged Epsom', noted that the same sideshows had returned.[83] Jellied eels, ice-cream, fish and chips or ham sandwiches, roundabouts and swings, acrobats and fortune tellers, bookmakers and backers, and occasional anti-gambling preachers could all be found there. Even at the small Cartmel course there was a fair, where dolls, coconuts, shooting galleries and other stalls paid 10s each to the race fund, while refreshments paid by frontage length, and donkeys were charged a shilling.[84] Most courses had a wide variety of entertainment. There was music in bandstands; indeed Ascot had three military bands in the 1930s. Refreshments and luncheons were popular. At Ascot the royal luncheon party was the highlight for guests in the Royal Enclosure, and many grandstands increasingly had dining facilities attached or nearby. For the less well-heeled, large numbers of booths and tents provided eating and drinking facilities, and alcohol provided a key socially-bonding lubricant for many through the day, although there was little or no evidence of prosecutions for drunkenness, suggesting that it was tolerated, or that little misbehaviour generally resulted. All descriptions of race meetings stressed the amount of time spent in booths, which also provided a refuge during inclement weather. Racing was a major context for convivial enjoyment of the social pleasures of ludism, laughter and liquor.

Stalls staff were often 'characters', well recognised by racing regulars. Women played an important role, although often within well-defined male limits. The journalist Clive Graham noted the death of 'Polly, the matronly figure with the fat chuckle and mass of red hair who used to preside behind the champagne bar at so many race meetings', commenting 'wonderful figures these racecourse barmaids'.[85] The sale of race cards was another significant item of revenue for most meetings, and the race-card sellers, again sometimes women, were also well known. A 1929 subscription list for 'Old Kate', born in the Stratford workhouse, who exchanged greetings with her many regulars at major meetings, was promoted by *Sporting Life* and headed by the king.[86]

Placing a bet was part of the fun of racing. Bookmakers' odds varied sufficiently to make it worthwhile looking for the best odds before placing a bet. After 1928 the Tote provided an alternative. It paid out better odds on longer-priced winners, and was also an attraction to those women racegoers who disliked the crowded betting rings. Most spectators saw on-course bookmakers as part of the carnival character of racing. All racecourses had special betting rings, with smaller, less-capitalised bookmaking firms taking smaller bets in the cheaper enclosures and on any free part of the course. Bookmakers employed their own racing slang, and firms shifted from enclosure to enclosure depending on their betting fortunes. Betting could be a battle of wits, and laying odds to best advantage required good knowledge of mathematics. Tic-tac men signalled information to their principals in a picturesque and mysterious manner, helping to lay off heavy bets and even up the betting, as well as relaying phone bets from the starting-price offices in London and elsewhere.

The national 'starting price' of each horse in a race was dependent on the final odds course bookmakers offered, so where off-course bookmakers had taken large amounts against particular horses they tried to reduce their liabilities by betting on the course itself over the telephone (aka the 'blower') through agencies who backed or laid horses on their behalf. The main two firms were the Victoria Blower, and the larger London and Provincial Sporting News Agency, founded by bookmaker F. Trueman and A. L. Forster, a racing journalist in London in 1921. Both also supplied continuous racing and betting information by phone from the racecourse to subscribing bookmakers throughout Britain. By 1929 the London & Provincial had become a limited company, and was being regularly used to 'lay off' money on the course and so shorten starting prices. It was chaired by Brigadier-General Kennedy, had branch offices all over the country, and provided private betting information to subscribers at 2 guineas a week.

Contemporary commentators believed that between the wars the number of course bookmakers was rising, and that the actual amount bet was growing, but in smaller individual amounts. So top bookmakers may have been less able to accumulate the wealth of the pre-war years. Even so, one of the major course bookmakers of the interwar period, Jack Burns, had 'amassed a fortune reputed to be on the £250,000 mark' between 1918 and 1937.[87] The top female bookmaker, Helen Vernet, a Ladbroke's representative from 1928, was socially well-connected, earning c.£20,000 a year, but had an expensive lifestyle and died comparatively poor, leaving an estate of under £8,000.[88] Most Ladbroke's representatives were ex-public school, sometimes ex-officers, with fathers who came from middle-class professions.[89] Certainly even in the early 1920s some bookmakers could afford cars and drove from course to course.[90] Most of the roughly five hundred on-course bookmakers were members of firms, which also employed clerks, whose wages, usually paid by the day, were estimated as from £10 to £20 a week during the summer months.[91] Bookmakers had to meet heavy charges. After the Racecourse Betting Act was introduced, executives could charge them anything up to five times the ordinary price of admission. Total costs, including clerk, runner and transport, could amount to about £25 a day.[92]

Most bookmakers were honest in their dealings, although insufficient money might come in to cover losses if a succession of favourites and second favourites won. At one such Derby meeting, a small bookmaker came with £230 on the first day and closed his book on the third day with only 3s 6d left.[93] The profession still had a reputation for welshing, largely ill-deserved, although there were some, usually beginners, who tried to avoid paying out on winning bets, and a few who did it more regularly. Most of these were probably on the open part of the course. Some claimed that numbers were growing because welshing was facilitated by the speed and startability of the small car.[94] It was certainly true that where welshers were prosecuted they rarely came from the locality, although few travelled as far as the welshing bookmaker at East Essex point-to-point races who gave a Glasgow address.[95]

For those spectators who knew little about horses, and wanted guidance, itinerant course tipsters provided colourful if often highly unreliable facilities. These apparently inspired prophets of the racing world sold their 'horse sense' predictions for future races to the gullible and naive at prices usually ranging from 6d to 2s 6d. They were tolerated by racing insiders as doing no harm to the game, contributing to the carnival atmosphere since to make money it was vital to attract attention. Some were course characters. Some were knowledgeable about horses. Most only pretended such knowledge, and resorted to a variety of strategies to imply their expertise. Some posed as ex-jockeys or stable lads. At Redcar races in 1922 several tipster pitches even had 'another man in the multi-coloured garb of a jockey to help in the operations and give a palpable touch of veracity'.[96]

Racing provided employment opportunities for ethnic minorities often marginalised in wider society. In the East End of London, many leading bookmakers were Jewish. Most were well regarded, though some, like the East End Jewish and Italian gang members involved in the turf wars of the early 1920s discussed later, existed on at least the fringes of criminality. A number of tipsters were black, like 'Ras Prince Monolulu', self-described as 'The Prince of Tipsters', whose instantly recognisable appearance in feathered headdress, colourful costume and waistcoat, and shout of 'I've got an 'orse', was a familiar sight to thousands of racegoers, especially at major courses like Epsom, Ascot and Doncaster.[97] They were more noticed because they stood out. The *Liverpool Post*'s reporter describing the arrival of the 'Bookie's Special and its Load' for Aintree noted the 'towering African in gaudy robes carrying a baby nearly as white as the young Englishwoman at his side'.[98]

Gypsies had followed the racing crowds at the big meetings for at least a century, and press coverage of the Epsom Derby usually made reference to them. It was one of their traditional meeting places, with parking on the Downs, and opportunity to make money from palmistry and other activities. With the advent of motor traffic a few found a new source of income, extorting sums of money for parking, but generally most behaved well. Although prejudice ensured that they were perceived as a problem, the Epsom executive even offered caravan-dwellers awards each year in an effort to encourage good behaviour and tidiness. But the introduction of an Epsom and Walton Downs Regulation Act in the mid-1930s allowed the formulation of bye-laws to control the conservation area. Licences had to be obtained to erect caravans or tents and caravans were banned during Derby Week. Initially this was difficult to police and had little effect. In 1938 seventy-three-caravan dwellers sent a solicitor's letter offering to pay £1 each for the privilege, and gypsies were still very much in evidence on the course.[99]

Racecourse crime

Reformist, respectable morality was also challenged by the more overtly criminal element attracted by the large crowds and the liminality of the course. Petty crime was to be found almost everywhere. During the interwar period pickpockets, three-card tricksters and other con-men gangs, like the welshers, found the racecourse a useful source of revenue. Such activities, though well known to regular patrons, attracted a large crowd, some naive and some more maliciously enjoying seeing people rooked. At York in 1925 a 26-year-old Castleford miner running the three-card trick attracted a crowd of thirty or forty people, placing bets of between £1 and £5. Such men were often highly skilled. Another trickster arrested at the same meeting was indignant, explaining and demonstrating to the magistrate that he was so clever in the manipulation of the cards that he 'had no need to cheat'. He was fined £5 anyway.[100] Some pickpockets, like the Aldgate gang, operated in larger groups and used techniques like 'steaming' where they rushed in and knocked people.[101] Crowds aided criminality. Passing forged notes, especially large-denomination ones, was easier at the races.[102]

It was hard to catch such criminals in the act so police usually dealt with them by arresting them as 'a suspected person'. Most major meetings had large numbers of police. Ascot, for example, had five hundred Metropolitan police and extra CID men in 1933. They were supported by travelling urban detectives with specialist knowledge of names and faces of local villains. At most courses the vast majority of those arrested were aged between the mid-twenties and mid-forties, possibly because they had been in the occupation long enough to be easily recognised. Most were not local, or even racing men, but mobile urban criminals who also frequented fairs and other crowded venues. Pickpockets arrested in York in 1936 included a 70-year-old from Harrogate, six Londoners with an average age of 31, and two others from Salford and Manchester. Four Manchester men aged between 26 and 37 were arrested for running American Take a Pick, a game of chance using straws with numbers and a board displaying winning ones.[103]

When attendance at fixtures boomed after 1918, there was a concomitant rise in racing crime. As early as January 1920 *The Times* was complaining that 'the racing world has become obsessed with pests of all kinds - blackguards, imposters, thieves and welshers - who carry out their nefarious operations in the race trains, in race towns, at the races, on the streets, in London and provincial offices'.[104] This was a blanket, unfocused condemnation, in which racing was to blame for almost all crime, everywhere.

Much of this criminality was a minor part of course culture. It had little impact on the atmosphere, fun and attraction of the races for the public at large. This applied particularly to the activities of the so-called 'race gangs' which received much publicity in the London press.

The races were one of several locations for what were internecine gang wars, as protection gangs tried to raise money from bookmakers by a number of different rackets, leading to moral panic across the country with regular headlines on 'Racecourse Ruffianism'.[105] This theme was to create huge adverse publicity for racing, a publicity that in a period of fluctuating economic fortunes, it could ill afford.

Such reports hugely exaggerated criminality. In fact, despite or because of a large police presence, numbers of prosecutions were usually low even at major meetings with large crowds. This may have been partly due to tolerant policing, but good behaviour was also part of racing culture. Except where inter-gang disputes were involved there were almost no prosecutions for drunkenness, affray or similar violent offences at meetings throughout the period. Crowds were generally peaceable and friendly, as press reports were prepared to admit. In 1921, just eighteen months after earlier alarmist complaints, *The Times* reported that at Epsom all the police did was keep people off the course: 'There was nothing else for them to do on the course for a better behaved crowd cannot be imagined'.[106] Yet it still maintained headlines about violent racecourse ruffianism. At most well-policed meetings gang problems were either non-existent or unpublicised. Rather than praise racing, however, the police generally claimed the credit. According to York's chief constable, for example, York had never had any trouble from the race gangs, because it was well policed by the local force supplemented with a staff of detectives from most of the important towns, as well as many extra police from the region.[107]

The intimidation of bookmakers and their agents by race gangs, taking over the best pitches and then letting them or demanding 'protection', was common even pre-1914. Such techniques included preventing recalcitrant payers from attracting business, bogus subscription-list collections, claiming non-existent winning bets, selling bookies a race-card marked with dots and dashes to show form, or renting them the 'tools of the trade' like stools, chalk and water for their blackboards which they already had. Such business was profitable. A gang could clear £4,000 plus at Brighton, over £15,000 on Derby Day.[108]

By the end of the First World War some gatemen, ring officials and staff managers had been involved in the corrupt selling of bookmaker pitches, or admitting gang members free. After the war struggles to dominate bookmaker pitches on and off the racecourse became part of a far broader pattern of criminality, protection rackets, hardness and local and regional status. There were gangs based in Glasgow, Leeds, Mexborough, Cardiff and Newcastle with more than local reputations and the problems were nation-wide, but it was the problems on courses round London which received major coverage. These were widely reported elsewhere, creating a national sense of moral panic and a negative image of racing. Demanding money with menaces at courses round London was a feature of a number of prosecutions from 1919 to 1923.

Like reports of more recent football hooliganism, some of the reported violence linked to racing was a product of simplistic analysis. First, and importantly, much of it took place away from the racecourse, but press coverage almost always linked the trouble to racing. Partly this seems to have been because many gang members had large sums of money on them when arrested because of their criminal rackets, and usually gave their occupation as 'bookmaker' or 'professional backer' because it provided a ready explanation of the money.

Between 1919 and about 1923 much of the publicity related to the turf war between the Birmingham (or Brummagen) Boys and the London-based Sabini gang.[109] The 'Brummagem Boys' operated the Midlands race circuit, and although styled 'boys', few were young. The leaders of the Birmingham gang, Kimber and Townie, were effective organisers, intelligent hard men who gained a measure of respect from at least some policemen, although many of the gang were far more violent and not always controllable. Some came not from Birmingham, but London. They established control over a number of course betting areas, charged a half-profits fee, and for a while extended their activities to some northern and southern tracks.

After the war some southern tracks were controlled by various gangs based at Hoxton, Camden Town, and a mainly Jewish 'Aldgate Mob'. By 1920, the Sabini 'Boys', a gang whose origins lay in the Italian and Jewish communities in the Saffron Hill area of London, became leading figures in racecourse protection, pushing back 'Brummagen' power. Levels of violence between the gangs soon escalated, driven by status and territorial rivalries, and using a variety of weapons, from razors and spanners to guns. Birmingham incursions into London were seen as an affront. In March 1921 the Sabini's leader, Darby Sabini, was attacked at a Greenford trotting fixture by some Birmingham men, and defended himself by brandishing a revolver. At attempt by Kimber to calm things down by visiting Darby a few days later went wrong, and he was shot and wounded. In April 1921 at Alexandra Park a 42-year-old Birmingham man was chased by several of the rival gang and shot one of them. A few weeks later, Birmingham gang members badly beat up East End Jews taking bets in the silver ring at Bath. As rivalry escalated there were increased levels of violence, more shootings, and more individuals involved, while press coverage spread. The West Hartlepool press reported in June 1921 that a Bethnal Green 'bookmaker', with eighteen previous convictions, was arrested at Epsom for carrying a revolver, and linked it to 'the feud between London and Birmingham bookmakers'.[110] About the same time Birmingham men who had attacked a charabanc of Leeds bookmakers (in the mistaken belief that they were the London gang on the way back from Epsom) were charged with committing serious injury and carrying firearms. Between fifty and seventy Birmingham men were involved in the gang. By July the north-eastern press was reporting any southern violence that could be linked to racing, 'Racing Disturbances' in Salisbury streets by Londoners after the races, or 'Racecourse Ruffianism' at Sandown Park when a 53-year-old Whitechapel commission agent, Philip Jacobs, was battered with a hammer and later died.[111]

A Bookmakers and Backers Racecourse Protection Association (BPA), was formed in August 1921 in London and initially dominated by southern course bookmakers. Its members were later seen as 'men of integrity and fair dealing' by the senior Jockey Club supervisor of racecourse detectives.[112] The BPA saw the Birmingham gangs as the major problem and employed toughs as 'stewards' in response. Initially Darby Sabini and leading members of the Jewish underworld were among them, but by May 1922 they were sacked. Through 1922 a vicious battle for territorial supremacy was fought at courses, car parks, pubs, clubs and railway stations, with the police often onlookers, since assaulted gang members often 'forgot' details, and intimidated witnesses would not then give evidence. Course bookmakers at this time had to be able to stand up for themselves or employ tough minders, and leading members of the BPA, such as the president, Mr Yeadon, were attacked. While the BPA's membership grew, to the police the BPA 'steward' protectors, often with criminal convictions themselves, were as bad as the gangs. Four badged 'stewards' mainly from the Leeds area, prosecuted by the police at Beverley in May 1922, defended themselves as being there to try and stop 'rowdyism' on behalf of the BPA.[113] There were major incidents at Doncaster and Yarmouth meetings later that year. Part of the Jewish and Italian membership broke away from the Sabinis, who agreed to divide the racecourses with Kimber to deal with the new threat.

The Jockey Club Senior Steward in 1922 introduced discussions between the Home Office, Scotland Yard and the racecourses, and wanted the Jockey Club to appoint their own officials to supervise and tighten racecourse arrangements. There was opposition from some racecourse companies. Even when Lord Jersey, the next steward, pressed it, little progress was made. There were numbers of gang fights through 1923, 1924 and early 1925 in the clubs and streets of London, linked to protection rackets and bookmaking. Other parts of the provinces now had 'copy-cat' gang warfare. At a National Hunt meeting in Cardiff in December 1923 there were similar fights between rival gangs. Violence was becoming less reported by 1924 and at the beginning of the 1925 flat season the Jockey Club, after a long period of relative apathy, finally set up a mobile team of about sixty knowledgeable ex-CID men to patrol and supervise the betting rings. Britain was divided into two areas, North and South, each with a supervisor. Corrupt gatemen, ring officials and staff managers were identified and dealt with, while the Jockey Club ensured ring-keepers employed by the courses were licensed. The entrance gates were better supervised to try to keep out known undesirables.[114] The National Hunt followed suit.

Initially the police were not always cooperative. There were unsubstantiated allegations that some officers were receiving bribes from the gangs. Some minor racecourse officials were certainly corrupt and unhelpful. The major gangs exercised a significant measure of control over bookmakers and pitches right through the 1920s, but their intimidation was diminishing. The BPA prosecuted some of the violent attackers, despite threats. Its membership grew, and it did more to point out dishonest bookies and welshers. The various regional branches formed Pitch Committees, so as to make the allocation of pitches fairer.[115] Second, violence was further reduced in 1924 by the intervention of the home secretary, alarmed by the rival gang warfare. Convinced by the media hysteria and the grip of American gangster language that every mob was a race gang, he ordered the Flying Squad to make racecourses safe. The squad had a very tough reputation and targeted courses where they thought trouble was likely. Third, the Jockey Club and NHC finally took more direct responsibility for bookmakers' pitches. In 1929 they decided that pitches would be allocated by the racecourse personnel who would act in liaison with the local BPA. Bookmakers would have to apply to them, would be vetted, and would have pitches allocated on a seniority basis. Protection rackets at the courses continued through the 1930s, a seedy, sordid world later captured in Graham Greene's 1938 novel *Brighton Rock*, but Chinn takes the view that intimidation by the race gangs was by then in decline.[116] Greene's book was influenced by a 1936 clash at Lewes racecourse, when a gang ran riot, attacking bookmakers friendly to the Sabinis, when they failed to find them. As a result the Sabinis kept their West End dominance, but handed over control of the Kings Cross area to their rivals.

Such criminality was a minor part of course culture. For most contemporaries, especially the casual spectator, racing was simply a carnival, a chance to enjoy oneself. It was also, as this chapter has reminded us, a place of work for bookmakers, course officials, racecourse workers and employees of various branches of the catering and entertainment industries. The culture of the course was however only part of the world of racing. Jockeys and trainers, owners and breeders, all spent much of their time elsewhere. Much of the preparation for racing took place at specialised racing stables, which had their own life, culture and vitality. Most jockeys, but not all, learned their trade there before riding full time. Yet little research has taken place into the lives of trainers, stable lads and jockeys, and it is to these that we now turn.

Notes

1   *Liverpool Echo* (*LE*), 24.3.1922.
2   *LE*, 26.3.1930; *Sporting Chronicle* (*SC*), 28.3.1935.
3   *Doncaster Gazette*, 12.9.1929.
4   Jack Fairfax-Blakeborough, *The analysis of the turf* (London: Philip Allan, 1927), p. 96.
5   *Sporting Life* (*SL*), 28.5.1924.
6   *SL*, 26.5.1924; *Yorkshire Evening Press* (*YEP*), 25.8.1936; *Daily Express*, 27.7.1937.
7   *YEP*, 28.8.1929; *ibid.*, 27.8.1931.
8   See for example, *SC*, 8.3.1927.
9   Jack Fairfax-Blakeborough, *Northern turf history volume III: York and Doncaster* (London: J. A. Allen, 1950), p. 462; *LE*, 26.3.1930.
10   C. R. Acton, *Silk and spur* (London: Richards, 1935), p. 182.
11   *YEP*, 25.8.1936; *ibid.*, 9.9.1936.
12   *Ibid.*, 9.9.1936.
13   Dorothy Laird, *Royal Ascot* (London: Hodder and Stoughton, 1976), p. 193.

14 *Yorkshire Herald* (*YH*), 27.8.1938.

15 Arthur FitzGerald, *Royal thoroughbreds: a history of the royal studs* (London: Sidgwick and Jackson, 1990), pp. 182–99.

16 *The Sportsman*, 24.3.1924.

17 *The Times*, 2.6.1938.

18 David Cannadine, *Class in Britain* (New Haven: Yale University Press, 1998), pp. 137–43.

19 A. Edward Newton, *Derby day and other adventures* (Boston: Little, Brown and Co., 1934), p. 22.

20 *North-Eastern Daily Gazette*, 22.8.1922.

21 *YEP*, 27.8.1936; *YH*, 27.8.1938.

22 *LE*, 26.3.1930; *ibid.,* 27.3.1930.

23 *The Times*, 14.9.1933.

24 For example, Northumberland Record Office, NRO. 432/1, 2, Rothbury Steeplechase Committee minutes, where the duke of Northumberland lent support.

25 Leicestershire County Record Office, DE 1436/59, Melton Hunt steeplechases balance books.

26 Mike Huggins, 'Culture, class and respectability: racing and the English middle classes in the nineteenth century', *International journal of the history of sport,* 11:1 (1994), 19–41.

27 Company File, Haydock Park Race Company, quoted by Mark Clapson, *A bit of a flutter: popular gambling and English society c.1823–1961* (Manchester: Manchester University Press, 1992), p. 112.

28 G. Bonney, 'The Epsom Derby' in Ernest Bland (ed.), *Flat racing* (London: Andrew Dakers, 1950), pp. 137–9.

29 John Hislop, *Far from a gentleman* (London: Michael Joseph, 1960), pp. 46, 66.

30 The Come to Sussex Association, *The come to Sussex county guide* (Chichester: CTSA, 1934), p. 112.

31 See lists in *Liverpool Post,* 24.3.1925, and comments in *LE,* 24.3.1938.

32 R. M. Bevan, *The Roodee: 450 years of racing in Chester* (Northwich: Cheshire Country Publishing, 1989), ch. 12.

33 Seebohm Rowntree, *Poverty and progress: a second social survey of York* (London: Longmans, Green, 1941), p. 400; *YEP*, 24.8.1932.

34 Philip Welsh, *Stable rat: life in the racing stables* (London: Eyre Methuen, 1979), p. 26.

35 *Sporting Chronicle*, 30.5.1935.

36 *YEP*, 25.8.1925; *ibid.,* 25.8.1936.

37 Kate Fox, *The racing tribe: watching the horsewatchers* (London: Metro Books, 1999).

38 Jeff Hill, 'Rites of spring: Cup Finals and community in the north of England', in Jeff Hill and Jack Williams, *Sport and identity in the North of England* (Keele: Keele University Press, 1996).

39 Stanley Jackson, *The Aga Khan: prince, prophet and sportsman* (London: Odhams Press, 1952), p. 148.

40 'The Scout' (Cyril Luckman), *The Scout's guide to racing 1937* (London: The Express, 1937), p. 9.

41 Bernard Darwin, *British sport and games* (London: Longmans, Green, 1940), p. 40.

42 The Aga Khan, *The memoirs of Aga Khan: world enough and time* (London: Cassell, 1954), p. 99.

43 Newton, *Derby Day*, p. 24.

44 Leonard Jayne, *Pony racing, including the story of Northolt Park* (London: Hutchinson, n.d.), p. 14.

45 *YH*, 21.5.1938.

46 John McGuigan, *A trainer's memories: being 60 years turf reminiscences and experiences at home and abroad* (London: Heath Ganton 1946), p. 12.

47 *SC*, 30.5.1935.

48 *Daily Telegraph*, 14.6.1933.

49 *Daily Mirror*, 23.3.1922.

50 *Ibid.*, 19.3.1921.

51 *Daily Sketch*, 30.5.1925.

52 *London Evening News*, 4.6.1937.

53 *Daily Mirror*, 27.5.1925.

54 *SC*, 7.6.1935.

55 Bevan, *The Roodee*, p. 121.

56 *The Times*, 30.10.1933.

57 John Stevenson, *British society 1914–45* (Harmondsworth: Penguin, 1984), p. 117.

58 *North-Eastern Daily Gazette*, 24.5.1920.

59 *The Times*, 3.6.1920 and *ibid.*, 16.6.1920.

60 *YEP*, 9. 9.1936.

61 *LE*, 24.3.1938. Reg Green, *A history of the Grand National* (London: Hodder and Stoughton, 1987), p. 212. J. K. Pyke, *A Grand National commentary* (London: J. A. Allen, 1971), p. 97.

62 *Liverpool Post*, 24.3.1925.

63 *LE*, 26.3.1930.

64 Bevan, *The Roodee*, pp. 112, 121.

65 Leicester County Record Office, DE 2805/10, The New Leicester Club and County Racecourse Co. Ltd. Directors' Reports and Accounts 1919–39.

66 For details of the relationship between the demand for leisure and the British economy see Stephen Jones, *Workers at play: a social and economic history of leisure 1918–1939* (London: Routledge and Kegan Paul, 1986), ch. 1.

67 *SC*, 30.5.1935.

68 *Cleveland Standard*, 6.6.1936.

69 *The Times*, 10.1.1938.

70 Leicestershire County Record Office, DE1436/59 Steeplechase balance sheets 1919–38.

71 Chris Pitt, *A long time gone* (Halifax: Portway Press, 1996), p. 244 provides Tote figures for comparison.

72 W. Vamplew, *The turf* (London: Allen Lane, 1976), p. 72.

73 Ross McKibbin, *Classes and cultures: England 1918–1951* (Oxford: Oxford University Press, 1998), p. 355.

74 For example, *Bloodstock breeders' review,* 1922, quoted in Leo Rasmussen and Miles Napier, *Treasures of the bloodstock breeders' review* (London: J. A. Allen, 1990), p. 44; Quintin Gilbey, *Champions all: Steve to Lester* (London: Hutchinson, 1971), p. 7.

75 See A. W. Coaten, 'Evolution of racing' in Earl of Harewood and P. E. Ricketts (eds), *Flat racing* (London: Seeley Service, 1940), p. 160.

76 *YEP*, 25.8.1925.

77 *SC,* 30.5.1935.

78 *Beverley Guardian*, 25.6.1938; *ibid.*, 29.4.1939.

79 *The Times*, 7.1.1935.

80 *SL*, 26.5.1924.

81 George Hamlyn, *My first sixty years in the ring: a racing and training autobiography* (Hungerford: Sporting Garland Press, 1994), p. 10.

82 'Racing under pony turf club rules', *Bloodstock breeders' review*, 1937, p. 273.

83 *The Times*, 1.5.1919.

84 Rollo Pain, *Why Cartmel? Survival of a small racecourse 1856–1998* (Kendal: Lakeland Health, 2001), p. 65.

85 *Daily Express*, 27.7.1937.

86 *Bloodstock breeders' review*, 1931, p. 119.

87 Clive Graham, 'The pencillers', in *The Scout's guide to racing 1937*, p. 72.

88 Laird, *Royal Ascot,* p. 191.

89 Richard Kaye, *The Ladbroke's story* (London: Pelham Books, 1969), p. 61.

90 1923 House of Commons Select Committee on Betting Duty, minutes of evidence, Q241 (Dowson).

91 Graham, 'Pencillers', p. 78.

92 Eric Rickman, *On and off the racecourse* (London: Routledge, 1937), p. 221.

93 Ras Prince Monolulu, *I gotta horse* (London: Hurst and Blackett, n.d.), p. 91.

94 See Robert Graves and Alan Hodge, *The long weekend: a social history of Great Britain 1918–1939* (New York: W. W. Norton and Co., 1963), p. 293.

95 *The Times*, 14.3.1933.

96 *North-Eastern Daily Gazette*, 5.6.1992.

97 For an account of his life see Ras Prince Monolulu, *I gotta horse*. See also personal reminiscences of Phil Welsh: *Stable rat: life in the racing stables* (London: Eyre Methuen, 1979), pp. 92–7.

98 *Liverpool Post*, 26.3.1925.

99 *The Times*, 24.5.1938.

100 *YEP*, 28.8.1925.

101 Carl Chinn, *Better betting with a decent feller: bookmakers, betting and the British working class 1750–1990* (Hemel Hempstead: Harvester, 1991), p. 198.

102 Forged £20 notes were given to a bookie at Kempton, *Northern Daily Mail* (*NDM*), 24.5.1921.

103 *YEP*, 26, 27, 28 and 29.8.1936.

104 *The Times*, 15.1.1920.

105 Michael Seth Smith and Roger Mortimer, *Derby 200: the official history of the Blue Riband of the turf* (Enfield: Guinness Superlatives, 1979), p. 46. For examples see *The Times*, 5.4.1921, 12.4.1921, 26.7.1921; 18.8.1921.

106 *Ibid.*, 2.6.1921.

107 *YEP*, 26.8.1925.

108 Chinn, *Better betting*, pp. 198–200; Raphael Samuel, *East End underworld: chapters in the life of Arthur Harding* (London: Routledge, 1981), p. 184.

109 Chinn, *Better betting*, pp. 201–3 deals with this gang war well, using oral evidence from Birmingham. James Morton, *East End gangland* (London: Warner Books, 2001), pp. 142–68, is strong on London evidence.

110 *NDM*, 2.6.1921.

111 *NDM*, 2.7.1921; *ibid.*, 17.9.1921.

112 W. Bebbington, *Rogues go racing* (London: Good and Betts, 1947), p. 118. Bebbington provides a fascinating personal view of the gang wars.

113 *North Eastern Daily Gazette*, 30.5.1922.

114 Bebbington, *Rogues go racing*, p. 16.

115 See Chinn, *Better betting*, pp. 203–4.

116 Chinn, *Better betting*, pp. 204–5.

6

Jockeys, trainers and the micro-world of the stable

The top jockeys and trainers, often working-class in origin, enjoyed a middle-class income often equalling that of lawyers or doctors. To the public, jockeys were the object of either venom or veneration as they lost or won. Within racing's social elite, trainers and jockeys were often looked down upon. As the *Times* racing correspondent in 1933 commented, 'the very word "professional" arouses suspicion'.[1] Significantly, while lists of breeders and owners in *Ruff's Guide* or the *Racing Calendar*, like racing officials, attracted the honorific title 'Mr', trainers and jockeys received only surnames and initials. Yet 'leading trainers' occupied an ambiguous and socially higher position than professional jockeys. In separate lists, like lists of *amateur* jockeys, their names attracted the socially significant honorific, as when they were breeders or owners. Even top jockeys accepted this social seniority. Steve Donoghue, eight times champion jockey, addressed trainer Fred Darling as 'Sir' and spoke humbly to him.[2] Such hierarchy was reflected in some major event trophies. For example, the 1933 Grand National trophy for the winning owner was worth £300. The trainer received one of £50 value, and the jockey one worth just £25.

Jockeys

The social status of jockeys was ambiguous. Some were paradigmatic examples of one of the key sporting myths, that of the 'self-made man', enjoying upward social and economic mobility, through talent, hard work and self-sacrifice. Yet jockeys could be despised as decidedly inferior: simply servants, hired to do a job, expected to be tactful, respectful and diplomatic. Some owners resented their increasing popularity and public notoriety. As Fairfax-Blakeborough remarked ruefully, it was 'an age of grovelling, almost toadying, and syco-phantic jockey admiration', and the 'tendency to place successful jockeys on pedestals and fall down and worship them is just a little nauseating to some of us'.[3]

The press and public, by contrast, gave them status and adulation. Most did not see the effort, the wasting and the work, or the conflicts and tensions. They saw heroic and glamorous figures who did little menial work and simply arrived in the parade ring, mounted the horse and rode for a few minutes in brightly-coloured silks before winning. The two most popular, often knowingly referred to as 'Steve' or 'Gordon', provided sharp contrasts. Steve Donoghue, the leading jockey of the 1920s, was a colourful celebrity, lionised by the press, who transformed his great performances into heroic myths. He was 'the world's most famous jockey'.[4] Popular with crowds and punters, he was an extrovert celebrity, bold, stylish, admired and envied, over-generous, humorous, but naive. Gordon Richards first won the championship in 1925 and dominated the 1930s as champion jockey, but was more insecure socially. Although he acquired a dinner suit, learned to play golf and holidayed in Switzerland, he found the social side and publicity more difficult. When he married in 1928, he kept quiet about it and initially lived in secret.[5] He was presented as a reliable, steady and modestly-reserved person showing goodness, decency, honour, courage and will power, grit and determination, and the ability to overcome setbacks.

Jockeys acquired name tags, personal nicknames reflecting appearance or character: 'Moppy' or 'The Champ' for Gordon Richards, 'The Little Swell' for Tommy Weston. Success often came very early. 'Boy jockey's brilliant win on Battleship' summarised 17-year-old Bruce Hobbs's achievement in winning the 1938 Grand National.[6] Fan following was very evident. When Richards created a new record with his two hundred and forty-seventh winner of the season in 1933, journalists from across the world chased him to get a first-hand story and there was a 'stampede' of women to welcome him back to the winner's enclosure. He even received a telegram from the king, expressing 'hearty congratulations'.[7] Not only girls, but 'women in good society' were susceptible to jockeys' attractions, and jockeys enjoyed 'considerable success with the opposite sex'.[8] They also received innumerable letters from strangers, some on 'most intimate subjects', written as if they knew the jockey personally, wishing them luck, perhaps asking for tips or loans, or abusing them and accusing them of cheating.[9] Top jockeys had a top lifestyle, with fast cars, fast women and fashionable clothing. They were expected to supply comments and tell their stories to the racing and popular press. They took part in social and charity events. They presented prizes and gave speeches. Freddy Fox, for example, presented the prize at the Greyhound Grand National at the White City in 1935.[10]

The heavier jump jockeys, who took more risks riding over fences, perhaps had more riding skills as a result, while the lighter flat jockeys, who had to starve themselves more, saw themselves as more professional because of their longer season and higher number of rides. But there was a mutual solidarity arising from the shared experience of racing and often shared backgrounds. Jockeys loved racing and horses, and the language of jockey autobiographies is very revealing here. Hislop, for example, talked about his horses as 'noble', 'magnificent', a 'beautiful picture', and found racing had 'a freshness and interest', an 'exhilarating' 'new world' of 'romance and risk'. Rae Johnson, on his first ever visit to a racecourse, 'got drunk … on the atmosphere', enjoyed its 'excitement', 'thrill', 'applause' and 'glamour'.[11] One division was created by the highly efficient racecourse valet system, which looked after and transported jockeys' gear from meeting to meeting. Hislop saw his valet as one of the most important people in his life. Valets and clients, he suggested, formed separate individualistic coteries, 'rather in the manner of houses at a public school'.[12]

How many jockeys were there? Jockeys and apprentices had to be licensed by the Jockey Club, so detailed statistics were listed in publications like *Ruff's Guide* or the *Racing Calendar*, although figures vary slightly. In 1938, while the *Racing Calendar* quotes 180 flat jockeys and 209 apprentices, *Ruff's Guide* lists a higher figure of 188 jockeys but only 179 apprentices. Professional jump jockeys were licensed by the NHC, but there were also many 'gentleman amateurs' who did not need to be licensed, although after having ridden ten winners in races open to professionals they needed the stewards' permission to continue. The figure for amateur riders given in Table 6.1 is therefore a serious under-estimate. In 1932 the list only gives 56 licensed amateurs but there were 114 who were successful enough to ride winners.

Table 6.1 Numbers of jockeys, 1920–38

	1920	1923	1926	1929	1932	1935	1938
Licensed jockeys: flat	305	277	255 (78)	236	212 (77)	162	188 (78)
Jockeys: National Hunt	360	359	362 (160)	347	313 (147)	299	329 (167)
Amateurs	106	51	76	77	56	72	51

Source: Ruff's Guide to the Turf
Note: Figures in parentheses show number of jockeys who rode winners

Each year a majority of jockeys never had a winning race yet despite their differences jockeys possessed a significant degree of cameraderie. Most defended each other in public, criticising rarely, although personal rivalries and antagonisms occasionally surfaced. Some changed, rode and travelled from course to course, lodging together, developing a close bond strengthened by shared experience, risks and diet. This extended to jockeys who came from overseas. Ever-increasingly jockeyship was cosmopolitan. The so-called 'Colonials', to distinguish them from the European 'Continentals', often rode slightly shorter, with a looser rein.[13] Australians like Wootton, Frank Bullock, Rae Johnstone and 'Brownie' Carslake, or South Africans like Buckray, were highly successful in Britain and Europe.

All jockeys needed courage and endurance, but this shared bond was particularly strong amongst jump jockeys, who were as a result perhaps more rough and ready. One consequence of this was that the social and cultural differences between amateur and professional riders in National Hunt racing were less strong than in other sports, and many believed 'these rules that one is a professional and another is a gentleman rider mean very little'.[14]

While the number of 'gentlemen/amateur' riders in this period was significant, there were regular debates whether all actually paid their own way. They had to prove they could afford to ride without needing expenses or presents, but some were 'shamateurs'. Only a few rode in flat races, presumably because of the difficulties of keeping to a weight of below 8.5 st., and only twelve won a flat race in 1921, with none riding more than ten times. Most first rode hunters and point-to-points before entering National Hunt racing, where weights were higher. Here they had some chance of competing successfully with professionals. Serving and former officers provided a consistent nucleus. Harry Brown, the champion National Hunt rider of 1919, an old Etonian and former soldier, rode as an amateur, and later became a successful trainer. In 1926/7 over 150 different amateurs rode winners, although in 1937/8 this had fallen to 99. Many with middle-class backgrounds, like J. R. Antony or F. B. Rees, used this as a quick route into the professional ranks, and lost nothing socially. Rees, champion jockey four times, was the son of a South Wales veterinary surgeon. Others, who had no such ambitions, still rode as well as the professionals. Captain Bennet, a veterinary surgeon, winner of the 1923 Grand National, was level at the head of the winning jockey list with sixty-two victories when he died of a fall at Wolverhampton in 1924.[15] Bill Dutton, a Chester solicitor, rode the 1927 National winner. Riding in prestigious point-to-points even temporarily attracted the future Edward VIII, though his own riding was never outstanding. Big races like the Grand National even attracted amateurs from abroad.[16]

In the nineteenth century, a career in the racing stables had been an attraction for many lightweight youngsters from surrounding rural areas, or from towns like Manchester with regular race-meetings. By the twentieth century educational legislation, higher weight caused by better living standards, and ever-increasing urbanisation all placed more limits on jockey recruitment. It had a long, badly-paid apprenticeship. The chances of becoming a top jockey were limited. Parents were therefore often reluctant to let their sons enter the stables, a reluctance exacerbated for some by concerns about the respectability of racing. Richards, although keen to be a jockey, left school at 13 to become a warehouse boy, and had to overcome considerable resistance before his parents signed his indentures in 1920.

The number of apprentice jockeys listed fluctuated, as Table 6.2 shows, but was generally less in the 1930s.

Table 6.2 Numbers of apprentices, 1920–38

	1920	1923	1926	1929	1932	1935	1938
Apprentices	195	224	234	192	153	146	179

Source: *Ruff's Guide to the Turf*

Apprentice jockeys learnt to ride taking out horses on 'work' gallops, where racing conditions were simulated. Experienced jockeys were usually helpful with advice, and showed little jealousy. Up to 1914 jockey apprentices had little education but after 1919 they were increasingly well-educated and keen to succeed. Welsh remembered his first ride in public vividly: 'It was intoxicating. I'd never known anything like it'.[17] Most apprentices tried desperately to improve. If they could show the 'guvnor' that they had adapted well they got rides, avoided the rigours of afternoon work, and met famous jockeys, whose styles they would emulate. They would also copy the changing-room technique of depreciating their own chances.

Chances of getting a race were quite reasonable. Some races gave a 5lb. weight allowance to apprentices. All courses had at least one specific 'apprentice' race a year. So good light apprentices could temporarily get large numbers of rides. Success was elusive, but in 1932 a third of all apprentices listed in *Ruff's Guide* achieved a winning ride, and, in 1938, 27 per cent. Successful apprentices had a reasonable opportunity of initially becoming jockeys, but more limited opportunities of remaining in the job, as there was a vast oversupply of labour.[18] Of listed apprentices in 1920, 46 per cent became jockeys, but only 16 per cent lasted more than three seasons. The picture in 1930 was similar: 44 per cent became jockeys, but only 16 per cent lasted more than three seasons.[19] Riding accidents were relatively common, even in flat racing. Donoghue suffered broken wrists, two broken legs and a smashed arm socket amongst other injuries. Jump jockey Billy Stott had broken almost every bone in his body when he finally retired, in a very poor state of health, to invest his money in an Epsom laundry.[20] Steel helmets were starting to be worn by steeplechasers by 1923 but were still scorned by flat-race jockeys in 1939.[21] The Jockey Club and NHC operated Jockeys' Accident Funds, using part of the licence fee together with 'Fund Money' contributed by jockeys from their riding fees. Contributions from the Racecourse Betting Control Board were also used. Funds paid out benefits of £1,000 on death and £3 weekly for racing accidents.

Although some, like Richards, were natural lightweights, many others rode about 2 st. heavier off-season. They lost weight by 'wasting', achieved through constant physical exercise wearing many clothing layers, using Turkish or electric baths, or dosing with purgative medicine. Without success few were able to maintain this self-discipline and the consequent strain of dehydration, malnutrition or bulimia. To ride into his mid-fifties Carslake needed a starvation diet, with only one meal a day – often a boiled egg, a piece of dry toast, a cup of tea. Some jockeys moved from the flat to steeplechasing where weights were higher, as did Frank Wootton who topped the steeplechase list in 1921. Wasting could bring on lung diseases, arthritis and other long-term health problems. William Higgs's wasting 'left its mark on his digestive powers'.[22] It perhaps caused the early deaths of others like Wootton or Carslake. It carried a punishing mental toll. But those who could 'do the weight' could have a long career. Many top jockeys rode for thirty years or more. Joe Childs won races from 1900 to 1935 despite never being champion jockey. Freddy Fox, champion jockey in 1930, rode for thirty years. Donoghue rode his first winner in 1905 and his last in 1937. Richards, who could ride at 8 st. without wasting, rode his first winner in 1921, his last in 1954.

Knowledgeable commentators believed that the general standard of riding improved during this period. Acton suggested that there was 'not eight pounds difference' between good apprentices and most first-class jockeys after 1918.[23] Jockeys needed a daunting combination of athletic skills: good 'hands' to communicate through the reins, balance, bravery, competitiveness, racing instinct, ability to use the whip with either hand while keeping a half-ton of pitching horseflesh straight and doing its best, riding a good start and finish, physical strength, coordination and mental toughness. They had a knife-edge to tread in trying to follow owners' and trainers' instructions while also using their initiative without causing annoyance. This was difficult. Horses varied in character, from those who did better with shouting crowds to those who hated noise; from those who loved to lead to those who hated being in front. Other jockeys' riding instructions might also adversely affect the race.

These specialist talents were rare. In flat racing a small group of around 15 jockeys always had a high proportion of the rides, and the number of rides they could obtain was increasing. In 1929 47 per cent and in 1938 50 per cent of all races were won by the 12 leading jockeys. In 1921 only 4 jockeys had over 400 rides but by 1938 15 jockeys and one apprentice had over 400 rides, while a further 33 jockeys and 5 apprentices had over 100 rides in the season. The top jockeys rode the top horses, so success bred success. In 1921 Donoghue topped the table with 694 rides, but by the 1930s Richards regularly got over 900 mounts a season, rode 1,000 in 1936, and once, in October 1933, rode 12 consecutive winners. Informed commentators later saw the interwar years as 'an age of exceptionally good jockeys'.[24] Southern English jockeys benefited most, although Bill Nevitt, who once rode 10 winners in 3 days as a youngster, dominated the northern courses for Peacock's Middleham stables, and was often second in the jockeys' lists in the 1930s. National Hunt jockeys rode far fewer races. Only 13 steeplechase jockeys got over 150 rides in 1938 and the top rider, G. Wilson, got a mere 379 rides.

Elite flat-race jockeys earned the most. Minimum fees were 5 guineas per win, and 3 guineas for losing races (NH races had higher fees of 10 guineas and 5 guineas except for races with prizes of under £85). Where jockeys had to travel, the cost of first-class travelling expenses and £1 a day for living expenses was shared amongst owners, although apprentices travelled third-class, reflecting their lower status. Jockeys would also be paid for riding 'work' and for trials of horses. Top jockeys could be offered an annual four-figure retaining fee for a prioritised 'first claim' on their services from owner or trainer, and could have then have 'second', 'third' or more claims. For Donoghue or Richards a first retainer could be £5,000 a year. In many seasons Richards had five retainers, half of each paid in advance. Owners also regularly offered large financial inducements for success in major races, while some contracts specified a percentage of up to 10 per cent of prize money won.[25] Only the best had retainers, and only the very best had several retainers. More than half of all jockeys were freelance. In 1938 only four jockeys had three retainers or more, and only fifteen jockeys thought it worthwhile to publish a telephone contact number. Presents from generous winning owners or backers varied but could be quite handsome. Amongst jump jockeys presents were rarer, though William Watkinson once got £70 for winning on a chance ride in 1920, and when he rode the 1926 Grand National winner, Jack Horner, he got £1,000 from the owner, while a winning punter sent him a further £600.[26] Ordinary jockeys got few such chances. As jockey Snowy Shepherd complained bitterly, one millionaire had 'no end of winners', but 'never said "Thank you" to me, not once … never mind about a drink … Sod him'.[27]

The most successful could ignore traditional expectations of loyalty, continuity and commitment in their quest for winners. Donoghue broke contracts, evaded engagements, ignored retainers of top owners, and picked and chose between top horses, 'jocking off' less-skilled jockeys in the process. He won the Derby in 1921 on Humorist for J. B. Joel, and received a cheque for £2,000, but broke his £3,000 retainer with Lord Derby to do so. It was not renewed.[28] He broke Lord Woolavington's retainer of *c.* £4,000 in 1923 to ride another Derby winner. Despite this his talents brought plenty of rides as a freelance. In 1925 he won the Derby for the bullion broker Henry Morris, charging him his 'usual fee – £250 for the ride and £5,000 for the win'.[29] As his skills faded his behaviour palled. His income had dropped to *c.* £2,000 per annum by 1926–8, not enough to maintain his lifestyle.

Jockey ebullience, rudeness or vulgarity could all be tolerated for the sake of success. The steeplechase jockey F. B. (Dick) Rees, a former amateur, having once 'wined and dined too well', fell off at a water jump, gave a rude sign to the crowd and then urinated facing the stand, but was still champion jockey five times.[30] Most top jockeys had sufficient social skills not to offend the owners for whom they worked, and were seen as 'little gentlemen, brimming over with goodwill and kindliness'.[31]

A champion could earn what was estimated in 1934 as 'up to £15,000 a year', and not much less than £20,000 in 1935.[32] This could be supplemented by earnings abroad in the off-season, or the buying and selling of horses. Top jockeys on the British circuit could be found riding in India, South Africa, Europe, the United States and elsewhere, travelling mainly by boat, although increasingly by aeroplane from London. In Newmarket wealthier jockeys were earning enough to retain the services of bank clerks to manage their financial affairs. While successful their annual income fuelled an upper-middle-class lifestyle. Donoghue had a large house, chauffeur, gardener and cook by the time he was in his early twenties and also maintained a flat in Park Lane, London, with a valet and housekeeper.[33] Jockeys often socialised together in winter, spending summer's money in high living, holidaying in St Moritz or the Caribbean, or mixing with 'society', the wealthy, famous or notorious international set. They lived hard and sometimes played hard too. Out of season Rae Johnstone was a connoisseur of good wine, good food and attractive women.[34] Sometimes, too, personal rivalries led to fights, such as Ingram's assault on Donoghue in August 1923.[35]

Jockeys were banned from betting by the racing authorities, but many used their privileged information about horses to do so; indeed Ras Prince Monolulu claimed 'jockeys do bet: always have done, always will do'.[36] Charlie Elliott bet in large sums to finance his taste for the high life, although his betting, as with Donoghue, eventually became a road to heavy losses. Some bet directly with bookmakers. Donoghue once contacted the betting firm Ladbroke's by phone, apparently over his account, while two members of the Jockey Club were having a drink with its chairman. The operator passed on his message very loudly, but nothing transpired.[37] Some, like Johnstone, worked with a confederate; others expected owners and trainers to bet on their behalf.

Since jockeys were competing for rides racing careers could be short and income low. In 1920 twenty professional flat-race jockeys who had won a race that year had less than twenty rides, although some may have been based overseas. Their income was perhaps below the national annual average wage of £170. And some never won! National Hunt opportunities were fewer still. In 1939 sixty-three jockeys had less than twenty rides. Riding was high-risk, with the constant danger of death or serious injury. Steeplechasing was more dangerous than the flat, and point-to-point more dangerous still. But even flat jockeys faced damage and potential earning loss. Injuries were common. Harry Wragg's compound fracture of the leg in 1928 cost three months in a nursing home.[38] Then there was loss of form, or bad luck. Donoghue rode forty-nine consecutive losers in 1919, the South African jockey Nichol rode seventy-one in 1933.[39] Unsuccessful jockeys got few rides. Beginner 'chalk jockeys', so called because their names were chalked on the runners and riders board because insufficiently famous to be painted, and at a meeting for perhaps only one race, would scout round desperately, listening to conversations, touching their cap to owners and trainers, in hopes of a 'spare' ride. Others might turn up just in the vain hope of one. Savings could soon go, and ordinary jockeys struggled to make a living. One jockey, looking back, bitterly claimed that if he had his life over again and his father had suggested being a jockey, he would 'cut his head off'.[40]

Pressure for success meant jockeys' riding behaviour and honesty varied. Doug Smith described how one jockey deliberately caught hold of his foot and pushed him aside. Owners rarely complained, he suggested. By the interwar period there were fewer complaints about jockey dishonesty, but certainly jockeys were always beset by temptation. Allegations were hard to prove, and were only reluctantly made. As Lord Zetland accepted, 'we may have suspicions of malpractice by jockeys, and others which may amount to almost certainty in our minds, but that is not sufficient'.[41] A jockey remembered 'a few dodgy ones … there would be a few red faces … some pulled some strokes', but felt 'it wouldn't do' to say anything.[42] Acton, while believing that modern jockeys were 'more honest', accepted that some dishonesty continued.[43] It was largely trainers and owners who manipulated the horses, and their instructions which revealed whether a horse was to be judiciously reserved for another occasion, or held back if it could not win. Jockey autobiographies suggest occasional approaches by other parties. Rae Johnstone claimed he had only twice been approached to stop a horse (by bookmakers), but suggested that it was not worth it, since 'a jockey's most valuable ally is a reputation for dependability, for doing what he is asked'.[44] Leach only remembered one instance. Even for the top riders there was the danger of being caught out and warned off. Charlie Smirke, for example, was banned for allegedly pulling a horse called Welcome Gift, although the horse was a rogue one and it may not have been Smirke's fault. He lost five years of his career.

One top racing commentator estimated that by the 1920s many of the better jockeys had '£20,000-£50,000 to their credit in the bank when they gave up riding'.[45] For top jockeys, collections further eased the pain, and retirement was another ritual, involving grateful owners, trainers and grateful jockeys too. Lord Milton chaired Donoghue's 'dinner committee'. When Charlie Fox retired in 1936 he abandoned plans to train, bought a country estate, rode to hounds and became a JP.[46] The steeplechaser W. J. Speck, who died in April 1935 after a fall, left £19,000, although this was seen as 'a lot of money for a jumping jockey'.[47] His Cheltenham funeral procession illustrated the prominent cultural position of jockeys in racing communities. It was supposedly 2 miles long, and, Sutton Hoo-fashion, his saddle, whip and colours were buried with him.[48] Joe Childs bought a stud farm in Essex in 1926. Of those more successful jockeys who had managed to save money, many rented premises and went into training on retirement, although only a minority were successful. But few jockeys ever achieved a trainer's licence. Only 7 per cent of jockeys licensed to ride in flat racing in 1920 did so.

Retirement from the racetrack was due to lack of success and rides, increasing age, increasing weight or health problems. What was more rarely voiced publicly was when normal apprehension became loss of nerve. Even Dick Rees finally lost it. Frank Bullock never got on a horse again once he retired. Younger former jockeys perhaps turned to work in the stables, or as labourers round the racecourse, or to writing reports on horses' progress to newspapers. Many found the change difficult. When Donoghue first retired it was traumatic: 'I was cutting myself off from those lads, from the weighing room, from the courses on which I had spent my whole life, from the things which had filled every second of my career … I felt the wrench as I had never expected to feel it … it was some sort of an end'.[49]

It was a commonplace in racing books that some successful jockeys saved insufficient to retire in ease and comfort, let alone affluence. The early success and quick money that young jockeys enjoyed often made them cocky and impudent and so they spent their money as fast as they earned it. [50] Bill Rickaby was sacked at the end of 1936 because he was 'a rather wild young man'.[51] Jockeys got over-confident, and it was easy to become surrounded by hangers-on and false friends. The less bright or less streetwise were easy prey to these supposedly admiring adventurers. Some were 'easy-come, easy-go', although this was explained as 'kindly hearts and abounding generosity rather than personal extravagance', since they were expected to support charity demands and contribute to racing retirement or other presents. Some, like 'Tiny' Heppell, turned to drink on retirement, while others, like Johnny McCall, son of a Dunbar trainer, who ended his working life as 'boots' at the George Hotel, took what badly-paid jobs they could find.[52]

The world of riding and training was often portrayed as a man's world, with women appearing only as wives or girlfriends, washerwomen or landladies. Here again, however, conventional racing literature does women an injustice, since the period saw women's increasing involvement in riding and training. Yards occasionally used women workers during the 1914–18 war, but they were replaced afterwards. Around this time, Snowy Shepherd remembered some very good women riders in Newmarket stables, including Lester Piggott's mother, Iris Rickaby, whom he regarded as being as good as any man. Women were then allowed to ride in point-to-points, but rarely and almost always in separate races. Such races continued after 1918, and it was in the South, and especially in East Anglian point-to-points, that it would appear that women first began to ride against men, something seen as a 'startling innovation'.[53] The annual Newmarket Town Plate, a long-standing 'fun' event unrecognised by the Jockey

Club, now allowed lady riders. This was fine so long as they lost, but in 1925 a daughter of Solly Joel, the rich South African owner, won it racing against three men and four women, and was celebrated at the subsequent luncheon. Miss V. Selby Lowndes won a lightweight mixed race at West Street Harriers Meeting in 1929 under NH rules, riding sidesaddle, and other women were also successful riding astride the same month. This initially led to a change in rules in March 1929 in which women were no longer allowed to compete against men. But the reaction to this led a great many more hunts to introduce separate ladies' races into their point-to-points, which by the 1930s were being run increasingly fast. Women may not have been granted training licences, but trainers' wives and daughters were sometimes a behind-the-scenes power. Although Sir Robert Wilmot trained for over twenty years, for example, for much of the time the stable was 'carried on under the management of Miss Norah Wilmot', one of his daughters.[54]

Trainers and training stables

Jockeys may have had highest public status, but it was the specialist training stables who prepared their horses. These were complex businesses, employing jockeys, stablemen and stable lads and giving ancillary employment to vets, saddlers and other trades. Some even had a blacksmith's shop on the premises. The 1921 census showed that in England and Wales training stables provided on-site employment for 3,424 full-time racehorse trainers, jockeys, stable attendants, grooms and horsekeepers, and agricultural labourers. Of these, 3,116 were trainers, jockeys and training stable attendants.[55] All these were largely male occupations, with only 8 females employed in total.

The 1931 census listed 2,360 men and 2 managerial women working as racehorse trainers, jockeys and stable lads, apparently a significant fall. However, grooms and labourers had been excluded from the aggregative data. Reference to the Industry Tables shows their numbers had increased by about 21 per cent, so there was probably little change.[56] Certainly, a conservative estimate of over 2,500 stable lads would be needed to deal even with the flat racehorses in training at this time.

In the nineteenth century there were around 200 training stables. By the 1930s there were between 350 and 400. They were a significant source of rural, village and small-town employment, and contributed to rural culture.[57] Even in mid-winter, for example, Egerton House, Newmarket, had 55 racing staff.[58] Trainers, like jockeys, had to be licensed and paid an annual fee, without which they could not practise. Bad character, or being warned off by the Jockey Club or NHC, would be reasons for withholding such a licence. Some trainers specialised in flat racing or National Hunt racing, but many were licensed for both, although appearing separately in *Ruff's Guide* list totals in Table 6.3.

Table 6.3 Numbers of licensed trainers, 1920–39

	1920	1923	1926	1929	1932[a]	1935	1938
Trainers: flat racing	299	331	333	325	316	335	338
Trainers: National Hunt	251	271	264	257	244	266	281

Source: *Ruff's Guide to the Turf*

Note: [a] In 1932, according to *Ruff's Guide*, a total of 204 trainers were winners of whom 11 held military office and 2 had titles

They were scattered widely across the British countryside, often near current or former racecourses like Newmarket or Middleham. There were identifiable broader training regions and the largest concentration of trainers (*c.* 24 per cent) was in the Wiltshire/Berkshire Downs area, which had overtaken the two leading nineteenth-century training areas, the North and East Ridings of Yorkshire and Newmarket, which together provided *c.* 25 per cent. There were other concentrations in Sussex, Surrey, the South-east and Lancashire. Scotland's few trainers (*c.* 3 per cent) concentrated particularly at Ayr, Berwick, Dumfries and Dunbar, where they could train on turf and sand. Wales, where training was less popular, had fewer still (1–2 per cent). Trainers, lads and grooms moved stables fairly regularly. Trainers moved to get more or cheaper accommodation. Lads looked for better wages, or better treatment.

The names of top trainers were well known from media reports, racing nonfiction and cigarette cards. The public knew less about trainers' actual work. Trainers were given credit for successful horses, yet excuses were found for unsuccessful ones. Trainers were seldom blamed directly. Objective comparison between trainers was difficult, even for other trainers, because the factors that made a good trainer were unclear, although there was an unofficial trainers' championship, listing trainers in terms of annual prize money won, which was a goal of ambition. Some trainers, like George Lambton, Frank Butters and Fred Darling, headed this on several occasions, but their success was often distorted by two or three classic wins by one horse rather than all-round success. Good horses made good trainers appear still better. On that basis Joe Lawson, who headed his second championship with a record £93,899 in 1931 without winning a single classic race, was perhaps the best.[59] In terms of sheer numbers of winners Dobson Peacock, who trained fifty-two 'moderate' horses to win one hundred races from his Middleham yard in 1932 (they won ninety-eight races in 1931) was perhaps even better.

Trainers were specialists. They used experience, knowledge and understanding to train and feed horses individually according to their capacities, placed them carefully in races to maximise chances, and had sound socio-economic stable management skills. Some trainers trained privately for a single individual for a salary and a percentage of all stakes, while the owner paid stable bills and fees. Most were public trainers, training for any owners who placed their horses for a fixed fee per horse, but paying all stable bills. Top ones might have ten or more different patrons, on whose behalf they acted, while keeping them informed of progress, entries and their horses' chances. Trainers with a good eye for a horse might be asked to visit throughbred sales and purchase horses for owners.

Trainers came from a variety of socio-economic backgrounds. Their personal and professional rivalries were coupled with interwoven social lives and family trees. The majority were either the sons of trainers, or were former jockeys who turned to training because they felt they might get former patrons' custom, although jockey-trainers were often less educated and less literate. There were also increasing numbers of 'gentlemen' trainers, although their numbers should not be exaggerated. Of 406 trainers in 1937, only 8 were titled and 31 claimed military rank.[60] Many training families had been training for generations, a reflection perhaps of the paternalistic and Darwinistic beliefs of some well-bred aristocratic owners. Their trainers, like their horses, should come from good stock. Training was dominated by training dynasties, often with strong jockey-ship connections. Intermarriage with other leading training dynasties was common. As Birley has reminded us, 'racing family dynasties had grown up as much amongst the prosperous yeoman class as amongst the aristocracy'.[61] Fred Darling (1884–1953), for example, who was leading British trainer in 1926 and 1933, was the son of trainer Sam Darling (1852–1921), whose classic successes helped him leave an estate of £38,603, the brother of Sam Henry Darling (1881–1967), another successful Newmarket trainer, and the great-grandson of the jockey who won the 1833 St Leger. The Jarvis family, amongst the oldest of Newmarket training families, had intermarried with the Ryans, the Butters and the Waughs, also leading Newmarket trainers. In steeplechasing the Antony family had been farming and training steeplechasers at Tenby in the nineteenth century, and both Ivor and Owen Antony had ridden as Hunt jockeys, with Ivor champion jockey in 1912, before they too turned to training.

Sons of successful trainers were generally well educated, some having been sent to public school. During the holidays they gained experience of key skills: going through entry sheets placing horses to maximise their chances, or mastering stable management and finance. Even a small stable's administration of entries, forfeits, accounts and correspondence was time-consuming, and an average-size or larger stable often employed a secretary, but well-educated trainer's sons often learned this too. They rode out with and helped their fathers. On leaving school if they wished to enter training they often entered pupilage with another trainer. Sometimes they were formally apprenticed but sometimes this was a less formal arrangement.

The entry of 'gentlemen trainers', from more privileged backgrounds, had begun before 1914. By 1920 an older trainer was complaining, 'now that noblemen and gentlemen have in so many instances, taken the place of the old timers, we rarely meet any of them' (in Newmarket's public houses).[62] In fact they had a different social life, 'dined out' at each other's houses and mixed with the hunting/fishing set.[63] They were described as 'gentlemen by birth, with a public school education and a natural love of horses'.[64] 'Amateurs' who had turned professional, they came predominantly through a background in hunting field, point-to-points, Bona-Fide meetings and National Hunt racing, riding and training first their own horses, then others'. The Hon. George Lambton (1860–1945) trained very successfully for the seventeenth earl of Derby.[65] Lord George Dundas was the younger son of the first marquess of Zetland, for whom he went on to train. Other gentleman trainers came from Ireland as its political situation deteriorated. Several trainers had held military rank. Captain Sir Cecil Boyd-Rochfort (1887–1983) bought Freemason House as a training centre in 1922, took out a licence for 1923 and went on to achieve thirteen classic wins. They had enthusiasm and 'the right sort of friends'.[66] The increasing respectability of training can be seen in the way some young men of landed or upper-middle-class backgrounds were prepared to adopt a pupilage approach, parallel to the learned professions. Neville Crump, after studying at Marlborough School and Balliol College, paid trainer Sonny Hull 'a premium' to study with him.[67] John Hislop did the same thing.[68] Trainers with more middle-class backgrounds, sons of farmers, veterinary surgeons, even lawyers, sometimes entered steeplechasing. The former solicitor and amateur jockey, William Dutton, set up a small stable at Hednesford in 1932.[69]

Books by racing insiders often glossed over the difficulties of early years in training, before a reputation was gained. Jack Jarvis started with a yearly tenancy and three horses.[70] Ryan Jarvis, whose father was trainer for George V, still struggled when starting as a young trainer in 1936 even though his father bought him a small Newmarket yard. He only had four horses in his first season, when he trained for a banker and one of the Rothermere family, and had only one winner. By late 1939 he had only won twelve races, although he had expanded his still 'moderate' string.[71] The 'popular ex-jockey', Whalley, had only two horses in training when he got his first winner at Alexandra Park in 1929.[72] It was at this early stage that training was at its most pressured and arduous. The old maxim, 'tis only a trainer who knows a trainer's cares' was a reminder that nervous strain and desperation for scarce success could lead to much stress. Jack Leach, for example, was 'worried all the time', 'Too much work? Too little? Had I done this', with 'always something going wrong'.[73] By contrast 'star' trainers would have forty or fifty horses, with occasional examples of strings of nearly eighty, which created other worries.

Social relationships between owners and trainers were complex. Trainers could be of relatively high social status, and certainly as regards prosperity there was little to choose between the 'gentlemen' and 'trainer' routes. Differences were purely social, since they mixed in separate spheres in their training towns. Successful trainers relied on their track record, but that varied year-on-year, and trust and personal charisma also played a part. The racing world was largely conservative, monarchist and traditional in outlook, proud of serving royal and aristocratic masters. Jack Jarvis had 'always felt it a great honour and privilege' to train Rosebery horses.[74] Joe Child would toast George V in champagne every time he won him a race, exclaiming 'He's a gentleman', while William Jarvis became quite depressed at his failure to win the Oaks in 1938 for 'his much loved sovereign'.[75] Their owners often reciprocated, and trainers were well regarded. The Aga Khan, for example, praised his trainer, Frank Butters, as 'my very dear friend', a man who was 'one of the most delightful human beings one could ever hope to meet', and for whom all his family had 'the greatest affection'.[76] George V and Queen Mary sometimes dined with William Jarvis at Egerton House Lodge after going round the stables, gave him a silver cup when he made a private visit to Buckingham Palace, and made him a member of the Royal Victorian Order in the early 1930s.[77] Of Harry Cottrill it was said, 'one might almost think he was a member of the Jockey Club, such is his popularity with … the swells'.[78] Owners could become personal friends, addressed by their Christian names. Successful trainers were treated with respect and even deference by many of the owners who employed them, whether formally of higher or equal social status. At the same time trainers usually behaved with courtesy, civility and attentiveness towards owners. Losing a horse meant losing income, so trainers would rarely tell an owner that a horse was useless. A horse could be placed in a race against even worse horses, whilst a variety of excuses could be offered, from a bad draw to poor going, for a horse's lack of success. Most kept owners regularly informed by letter and telephone, and the diplomatic and social side of acquiring and keeping owners was vital to the success of all but the most talented. Owners could be stubborn. When Lord Rosebery's horses were unsuccessful at Ayr on the first two days of a meeting, Jack Jarvis received a telegram sending the horses back to Newmarket. When Jarvis sent a telegram saying that one of Rosebery's runners on the third day had a very good chance and requesting permission to run her he got a frosty response.[79]

Relations sometimes became strained. Some owners regularly changed their trainers. Others sometimes had doubts about particular running, or objected to other owners in the stable. Objections were rarely voiced in print, however. A series of undisclosed 'difficulties' led to the Aga Khan removing his horses from R.C. Dawson in 1931, but neither man would comment publicly. One owner at least actually took his horse away when his horse won, thanks largely to other jockeys' mistakes, because he believed that his trainer had misled him about his chances.[80] The eccentric owner Dorothy Paget broke with her steeplechase trainers regularly and moved her strings in sudden swoops around the country.[81]

Trainers' relationships with their own staff were usually formal, and their outward demeanour often serious and stern. In later life the jockey Gordon Richards recalled Fred Darling as a stern disciplinarian, well organised, with high expectations about smartness, ruthless with both horses and men. Boys had to ride out with polished leggings and boots, and properly-brushed hair. Bedding had to be neatly folded. Darling inspired a combination of fear and an immense affection in the staff who met his exacting standards.[82] Others would use physical violence, a cosh or stick to instil discipline. Some of the most successful yards gave few opportunities for their apprentices to ride their horses, preferring top jockeys, while by contrast Stanley Wooton was described as the 'fairest, most conscientious and painstaking trainer … with regard to apprentices'.[83]

Trainers had mystique, and kept their 'secrets' largely to themselves. Even many years later Ryan Jarvis was reluctant to tell stories about 'funny' events in racing, claiming 'anything I might say might be actionable, so I think I'll be careful'. The nature of work and stable relationships made trainers careful of mixing in pubs with the racing crowd, to whom they often appeared reserved. Competition meant inter-trainer rivalry was both obvious and sometimes acknowledged, while constant pestering for tips proved problematical. Some socialised well away from the stables and racing towns. Fred Darling, for example, while unwelcoming even to his owners, loved parties and girlfriends, but found them not in Marlborough but in London, motoring down and visiting nightclubs. However, he would hire the Marlborough Town Hall to give a party for his staff to celebrate his classic successes, to which they could bring partners.[84] Trainers' hobbies ranged from shooting, hunting or golf, to training greyhounds, playing tennis on Sunday afternoons, or buying, selling and breeding horses for themselves or for owners.

The successful adopted a wealthy and gentlemanly lifestyle, and became smart men of the world, a life that could last many years and was open to all who could develop the skills. Former jockey Harry Wragg, who had started working life in a Sheffield flour mill, and later turned to training, was helped by his wife, who made his home one of the centres of Newmarket hospitality, organising dinner parties and delighting in their social rise. They employed a cook, nanny, scullery-maid and gardeners.

Attitudes to betting amongst trainers varied, even in a single racing family. Colledge Leader (1883–1938), Lord Derby's private trainer at Stanley House, Newmarket from 1933, reputedly never bet. Yet his brother, Harvey (1893–1972), apparently enjoyed considerable success with his betting.[85] Betting was rarely excessive. Marcus Marsh would bet £5 or £10 for a sporting chance, £25 for a good chance, and £50 if it should win. Betting could influence stable policy, since betting stables were more likely to conceal the form of horses in handicaps, run horses in and out, engineer betting coups, or set out to win a small race somewhere with a horse trained up for the occasion. Small trainers might bet just to try to make ends meet.

The income of a trainer with a larger string was of upper-professional middle-class level, and the annual *Bloodstock Breeders' Review* 'memorative biographies' show many left substantial sums on death. Alec Taylor had trained the winners of 1,003 races worth £839,070 when he retired in 1927, and left nearly £600,000 on his death in 1943. Dobson Peacock left estate of £60,364 in 1935. Even a middle-ranking trainer like Fred Leader, who had never won a major race when he died, aged 52, in a car crash, left property of £22,370 in 1933. As well as profiting from weekly charges, income from fees could be augmented by presents given by grateful owners. Top trainers usually got a percentage of winnings and by the 1930s a bonus payment of 10 per cent of prize money was increasingly fashionable.[86] Frank Butters won £518,868 in prize money in ten years, so bonuses were a substantial extra income. Trainers could supplement income in other ways too. Almost all kept two or three pigs. Straw and horse droppings would eventually be sold to farmers. Some perhaps maintained a small farm, or kept breeding mares or stallions. But there were costs too. The trainer had to pay wages, fodder, bills, usually rent for the training stables, and all other entrance charges, vets' fees, etc. Most trainers had to pay a fee for use of local gallops. At Newmarket, for example, in 1934 the Jockey Club charged a heath tax of £10 for every racehorse and 3 guineas for every yearling that used the Heath.

Expensive horses needed good-quality accommodation, and training stables were very costly to set up, modernise, buy or rent. When Captain Boyd-Rochfort bought Freemason Lodge training stables and fairly modest house in Newmarket, it cost him over £12,000.[87] Bedford Lodge sold for £5,000 in 1930, and Bedford House for £15,000 a year earlier.[88] Better stables could fetch up to £50,000 in Newmarket, while the owner James White reportedly spent over £100,000 upgrading the Foxhill stables.[89] In the North trainers got larger premises for their money. The large Highfield House stables in Malton sold for £30,000.

Local status came from success at local meetings and in major races. Newspapers at Malton, Middleham, Newmarket or Epsom would celebrate training successes, as would the village itself, although even here jockeys were now getting the plaudits more than the trainer. As his trainer later remembered, when Grakle's jockey came back to Lincoln after his 1928 Grand National success, six thousand people filled the station yard and carried him shoulder-high to the Albion Hotel.[90] But trainers with long careers could expect final ritual recognition. When Richard Marsh retired after fifty years of training at Newmarket, he received a cheque for £3,435 as the proceeds of a testimonial, while fellow trainers gave him a silver cup and a cabinet of cigars.[91]

Most 'star' trainers, often absent from their stable, relied on a well-respected, experienced, truthful and honest head lad. He could make or break a yard, and was 'the greatest help a trainer can have' according to Richard Marsh.[92] He kept an eye on feeding, horse behaviour and leg defects, and knew a range of cures for most problems. Although some older trainers fed their own horses, head lads were usually responsible for preparing the specific feed, with Scottish oats being a mainstay, along with hay, bran and beans. Ideally they lived on the premises, but some lived nearby. They earned about £3 a week, if living in an on-site cottage, plus presents of *c.* £3 a winner.[93] Most yards also employed a travelling head lad who went to races with horses and grooms, and ensured that they were looked after on the course and loaded on and off the train safely.

Stable lads and grooms were at the bottom of the ladder. They would come from all over the country. Their parents had a variety of backgrounds, often skilled or semi-skilled like coachman or joiner, some more middle-class. The parents of several were farmers. Stafford Ingham was the son of a Penge chemist. As many came from urban as from rural environments. Tommy Weston, for example, had been selling newspapers and working in a foundry.[94] Most boys came to the stable on leaving school, with the key criterion being their light-weight build. Many were attracted by the apparent glamour of becoming a jockey, love of horses, and ideas of making money. Some already had brothers in racing, or came from racing families.

Most ambitious lads wanted to be jockeys, but only a few succeeded. Cyril Luckman suggested that 'only one in a thousand', Rickman that 'one in a hundred' became established jockeys.[95] Some could already ride but this was not vital. Harry Wragg knew nothing about stable work and had never seen a race-horse when he arrived in Newmarket.[96] Lengths of jockey indentures varied, most usually five years, but ranging from three to eight years. An initial 'trial' period was relatively calm. Lads did odd jobs and looked after ponies and hacks. Once indentures were signed they were often treated more harshly. Doug Smith had a 'spartan and cheerless' apprenticeship near Wantage, which he described as 'very tough', with strict physical discipline.[97] Stable food could be poor. Lads soon learned to keep quiet and be civil, addressing head lads, jockeys and other senior figures as 'Mr' rather than using first names. New lads were often the butt of practical jokes: water-buckets on top of a door or loosened bed frames. Stable initiation rituals, usually involving greasing and chaffing of genitals, conferred their racing nickname and supposedly qualified them to learn the finer points of horsemanship.

In stables lads lived in dormitories, accommodating from three or four up to thirty. Older 'board wagemen' out of apprenticeship lived in. Married men lived out and came in from their homes. Most earned around £2 a week if married, though less if single. Winning owners sometimes gave presents to the stable lads who 'did' their horses, which for a lucky few increased their earnings. Each trainer negotiated wage settlements separately, and lads' wages were tradition-ally very low, although most lived in at the stables, so accommodation and meals were free, and any doctors' bills were paid. Doctors' bills were necessary, since injuries were common: horses bit, kicked or threw their riders. One ex-jockey, Tom Aldridge, died at Durdans when his horse shied at some donkeys.[98]

Indentured lads got little money until they had served their time. Jack Morris initially got only £6 a year, paid to his mother, so he survived by scrumping, doing tack or washing jobs for older stablemen, taking beer bottles back – or 'you had to thieve it'.[99] Doug Smith was initially paid 2s 6d a week, which slowly went up first to 5s and finally to 10s a week. He shared with two others a room 'more or less like a coal cellar, decorated up', jointly using a hard bed in very cold conditions.[100] Shepherd, who even paid for washing, although work clothes were supplied, slept in a open-windowed loft with bare boards, to which his boots froze in winter, and used horse rugs for warmth. He admitted that it was 'only the horses' that kept him there.[101] Harry Wragg initially received only a shilling a week, eventually rising to three. His trainer, Bob Colling, was renowned for parsimony. All trainers charged owners for apprentices' riding fees, and often winning percentages or 'presents' too. Some kept the lot. Wragg got nothing from Colling, although he won many races for him. In the North wages were similarly low. At Manor House, Middleham, lads reputedly got a shilling a week, slept three to a bed and got only Christmas week off.[102] Lads generally had little free time, except on Sunday, when horses were not exercised, though in some yards churchgoing was compulsory, and evening stables were still expected.[103]

Lads commonly took care of two horses, and occasionally three, once they proved reliable. They were wakened by the head lad somewhere between five and half past six, and began by cleaning out the boxes and stalls. Wooden skips or sacks would be used for 'mucking out'. The horses were 'dressed over', vigorously strapped with wisp and rubber, and got ready for riding out with the rest of 'the string' or first 'lot' from six to seven o'clock. Then lads might have a slice of bread and a cup of tea. Tack would be put on, and horses sheeted up. Trainers would accompany the string to the gallops to supervise exercise, usually from hacks, thoroughbreds or trap, while wealthier trainers sometimes used cars. Gallops lasted up to an hour and a half on nearby laid-out heath or moorland. Usually two days were 'fast work' or galloping days, over the horse's best distance. Trainers would vary training according to a horse's characteristics, habits, condition and feeding, drawing on their experience and practice. Too much work would lead to poor eating. On the other days only trotting and cantering were required. Back in by nine, horses would be groomed over, boxes set fair and the horses fed, and lads would get breakfast. A second lot would be turned out by around quarter to eleven, and would be back in and done up by twelve thirty, unless it was wet, when they would have to be dried off. Older grooms would often be given time off in the afternoon, but at many yards apprentices would clean windows, weed, sweep and tidy the yard and drives, crush corn and cut chaff, and do odd jobs like tack and brass cleaning or washing out saddle rooms. Evening stables were around half past four. At Stanley House stables this was 'rather like a military inspection, with sawdust laid down everywhere ... at the entrance to every box brilliantly polished brasses, and every lad dressed in a white jacket to show off his horse'.[104] Boxes were tidied up, horses groomed, the trainer would inspect them and then they would be fed and finally done up about six-thirty, although the trainer might check later.

In winter National Hunt trainers were still busy, but others went into hibernation. Horses ceased fast work. Some would be sent back to be stabled at their owner's property. New yearlings came in late August or September to be broken in, backed and ridden under the supervision of the head lad. Exercised horses now wore a hood, breast-cloth and a big sheet, with a rug on top, to keep them warm. At Christmas staff might receive a cash bonus based on the stable's success. In early spring 2-year-olds would be tried to assess their merits and potential. Jockeys would sometimes be brought in specially, and special trial gallops hired. Trainers (and owners) kept a trial book to record this. Sometimes lads would wear the owner's silks over their shirts to aid identification.

Most lads were loyal to and really knew the horses they did, although over time the 'grand colt' might become a 'twisting bastard' with consistent failure. They learnt strategies to deal with their 'rogue' horses.[105] A constant image in oral testimony is that a horse was 'like a child', and had to be individually treated. Lads would go to great lengths to 'mother', encourage to feed and bring on 'their' horse. Indeed the letters of Snowy Shepherd's brother, about his horses, not his mildewed clothing, attracted Snowy to the same stable.[106] When they came back from holiday they would grumble about the poor treatment of 'their' horses, swearing and insulting their replacement: 'two rides from you is enough to f... any horse for life, the way you ride'.[107]

Although not physically hard, hours were from early morning to late evening if horses returned late from meetings. But stable life was regulated and predictable. Lads were subject to semi-feudal authority exercised by the trainer, the head lad or occasionally the trainer's wife. Trainers did not suffer fools gladly and some had, as Shepherd remembered, 'terrible mouths', and 'messed the men about' when not with owners. Generally lads accepted the discipline as a fact of life. 'Hard but fair', as Phil Welsh summed up his trainer, indicates a common view.[108] Photographs of staffs show them looking neatly presented and almost all wore well-fitting riding breeches, leather leggings or jodhpurs, shirts and short coats. Some wore collar and tie, others wore mufflers. Trainers expected tidy and clean appearances, and apprentices would often be supplied with breeches. In big stables there was particular emphasis on status. This showed itself not only in lads' appearance, but in horses too, and before a race horses were extra carefully groomed and manes carefully plaited. Trainers' initials were on exercise sheets, a visible symbol of status in the training community, and there were visual reminders of previous famous classic and other stable winners around the yards.

Lads had a flourishing social life, sometimes respectable, sometimes less so. Larger training towns often had institutes or clubs where lads could spend their evenings playing more respectable games. They were expected back at the stables usually well before ten o'clock, otherwise they would be locked out, and punished with extra duties, although lads would sometimes sneak out late for dances and to meet girls. Newmarket Racing Lads Recreation Rooms had an hour's Bible class on Sundays. It had a library, provided writing paper and envelopes, three billiard tables, a snooker table, and sold tea or cakes for a penny. Some stables had a mess room and a games room. Virtually every stable lad bet at least occasionally. Outside the stables, the chief sporting recreations were billiards, boxing, football and cricket. At Newmarket there was a Stable Lads' Football League, and there were other stable teams elsewhere. In bigger training regions there were boxing competitions for stable lads at weights from 4.5 st. to 8 st. Morris was a skilled boxer, and had several fights at Newmarket, including one against a boxer from the Chantilly stables in France, for a purse of £100.[109]

Strong rivalries coexisted with a keen sense of identity. Both operated at several levels. There were powerful interyard rivalries within Newmarket, Lambourn or Malton. Newmarket's superiority complex meant sometimes strong competition with 'country' stables, while there was further separation between northern and southern stables. Racing towns were also divided by the equivalent of 'town-versus-gown' rivalries. As Welsh admitted, at Newmarket 'our enemies were the townies'. Welsh also provided a more detailed account of the zest and energy of play, fighting and sexual experience, claiming that lads had 'glib tongues through living away from home, so [were] able to charm most of the local girls', and that some lads had to change stables two or three times to avoid having to marry pregnant girls, and learnt not to 'give their real names' when 'playing away'.[110]

The conservative nature of the industry ensured that lads were largely ununionised. Racing was individualistic and conservative. Trainers were strongly opposed to unionisation, because of the need for flexibility when dealing with horses, and the belief that a union would 'develop into a clearing house for stable information'.[111] Despite this, there was significant industrial unrest, passed over almost entirely in conventional racing literature. Some trainers looked after and paid their lads badly. Social and cultural relationships could be problematical. There are suggestions that there was a trainers' blacklist of men dismissed for misconduct of one kind or another, which meant that 'a man's chance of gaining a living in a stable is gone'.[112] Lads' grievances at Epsom led to a strike there in 1919, and assaults on non-strikers.[113]

The depressions of the 1920s and early 1930s led to a fairly quiescent work-force but there was increased discontent from the mid-1930s, as wages remained held down. An unsuccessful strike at Lambourn over wages and conditions in 1936 resulted in some lads there secretly joining the Transport and General Workers Union (TGWU).[114] There was renewed disaffection at Epsom, Lambourn and Newmarket, where some interim increases were given which raised experienced lads' pay from between 40 and 42s to 45s. The Newmarket Trainers' Federation initially recognised the TGWU, paid holidays went from a week to eight consecutive days after one year's service, wages were increased to 48s, and one-third of the men were to be freed from Sunday evening stables.[115] In mid-May 1938 Trainers' Federations at Newmarket and in Berkshire, Wiltshire and Hampshire passed resolutions refusing further increases. When strikes were threatened they refused either arbitration or the intervention of the Conciliation Board. Small-scale strikes at Newmarket had spread to Marlborough, Lambourn and Weyhill by late May 1938. At Lambourn, where three hundred struck, those lads who continued to ride out had to do so with police supervision, with widespread intimidation right through the summer, in attempts to raise the pay of less-experienced lads to 38s. At Wantage three stable lads pushed about and kicked a non-striker who didn't 'see any good in it' as late as December 1938.[116] Eventually the intervention of the Conciliation Board, and newspaper pressure for 'a living wage', orchestrated by Ernest Bevin, who was now general secretary of the recently-formed Stable Lads' Union, led to minor increases.

Stable difficulties should not be over-stressed. Although many lads put on too much weight to ride out and had to depart, for lightweight stable lads long careers were possible. Unsuccessful jockeys often returned to the yard, while a bad employer could be left. There was a fair amount of mobility between yards, with opportunities to work abroad too, through recruitment advertisements for apprentice-served grooms of 8 st. who could ride out, offering 'good wages and presents'.[117] In many yards the atmosphere was quite jolly and happy-go-lucky, with much laughing and joking, along with the coarse language. And lads always had the horses, or the sight of the Heath on a work morning in high summer, to sustain them.

Notes

1   *The Times*, 9.11.1933.
2   Marcus Marsh, *Racing with the gods* (London: Pelham Books, 1968), p. 17.
3   Jack Fairfax-Blakeborough, *The analysis of the turf* (London: Phillip Allan, 1927), p. 102.
4   *Daily Mirror*, 7.6.1923. Donoghue managed two autobiographies: Steve Donoghue, *Just my story* (London: Hutchinson, n.d. but *c.* 1923); Steve Donoghue, *Donoghue up!* (London: Collins, 1938).
5   Gordon Richards, *My story* (London: Hodder and Stoughton, 1955).
6   *Daily Mirror*, 26.3.1938.
7   *Daily Mail*, 9.11.1933. Richards ended the season with 259 victories.
8   C. R. Acton, *Silk and spur* (London: Richards, 1935), p. 106; Quintin Gilbey, *Fun was my living* (London: Hutchinson, 1970), p. 147.
9   See Donoghue, *Just my story*, p. 225.
10   *Sporting Chronicle*, 8.6.1935.
11   Rae Johnstone, *The Rae Johnstone story* (London: Stanley Paul, 1958), p. 12.
12   John Hislop, *Far from a gentleman* (London: Michael Joseph, 1960), pp. 110, 185.
13   See Hotspur's comments in the *Daily Telegraph*, 15.6.1933. See also A J. Dickenson, 'Jockeys and jockeyship', in Ernest Bland, *Flat racing since 1900* (London: Andrew Dakers, 1950), p. 194.
14   *The Times*, 6.2.1928.
15   *Daily Telegraph*, 13.1.1924.
16   See Suffolk Oral History Project 1985–88, OHT 354, Snowy Shepherd.
17   Phil Welsh, *Stable rat: life in the racing stables* (London: Eyre Methuen, 1979), p. 68.
18   The situation is little different today. For an overview of the labour market for jockeys, see Wray Vamplew, 'Still crazy after all those years: continuity in a changing labour market for professional jockeys', *Contemporary British history*, 14: 2 (2000), 115–45.
19   Wray Vamplew, *The turf* (London: Allen Lane, 1976), p. 156.
20   Captain X, *Tales of the turf* (London: Partridge Publications, 1943), p. 57.
21   See report on their use in *The Sporting Life*, 21.2.1924. Chris Pitt, *A long time gone* (Halifax: Portway Press, 1996), p. 197 says they were first used at Cardiff in 1923. Roger Munting, *Hedges and ditches* (London: J. A., Allen, 1987), p. 141 says they were made compulsory that year. Pictures indicate that the rule was not always obeyed.
22   Meyrick Good, *Good days* (London: Hutchinson, 1941), p. 99.
23   Acton, *Silk and spur*, p. 23.

24 Letter from John Hislop, quoted in John Hislop and David Swannell, *The Faber book of the turf* (London: Faber, 1990), p. 195.

25 Rickman, *Come racing with me* (London: Chatto and Windus, 1951), p. 131. Sidney Gilbey, *Memoirs of a racing journalist* (London: Hutchinson, 1934), p. 264 refers to a present of £5,000.

26 John McGuigan, *A trainer's memories: being sixty years' turf reminiscences and experiences* (London: Heath Granton, 1946), p. 88.

27 Suffolk Oral History Project 1985–8, OHT 355, Snowy Shepherd.

28 Sir Alfred Munnings, *The second burst* (London: Museum Press, 1951), p. 143; Michael Tanner and Gerry Cranham, *Great jockeys of the flat* (Enfield: Guiness Publishing, 1992) p. 134.

29 Donoghue, *Donoghue up*, p. 166.

30 Tim FitzGeorge Parker, *The ditch on the hill: eighty years of the Cheltenham festival* (London: Simon and Schuster, 1991), p. 65.

31 Arthur J. Sarl, *Horses, jockeys and crooks: reminiscences of thirty years' racing* (London: Hutchinson, 1935), ch. 19.

32 Gilbey, *Memoirs*, p. 217; Acton, *Silk and spur*, p. 104.

33 M. Seth-Smith, *Steve: the life and times of Steve Donoghue* (London: Faber, 1974), p. 56.

34 See Johnstone, *The Rae Johnstone story*.

35 *The Times*, 10.8.1923.

36 Ras Prince Monolulu, *I gotta horse* (London: Hurst and Blackett, n.d.), p. 56.

37 Richard Kaye, *The Ladbroke's story* (London: Pelham Books, 1969), p. 55.

38 Michael Seth-Smith, *The head waiter: a biography of Harry Wragg* (London: Michael Joseph, 1984), p. 70.

39 *Bloodstock breeders' review* (1933), p. 95.

40 Interview with Frank Johnson, Newmarket, 1997.

41 Quoted in Jack Fairfax-Blakeborough, *The turf who's who* (London: Mayfair Press, 1932), pp. 476–7.

42 See Suffolk Oral History Project 1985–8, OHT 355, Snowy Shepherd.

43 Acton, *Silk and spur*, p. 107.

44 Johnstone, *The Rae Johnstone story*, p. 68.

45 Fairfax-Blakeborough, *The analysis of the turf*, p. 128.

46 Tanner and Cranham, *Great jockeys*, p. 155.

47 *North-Eastern Daily Gazette*, 7.6.1935; Michael Seth-Smith *et al.*, *The history of steeplechasing* (London: Michael Joseph, 1966), p. 112.

48 FitzGeorge Parker, *The ditch on the hill*, p. 64.

49 Donoghue, *Donoghue up*, p. 285.

50 Noel Fairfax-Blakeborough (ed.), *J. F-B. The memoirs of Jack Fairfax-Blakeborough* (J A Allen: London 1978) p. 185.

51 Bill Rickaby, *First to Finish* (Gateshead: Northumberland Press, 1969), p. 16.

52 Noel Fairfax-Blakeborough (ed), *J. .F-B.*, p. 185; McGuigan, *A trainer's memories*, p. 90.

53 Vian Smith, *Point-to-point* (London: Stanley Paul, 1968), pp. 22–3.

54 'Memorative biographies', *Bloodstock breeders' review* (1931), p. 119.

55 *1921 Census industrial tables,* p. 198.

56 *1931 Census industrial tables,* p. 719.

57 See Mike Huggins, 'Nineteenth-century racehorse stables in their rural setting: a social and economic study', *Rural History,* 7: 2 (1996), 177–90.

58 Richard Marsh, *A trainer to two kings* (London: Cassell, 1925), p. 322.

59 See 'Successful trainers: Manton stable's remarkable record', *Bloodstock breeders' review* (1931), pp. 98–100.

60 See 'The Scout' (Cyril Luckman), *The Scout's guide to racing 1937* (London: Daily Express, 1937), pp. 163–6.

61 D. Birley, *Playing the game: sport and British society 1910–1945* (Manchester: Manchester University Press, 1995), p. 155.

62 Billie Brown, *Also ran: the life story of Billie Brown, owner, trainer and jockey* (London: E. Hulton, 1920), pp. 66–7.

63 Hislop, *Far from a gentleman,* p. 145.

64 Charles Richardson, *Racing at home and abroad: British flat racing and breeding, racehorses and the evaluation of the thoroughbred* (London: London and Home Counties Press Association, 1923), p. 334.

65 Hon. George Lambton, *Men and horses I have known* (London: Thornton Butterworth, 1924).

66 D. W. E. Brock, *The racing man's weekend book* (London: Seeley Service and Co., n.d.), p. 55.

67 Tim FitzGeorge Parker, *Ever loyal: the biography of Neville Crump* (London: Stanley Paul, 1987), p. 31.

68 Hislop, *Far from a gentleman,* p. 151.

69 Seth-Smith, *History of steeplechasing,* p. 129.

70 Jack Jarvis, *They're off: an autobiography* (London: Michael Joseph, 1969), p. 34.

71 Suffolk Oral History Project 1985–8, OHT 421, Ryan Jarvis.

72 *The Racing World and Newmarket sportsman,* 9.7.1929.

73 Jack Leach, *A rider in the stand: racing reminiscences* (London: Stanley Paul, 1970), p. 29.

74 Jarvis, *They're off,* p. 42.

75 Marsh, *Racing with the gods,* p. 26; John Rickman, *Old Tom and young John: stories from a horseracing family* (Cambridge: Allborough Press, 1990), p. 12.

76 Aga Khan, *The memoirs of Aga Khan: world enough and time* (London: Cassell, 1954), p. 199.

77 Bridget Rickaby, *All about Bill* (Newmarket: R. and N. publications, 1990), pp. 30–31.

78 'The Scout', *The Scout's guide to racing 1937,* p. 56.

79 Jarvis, *They're off,* p. 52.

80 Gilbey, *Fun was my living,* p. 154.

81 Ivor Herbert and Patricia Smyly, *The winter kings* (London: Pelham Books, 1968), p. 76.

82 Richards, *My story,* p. 28.

83 McGuigan, *A trainer's memories*, p. 82.

84 Marsh, *Racing with the gods*, pp. 21–4.

85 R. Mortimer *et al.*, *Biographical encyclopaedia of flat racing* (London: McDonald and Jane's, 1978), p. 342.

86 *Bloodstock breeders' review* (1937), quoted in Leo Rasmussen and Miles (comp.), *Treasures of the bloodstock breeders' review* (London: J. A. Allen, 1990), p. 293.

87 Bill Curling, *The captain: a biography of Captain Sir Cecil Boyd Rochfort, royal trainer* (London: Barrie and Jenkins, 1970), p. 32.

88 Seth-Smith, *The Head Waiter*, p. 73; Andrew Sim, *English racing stables* (Addlestone: Dial Press, 1993), p. 46.

89 S. Theodore Felstead, *Racing romance* (London: Werner Laurie, 1949), p. 77.

90 J. G. Lyall, *Round goes the world* (Stamford: Haynes and Co., 1937), p. 92.

91 'Richard Marsh', *Bloodstock breeders' review*, (1933), p. 125.

92 Marsh, *A trainer to two kings*, p. 299.

93 Acton, *Silk and spur*, p. 168.

94 Tommy Weston, *My racing life* (London: Hutchinson, 1952).

95 'The Scout', *The Scout's guide to racing 1937*, p. 10; Rickman, *Come racing with me*, p. 134.

96 Seth-Smith, *The head waiter*, p. 8.

97 Mortimer *et al.*, *Biographical encyclopaedia of flat racing*, p. 572.

98 *The Times*, 23.6.1923.

99 Suffolk Oral History Project 1985–88, OHT 327, Jack Morris.

100 Suffolk Oral History Project 1985–88, OHT 522, Doug Smith.

101 Suffolk Oral History Project 1985–88 OHT 352, Snowy Shepherd.

102 Sim, *English racing stables*, p. 58.

103 Acton, *Silk and spur*, p. 62.

104 Rickaby, *First to finish*, p. 14.

105 For an example of how one such rogue was made a 'good boy', see Suffolk Oral History Project 1985–88, OHT 355, Snowy Shepherd.

106 *Ibid.*

107 Hislop, *Far from a gentleman*, p. 155.

108 Welsh, *Stable rat*, p. 29.

109 Suffolk Oral History Project 1985–88, OHT 327, Jack Morris.

110 Welsh, *Stable rat*, pp. 47–8.

111 H. S. Persse, 'Training' in Rt. Hon. The Earl of Harewood and Lt.-Col. P. E. Ricketts (eds), *Flat racing* (London: Seeley Service and Co., 1937), p. 325.

112 Captain Heath, *Racing annual 1934* (London: News Chronicle, 1934), p. 67.

113 *The Times*, 13.10.1919; *ibid.*, 27.10.1919; *ibid.*, 29.10.1919.

114 Trainers were generally anti-union. See Persse, 'Training', p. 324, who argued that 'Trade unionism in a racing stable is not feasible'.

115 'Stablemen's conditions', *Bloodstock breeders' review*, 26 (1937), p. 277.

116 *The Times*, 16–28.5.1938, 27.8.1938 and 30.12.1938, provides more details.

117 For example, *The Sporting Life*, 26.5.1924.

7

Breeders and owners

Breeders

England, particularly northern England, was the original home of the
thoroughbred horse, and thoroughbred breeding was a national industry of
great value. In former centuries England had maintained a global supremacy,
even though Irish, French and American horses were occasionally successful in
major races. Between the wars England struggled to retain its lead. Nevertheless
a firm belief that Britain was best, and that British breeding was superior, still
dominated the cultural thinking of British breeders. Edward Moorhouse, secretary of the Society for the Encouragement of Thoroughbred Breeding, claimed
that 'England is the home of the thoroughbred and it is only here that he can
retain his perfection … it is vital to maintain our superiority'.[1] A highly affirma-
tive image of British stud produce was also maintained by the racing press, and
some correspondents, such as 'Audax' (Arthur Portman) or 'Mandanko'
(Professor Robertson) were breeding experts. All the major racing papers published descriptions of their correspondents' visits to racing studs. Descriptions
of the horses included colour, breeding lines, shape, conformation and similar
details and were always couched positively. The foals described in 'a round of
the Burton Agnes Stud' in 1935, for example, were variously of 'great symmetry
and superb quality', 'very smart', 'strong and active', 'good', 'shapely' and 'neat'.
The Lordship stud horses were variously 'lengthy', 'handsome', 'active', 'compact', 'well balanced', a 'good mover', 'fine', 'rich' and 'free-moving'.[2] Poorer
ones were presumably not mentioned.

The ideal for all breeders was to breed stamina and speed in their horses, but
Britain, with its high proportion of 2-year-old racers, largely bred for speed at
the expense of stamina. English breeders almost never imported mares or stallions for breeding purposes, whilst exporting some of their best stock. One
result of this was that between the wars foreign horses began to achieve an

increasing proportion of successes in those British races requiring more stamina. New strains of outstanding prepotence were being established in France, America, Italy, Australia and South America. There were, for example, French successes in both the Cambridgeshire and Cesarewitch in 1938. British excuses were always found. When statistical articles appeared in the American-published *Thoroughbred Record* (Lexington, Kentucky) which appeared to suggest that English thoroughbreds were becoming inferior to those overseas, they were dismissed slightingly as 'ridiculous', 'based on false premises' and 'futile vapourings'.[3]

Breeders provided the thoroughbreds for flat racing, and were therefore indispensable. But although most of them bred for sale, and saw themselves as commercial businesses, the extent to which some actually made a profit was problematical. They did not support racing financially, but rather sought to gain from it by selling their stock. Breeders varied in their background, but a significant minority had titles or military rank. Breeding was an avenue which upper-class women were beginning to enter after the war and through the 1920s and 1930s. By 1938, Lady Beryl Groves, Lady James Douglas, Lady Wentworth and Lady Barbara Scott all sold five or more yearlings at the July Newmarket sales or the September Doncaster sales, which were the Mecca of yearling vendors and buyers. Lady Wentworth was sufficiently knowledgeable to write a book on breeding.[4] A majority of smaller breeders were farmers, and for many thoroughbreds were a sideline. If they paid their way, well and good; if they produced a profit, better still. Trainers with spare stable capacity might also become involved in breeding on a small scale, while veterinary surgeons some-times conducted a stud. Jock Crawford, for example, son of a blacksmith, who had trained as a veterinary surgeon in Glasgow, became interested in racing and breeding in India, and became involved in the British Bloodstock Agency and the Glasgow Stud at Enfield.

The number of yearlings sold by each breeder varied. At the earlier Newmarket July sales, small breeders, selling one or two yearlings, usually represented between 50 and 60 per cent of the vendors. This was probably an attempt to cash in on their assets as soon as possible. At the later Doncaster sales this figure was lower, usually around 40 per cent. Few breeders sold more than ten yearlings. In 1938 only the Aga Khan, Lord Furness, Mr J. W. Harris and four commercial studs, the Worksop Manor Stud, the Exning Stud, the Sledmere Stud and the Ballykisteen Stud in Ireland, sold so many.

Some breeders were breeder-owners, breeding and racing their own horses, and prepared to trade potential profit for the pleasure of ownership. Their motives varied, but some at least were less concerned with success *per se* than with trying to improve the breed. The duke of Westminster, for example, cared little for racing, but devoted 'his time, attention and money to breeding blood-stock' at his Eaton Hall Stud.[5] Kingsclere Ltd, a training stable syndicate in which he and the duke of Portland were involved, was not used between 1919 and 1934. Despite George V's large Wolferton Stud, of about twenty mares, its stock were only rarely successful on the racecourse, partly because for prestige reasons the king's racing manager and trainer in the early 1920s entered them at races where their majesties were more likely to be present. Even a change of trainer and racing manager had little effect. Indeed in 1927 and 1928 none of the foals bred at the king's stud won a single race. Yet the king had a very deep-rooted interest in breeding and the welfare of his young stock. On his arrival at Sandringham, his first tour of inspection was to go carefully round the stud. He enjoyed visiting the mares and young stock, and derived great pleasure from showing off to friends his leading stallion, Friar Marcus, at stud in Egerton.[6] By contrast George VI knew much less about breeding. Others bred because it was a 'traditional' part of upper-class life. At Wynyard Park, in County Durham, there had been interest in racing by successive Lord Londonderrys for many generations, and they continued to breed there, with only limited success, up to 1924. After 1933 they indulged their interest in breeding through membership of Apelle Ltd, a horse syndicate.[7]

Breeding provided great pleasure to many of those involved. To John Crawford, for example, 'his love and life was the throughbred. It was a joy to him to be able to dispense his unusual heritage to those whom he thought he could aid, or who desired his assistance'.[8] William Fawcett, the hunting and racing editor of *The Field*, clearly really enjoyed his 'joyous days in sun-lit pad-dock and shaded stud farm', amongst many 'friends of long standing'. He felt that 'to see the horses that you have bred yourself, to make plans for the mating of your mares, to weigh up and examine the winning strains in the different bloods, to find out that your theories have worked out correctly – there is a joy in all these things that increases with the passing of the years'.[9] Mrs Edward Clayton had a few horses in training, but preferred breeding: 'her heart and mind love chiefly the mare, the yearling, the foal and the sires at stud'.[10]

Some leading owner-breeders were very much involved in the study of breeding. At Lord Rosebery's stud, for instance, matings were made on his orders, not his manager's. For leading owner-breeders there was an element of competition to prove that their theories of breeding worked. Scientific advances in breeding theory came only slowly. Lord Astor claimed that he 'bred racehorses as some men breed other sorts of livestock or plants' and liked to test his theories 'against the best that others could produce'.[11] The Aga Khan's racing success was not just based on lavish investment and superbly equipped studs, and ability to pick good managers, trainers and jockeys. It was underpinned by an excellent knowledge of breeding, and a breeding philosophy based partly on mixing bloodlines of great stallions in carefully calculated percentages of inbreeding and outbreeding.[12] Inbreeding increased the influence of the ancestor to whom a breeder inbred. Other breeders, such as C. R. Acton, attached greater importance to the female line.[13] Lord Wavertree, a member of a well-known Lancashire brewing family, who had also made a profound study of breeding, attached little importance to the sire and great importance to his mares, and went further still, applying astrology to his racing and breeding interests. Breeders could follow a wide variety of breeding systems and theories: the stamina index, the Vuillier dosage system, the Bruce Lowe figure system and blood affinity all had their supporters. Most theories used data from the limited numbers of successful racehorses, not the far more plentiful bad ones or those offspring which never saw a racecourse.[14]

The breeding industry had always been economically risky and although it largely rode out the economic volatility of the 1920s and 1930s the period was fraught with anxiety for breeders, even though the drastic weeding out of useless horses that took place during the 1914–18 War had positive effects on the breeding stock. As the 1938 *News Chronicle Racing Annual* admitted, 'it is a hazardous game, this breeding'.[15] Least concerned were owners of top, fashionable, stallions whose offspring were winning races with substantial prize money, although stallion fees were taxed until Lord Rosebery succeeded in changing the law. For this minority breeding was more lucrative, although some kept their best yearlings rather than selling them. For others who wished to put their mares to a good stallion prices rose after the war. By 1936 the 'covering' of a mare by any of the top eight stallions would cost its owner over £400; in 1914 only three stallions had been priced so high. A top stallion was rarely allowed to cover more than forty mares a season, and in the mid-1930s the minimum covering fee charged for any of the top one hundred or so stallions was about 45 guineas, and a maximum around 500 guineas. There were around two hundred stallions appearing annually in the main section of the *Register of Thoroughbred Stallions*, and many more of minor importance in abbreviated form in the appendix.[16]

Breeding studs were scattered throughout the country, not just on rich estates, and many such as the Glasgow stud farm near Enfield, for example, run by the British Bloodstock Agency, were in locations which had been used for

Table 7.1 Percentage of stallions at different stud fees in guineas, 1920–39

	No. in sample	25g or less %	26–100g %	101–200g %	more than 200g %
1920	326	71	21	1	6
1929	223	56	29	4	12
1939	274	53	33	8	7

Source: Adapted from Wray Vamplew *The Turf* (London: Allen Lane, 1976), p. 193

many generations. There were areas of particular concentration, with the Newmarket area and the regions around York and Bedale being particularly significant. Many stayed in the same family for generations. Some changed hands regularly, but were rarely profitable. Lord St David spent more than £30,000 on his Newmarket Lordship stud in the ten years he held it but it could not attract an offer of £30,000 in 1936.[17]

Studs came under the category of agriculture. The routines of looking after the brood mares, and dealing with covering, foaling and rearing were attractive to some workers, and it was a semi-skilled occupation. Most commercial studs employed a specialised stud groom, who received accommodation, keep and salary, together with a 1-guinea fee paid by the owner of each mare covered, to ensure covering was successful. Stud grooms managed the stud, and often advised owners which foals to keep and which should be drafted and sold. Most studfarms employed grooms and stable lads too, some from long-standing stud-farm families. When John Lancaster joined a Newmarket stud, his father and uncle already worked there.[18]

Because owners could make money during a stallion's potent life, top stallions realised high prices. The great stayer Solario was sold for £49,350 on his owner's death in 1932, and maintained a stud fee of £525 thereafter, becoming champion sire in 1937. The Beech House Stud in Newmarket, owned by the bookmaker Martin Benson, paid £50,000 for Derby winner Windsor Lad in 1934, and £60,000 for Nearco, the Italian champion and winner of the Grand Prix de Paris, in 1938.[19]

Purchase could be risky. Nearco became a leading sire but Windsor Lad did not last long at stud. Call Boy, the 1926 Derby winner, cost £60,000 but proved virtually sterile, with scarcely any successful offspring. However these were excessive prices. Good stallions between the wars more usually sold for between

£7,000 and £16,000. Mares were a little cheaper. Mrs Chester Beatty paid £12,600 for a single mare that proved disappointing at stud, and the highest price paid during this period was £18,700. Lord D'Abernon sold five mares for £33,075 in the generally depressed market of 1929.

Not all breeders sold their stock. Traditionally the upper classes often kept their good yearlings to race. Top breeders such as the seventeenth earl of Derby or the Aga Khan, who could afford to have their mares covered by top stallions, were regularly successful in classic events with horses of their own breeding between the wars, although this was in part also a result of employing expert staff. Lord Savile (d.1931) carried on a small stud at Rufford, some seasons sending his yearlings to Doncaster, other times sending them for training.

A few of these rich breeders, who had access to the best stallions, mated their mares with their own stallions, but many sent nearly all their mares to stallions they did not own, paying high subscription fees for the privilege. A stallion was chosen for a variety of reasons, including the success of his progeny, conformation, temperament, speed or stamina, inbreeding or outcrossing, the blending of particular bloodlines, or just current fashion. Breeders were made well aware of their successes and failures. The racing press annually published lists of winning breeding stallions and mares based on the amount of stakes won at races that year by their offspring.

Prices of yearlings reflected both their perceived current market values, and attitudes amongst the wealthier classes who could afford the conspicuous consumption of racehorse purchase. Value was in part a product of the amount owners could afford to invest, and reflected current economic situations. It was also dependent in part on the number of yearlings available and this was linked to breeder confidence some two years before. The perceived annual quality of yearlings was also variable. So was the amount of prize money offered by courses, and this also influenced purchasers. Fashionably bred yearlings usually cost far more, and were bought by the richest owners. Lord Glanley bred more horses than he required but still sometimes bought two or three high-priced yearlings, as did Lord Woolavington. Indeed, the highest price paid for a yearling in the 1920s auction sales was 14,500 guineas paid in 1920 by Lord Glanely for Blue Ensign from the Sledmere Stud; the highest in the 1930s the 15,000 guineas paid by Miss Dorothy Paget for the colt Colonel Payne. However, some yearlings were sold privately by breeders. In 1926 the Aga Khan had spent lavishly on yearlings, paying in total £57,120. One of the yearlings, Feridoon, was purchased from the National Stud for £17,000 but was a complete failure as a racehorse and was eventually sold in France for about £13. This illustrates the point that potential racing success was a lottery, and not always related to price. Lord Glanley won the 1919 Derby with a horse bought for £470.[20]

Breeding was a high-status occupation, but the high prices paid for a few top-class yearlings concealed the high-risk nature of the industry, a gamble whether breeding for sale or personal racing success. Up to a third of mares would not foal successfully, some foals would be unsound, and some foals would not find a buyer, while a mare was a depreciating asset. In 1925, for example, of the 5,846 mares indexed in the *Stud Book*, 1,528 were barren and a further 112 slipped their foals. There was an early death rate of some 20 per cent of foals, and a further 20 per cent did not reach the sales. Research on nine-teenth-century breeding has suggested that a majority of breeders did not take such costings into account and actually made a loss, and the same may have been true of the interwar years, when taxes were higher.[21]

Vamplew argues that in the 1920s the cost of raising a thoroughbred year-ling, including costs attributed to the mare, was between £200 and £300.[22] To this should be added the covering fee for the stallion, and the stud fee of a more fashionable stallion, whose offspring were winning races and whose yearlings had more chance of achieving higher prices, was likely to be over £100. Each yearling sold had to shoulder an equal proportion of the stud fees, capital expenditure, charges and overheads of the stud. It should also be remembered that mares needed to be systematically replaced. In addition there was the high and growing burden of taxation. For studs to make a profit over time, there needed to bc high profits in some years to offset the inevitable losing years.

The apparently profitable average yearling prices concealed potential prob-lems for breeders. interwar specialists were well aware that breeding was 'a lot-tery', and that there was 'not the slightest doubt that very many … lose money over breeding livestock'.[23] In 1930 and 1931 many of the auctioned yearlings realised less or very little more than the stallion fee alone. So most breeders lost money. In the more favourable year of 1925, the 1,027 auctioned yearlings raised an aggregate sum of £613,078, representing an apparent mean poten-tially profitable average of £599 per yearling. But such aggregate figures con-cealed problems. Of the 'lots' (i.e. all yearlings sold) owned by particular breeders at Newmarket and Doncaster sales, more than 56 per cent sold for less than £450. Only about 20 per cent of all stallions whose offspring were auc-tioned achieved average prices of that figure or above. It was the large sums offered for the yearlings of these fashionable stallions like Phalaris, whose off-spring regularly achieved racing success, that drove up the average. At

Doncaster in 1938 a total of 357 yearlings were sold for a total of £244,120. But 58 of these yearlings sold for £1,100 or more, making together £140,385, or 57.5 per cent of the total. The others only averaged £347 each. At other sales, most yearlings were even cheaper.

Tattersall's auction house had a virtual British monopoly over the auction of yearlings, the main commodity in commercial bloodstock breeding, taking a 5 per cent commission.[24] They dominated other bloodstock sales and from 1927 also owned Manton, one of the foremost training stables. Their regular sales, held during race weeks, acted as a social centre for racing insiders. The first lots of yearlings came up for sale at Newmarket at the First and Second July Sales, which between 1919 and 1938 averaged 237 yearlings annually, with the First July Sales the more popular of the two. Their September Doncaster Yearling Sales sold on average 318 good-quality yearlings annually. Late yearlings, and those who had not found buyers earlier, would be sold at the Newmarket First October Sales, which averaged 118 yearlings annually, although a large proportion of these would be very moderate. Far fewer yearlings were sold at Newmarket's Second October Sales and the Houghton Sales, and the December Sales had very few yearlings. In Ireland the main sales of yearlings took place at the August Dublin Sales, where usually around 400 yearlings were sold. While the catalogue always had a significant proportion of poor-class youngsters, some top Irish breeders remained loyal to Dublin, so there were always many buyers from England and elsewhere. Some Irish breeders preferred to sell their stock in England, as did James Maher, perhaps the most prominent and successful breeder of his generation, having bred classic winners and a Grand National winner. He managed an average of 2,694 guineas for his 78 yearlings sold between 1919 and his death in 1935. Another Irish breeder, Peter FitzGerald, averaged 1,454 guineas for his 101 yearlings over the same period. These were well above the auction sale's annual average.

English auction figures suggest that the 1920s were a relatively prosperous period for breeders. The eleven years for 1919 to 1929 averaged 666 guineas per yearling with particularly high prices in 1919 and 1920, and again in 1925 and 1926, before reaching an interwar peak in 1928. However, there were also relatively poor years from 1921 to 1923. But the next decade saw a slump in fortunes, especially in the difficult years from 1930 to 1933, following the Wall Street Crash. Most disastrous of all was 1931, when the *Bloodstock Breeders' Review* admitted that the economic crisis had a 'malign influence' on the turf, especially the breeding side, and on yearling prices, although it still sounded positive, claiming a return of confidence in financial and commercial circles

Table 7.2 Tattersall's yearling sales at Newmarket and Doncaster auctions, 1919–38

	Yearlings sold	**Yield in guineas**	**Average in guineas**
1919	623	431,590	693
1920	709	516,916	729
1921	679	355,549	524
1922	722	367,470	509
1923	744	369,831	497
1924	712	470,249	661
1925	731	564,259	772
1926	748	545,016	729
1927	753	516,578	686
1928	780	653,932	838
1929	725	499,953	690
1930	672	300,965	448
1931	675	212,359	315
1932	613	217,959	356
1933	676	259,984	385
1934	681	409,741	602
1935	723	412,694	571
1936	741	414,266	559
1937	761	345,606	454
1938	714	340,280	477

Source: *Ruff's Guide to the Turf*

following the advent of the National Government.[25] Many owners sold their horses, reduced the number they had in training, or got rid of unprofitable breeding mares. There was less demand for yearlings. Even the National Stud, founded in 1915/16 thanks to the gift of the Tully Stud by Col. Hall Walker (created Lord Wavertree in 1919), which was sited in southern Ireland but run by the Ministry of Agriculture and usually ran in profit, sustained losses between 1930 and 1934, with a particularly heavy loss of £21,644 in 1931.[26]

The average price of a yearling in the period from 1930 to 1938 was only 463 guineas. Prices bottomed out at 315 guineas in 1931, and 1934 and 1935 were relatively good years but even then never reached the average of the previous decade. A more detailed analysis of the average price of a yearling at the prestigious Tattersall's Doncaster Yearling Sales held during the September St Leger Week between 1917 and 1939 also indicates that bloodstock prices showed violent short-term variation, although this was partly due to particularly high prices occasionally paid for horses from favoured studs. In 1917 the 269 yearlings fetched a mean of £413. In 1919 the 230 yearlings' average price was £1,020 although the sixteen yearlings of the fashionable Sledmere Stud, in the East Riding, raised £64,365 of this. This was in part due to the influx of foreign buyers and war profiteers spending their money. The following year the 271 yearlings averaged £1,063, with the eight yearlings of Maher's Confey Stud raising £17,010.

Sober reflection meant that Doncaster prices fell back slowly in the next three years to bottom out at £653 in 1923 but then began rising to a new and higher peak in 1926 when 325 yearlings averaged £1,115. The contraction of British staple industries, unemployment and the General Strike had had no effect on this comparatively wealthy group of purchasers. After a slight drop back in 1927, prices rose again in 1928 when 344 yearlings raised an average of £1,215, the interwar peak. But the Wall Street Crash in 1929 saw an immediate drop in prices, and they slumped further in 1930. The financial crisis of 1931 saw average prices drop even further to their lowest interwar point, with average prices of £500 at Doncaster. From then on confidence returned only slowly. Indeed, at Tattersalls staff salaries were cut by 15 per cent in 1933 because of depressed business.[27] At Doncaster average yearling prices rose slowly to reach £913 in 1934. The British market was increasingly flourishing while the Deauville Yearling Sales, the main continental competitor, stood still. However, for the next few years prices dropped steadily to a low of £650 in 1937, reflecting disturbed international relations, the threat of war and a gloomy view of the future of French racing by some French owners who were shifting some of their stables to England.[28] In 1938 the outlook seemed ominous. There were wars in Spain and China, there were misgivings about the future, and during the Doncaster Sales the British fleet was mobilised. At home unemployment was rising again, and there was still depression in many areas. Many in the industry expected a weak market. So it was surprising to many that Doncaster buyers seemed in an astonishingly complacent mood, raising the average to £684.[29]

Numbers involved in breeding during this period are difficult to calculate. By the 1930s winning breeders' lists giving races won and prize money gained by horses bred by them included over 600 names annually. This provides a minimum figure. Success in such lists generated competition. But not all breeders were successful. Breeders came from a variety of backgrounds, but we know more about the rich breeders like George VI, who maintained a royal stud at

Sandringham, although transferring his mares, foals and yearlings to the reopened Hampton Court paddocks in 1936.

Studs could be highly valuable capital commodities. Lord Manton's fifteen breeding mares and foals realised 70,100 guineas on his death in 1922. Larger racing stables often maintained an ancillary stud farm. The combined racing and breeding stud of Edward Hulton was disposed of for a total of 288,380 guineas in December 1925. Breeders' collective interests were looked after by their own organisation, the Thoroughbred Breeders Association, founded in 1917, a model for others subsequently throughout the racing world. It soon had over four hundred members. The specialist magazine devoted to the British thoroughbred, the *Bloodstock Breeders' Review*, was first published quarterly in 1912. This, together with the annual *Racing Calendar* and the *General Stud Book* produced every four years, both by Weatherby's, provided the background about pedigrees and racing success over different distances which breeders required. Weatherby supplemented the latter with regular returns of mares, lists of dams of winners, and other statistical records, while an annual *Register of Stallions* was published from 1910 onwards.

Irish horses sold regularly in Britain until 1932–33 when the British imposed punitive taxation of first 20 per cent and then 40 per cent on Irish bloodstock importations after the De Valera government repudiated liabilities respecting Land Annuities and other debts. Some Irish owners relocated their studs to England as a result. Such governmental intervention showed clearly that horseracing was a major international industry.

Britain held its position as a leading exporter of bloodstock, selling horses to the colonies, Europe, and other racing countries, although America and France were catching up rapidly. Indeed French-bred horses were being purchased for English studs by the 1930s. The American-owned and bred Battleship won the 1938 Grand National. Nevertheless, the details found in the annual supplements to the four-yearly *Stud Book* showed clearly the significant contribution of British stock to the export trade. Even in the early 1920s, approximately 150 mares were sold abroad annually, while a small number of stallions were also sold to support the breeding stock of countries abroad. Trade increased in volume thereafter, although reduced significantly in the early 1930s. By the year 1938, British thoroughbreds sold at auction were sent to 41 other countries. Most, but not all, had imperial associations: India took 115, South Africa 63, and Australia and New Zealand also took horses. France and the USA were by far the leading non-imperial customers. Although most thoroughbreds were of moderate quality, top-quality stallions reflected high prices. Here America proved a major purchaser. In 1936 the Aga Khan sold his 1930 Derby winner there for £45,000. When the 1935 Derby winner, Bahram, was sold to America in 1940 he raised £40,000. A number of commercial companies were set up to manage such international sales, including the British Bloodstock Agency Ltd, founded in 1911, which handled many interwar sales, and the joint Anglo-Irish Agency Ltd. Horses were insured during travel through Lloyds, and the more general extension of bloodstock insurance was another feature of the period. International links were fostered too by the Jockey Club, which from 1925 increasingly developed reciprocal arrangements with the racing authorities of the same group of countries for the enforcement of sentences passed on offenders.

Ownership

While within racing owners were a relatively high-status group, they received less coverage in the sporting press than horses, jockeys and trainers. Very rich owners like Lord Derby or the Aga Khan were exceptions. When press headlines like 'Great Day for Sir Abe Bailey' celebrated the success of the owner rather than the horse it was usually because a human-interest story was involved.[30] Ownership was more of a hobby in Britain than in most other countries. In Britain owners contributed over half the prize money of a race in stakes, forfeits and other entry fees. This was far higher than elsewhere. The British state, almost alone of almost any country where racing was carried on, gave no public money for its encouragement until some limited income from the Tote began to be dispensed in the later 1930s.

Owners were not easily categorised. Their approaches to betting, buying, selling and running horses could be very different. They were divided into three groups: those who owned steeplechasers, the largest group who owned the more expensive flat racehorses, and the smallest group who owned both. In steeple-chasing, very much the poor relation, owners in the early 1920s were suppos-edly divided into those horse lovers who raced one or two horses they had bred themselves, and gamblers manipulating their horses in the market.[31] However, the interwar period also saw an influx of rich Americans trying to win the Grand National, and an increase in the numbers of wealthier patrons like Miss Dorothy Paget or Lord Bicester.

Flat-racing owners were a disparate group with varied social backgrounds, education, interests and occupations, and ranged from members of the royal family and aristocracy to farmers, veterinary surgeons and small businessmen.

The royal family was not amongst the leading owners, but the monarchy's public support for racing should be seen as an important cultural marker. Its attitudes to betting, ownership and breeding varied. Edward VII enjoyed betting as much as ownership and breeding. George V took his responsibilities as an owner seriously, enjoyed the social life of a day's racing, was knowledgeable about breeding, but saw less appeal in betting. George VI maintained the royal stud and his racing stable, having five winners in 1939, but had no interest in betting.[32]

Breeding and ownership were largely inseparable. Interest in both was a pleasurable upper-class hobby, although betting among the upper classes had declined in both amount and importance.[33] Sporting, social and cultural motives for involvement were all important. Titled names dominated the winning owners' lists, as they did the Jockey Club. Lord Derby, one of the most successful owners of the period, with Lord Rosebery best represented the traditional racing aristocracy. Some of this group, like Lord Zetland, regretted that racing was growing ever more commercialised and businesslike, and wondered ruefully whether 'that spirit of good sportsmanship of which we are so proud plays as prominent a part in racing as we would like to think it does'.[34] Such local magnates often raced for racing's sake, and patronised their local meetings. Death duties were however increasingly having an effect on their involvement. The dukes of Richmond had a long-standing interest in the turf in general and in Goodwood in particular, but the eighth duke was so crippled by the crushing death duties which had to be paid when his father died that he could not afford to launch out as an owner on a big scale. He only had a few racehorses, and they were not of much account.

These long-standing aristocratic families were ever-increasingly joined in racing by newly-titled owners from lower-status backgrounds such as Lord Woolavington (a Scots-Canadian clerk and agent who became a wealthy whisky distiller), Lord Glanley (a former Cardiff clerk who founded a shipping company) and Sir Blundell Maple (the 'furniture king'). This new plutocratic meritocracy found racing suited to their ostentatious ambitions. They were often extremely wealthy. Lord Woolavington, for example, left estate of £7,150,000. Some envied the upper-class world, others enjoyed the surviving traditions of courtesy and respect with which trainers and jockeys treated them. Some loved horses, and spoke about them emotionally. Some were more dispassionate but very knowledgeable about racing and breeding. Others just gained pleasure from 'looking over their horses in the paddocks and paying an occasional visit to their training quarters'.[35] Some had a sentimental, sporting and irrational approach. Certainly they valued their involvement with racing highly. Lord Wavertree left his racing cups and trophies, together with his pictures of horses, to the Corporation of Liverpool.

It was wealthy owners who most often entered their horses for those races like the Derby with the largest money and status prizes. They could meet the very high entry fees, and had the cash and confidence to enter their yearlings for the classic races two years away before any evidence of their form. They could afford to get their breeding mares covered by the most fashionable stallions, buy the most well-bred yearlings at auction, have their horses trained by the top trainers and ridden by the top jockeys. They might even appoint a racing manager to supervise their interests. One usually reliable source suggests this alone could cost £2,000–£3,000 a year.[36] All this increased chances of success, at a high financial cost, since their stud farms would, like their incomes, be taxed. In many years they would be unsuccessful, a fate to be accepted, as part of the challenge and risk of racing. The Aga Khan spent 'a conservative estimate of £250,000 a year' on his racing, while Sir Abe Bailey was thought to have spent over a million pounds in total on his British racing involvement.[37]

As a group wealthy owners were by far the most regularly successful in winning the top races. Titled owners dominated the winning owners' tables in terms of prize money won. Rosebery, for example, was a highly successful owner, winning the Derby twice, and at one time or another won virtually all the chief flat race races. As a breeder he successfully aimed to produce classic winners and high-calibre stayers at his Mentmore Stud. He was the president of the Thoroughbred Breeders' Association and a senior steward of the Jockey Club.[38] The studs and racing stables of Lord Derby, Lord Woolavington, Lord Astor and the Aga Khan were also particularly prominent in winning Classic races. Such races, covering distances between a mile and a mile and a half, required a horse which had some of the skills of the sprinter, running races of less than a mile, and some of the stayer going in for races of 2 miles or more. It was hugely difficult to breed a horse with sprinting and staying power. Only a few individuals managed it more than once or twice. Although Lord Astor never won a Derby, his horses' other Classic successes ensured that his stable regularly paid its way. He was usually near the top of the table of winning owners. In 1925 he topped the list with prize money of £35,723 from seven winning horses, and in most other years his prize money was in five-figure sums.

He was a rare exception. Even richer owners found it very difficult to be consistently successful. Racing fortunes fluctuated violently from year to year. Sir

Hugo Cunliffe-Owen won £11,204 in 1921 and £24,292 in 1938, yet only £1,338 in 1925 from very similar-sized racing studs. Sir Abe Bailey won £15,648 in 1926, £23,279 in 1935 and £17,323 in 1938, yet only £1,423 in 1932.

Some rich owners maintained their own studs, others purchased their horses as yearlings. Some bought horses with proven expertise, either to race from, or as stallions for breeding. Such stallions were extremely costly. By contrast, the highest price paid for a steeplechaser was 10,500 guineas, paid for Silvo in 1925 by Mr Midwood. Even if such costs were ignored, for most owners the costs of having their horses trained and raced each year exceeded the prize money they would win. Annual training costs were probably around £400 per horse even at the start of the century, when trainers charged £3 or more a week just for basic training itself, and by shortly after the First World War the standing charge for training a horse for a week was between 4 guineas and £5 10s, plus further cash presents and bonuses to trainer, jockey and stable lads, veterinary charges, shoeing, transport and entry fees to races.[39] The Trainers' Federation, to which many trainers belonged, established minimum fees.[40] Top steeplechasing trainers were charging about 4 guineas a week in the 1930s, with small trainers charging a great deal less.[41] By the 1930s H. S. Persse, a well-known trainer, esti-mated that the full cost of keeping a horse in training for a year was at least £450 to £500, and this was probably a conservative estimate.[42]

Owners' chances of ever winning were quite limited. In flat racing published lists suggest that on average only about 600 owners, of the c. 2,500 owners who had registered their racing colours for flat racing, ever won a race each year. Of all horses put into training, about five out of six never won under Jockey Club rules: they were too slow, too unsound or too lazy. Of those winning owners listed in *Ruff's Guide* between 1932 and 1935, only about 25 per cent covered Persse's estimated cost of keeping their winning horses in training each year, and this takes no account of any horses they had in training which failed to win a race. Other owners' horses never won.

So why were owners in racing? They entered for a range of reasons. Lord Derby, who came from a long-standing racing family, simply enjoyed the pleasure of breeding and racing his horses at top-class events. Owners loved to see their horse win. The 'thrill' of winning was almost a cliché in racing. His biographer believed that the greatest thrill of Lord Rosebery's life was when his home-bred horse Blue Peter won the 1939 Derby.[43] The politician Lord Stanley said his winning of the Ascot Cup in 1936 had given him 'the greatest thrill' he would probably ever have.[44] Quintin Gilbey suggested that many enjoyed the meetings and found they derived 'a greater thrill from it than from any other sport'.[45] Some, like George VI, simply inherited a stud and continued to race. Some, even if relatively unsuccessful, just enjoyed it as a pastime. Lord Wyfold took a keen interest in his small stud, and gave real thought to the mating of his mares, whose produce he usually raced, as did Lord Cawley, 'a breeder of thoroughbreds in a small way, merely as a hobby'.[46] The seventh marquis of Londonderry (1878–1949) maintained a racing stud at Wynyard throughout the interwar years, and raced his own stock. He and his wife enjoyed following the successes and failures of their breeding stud, keeping it well archived, with accounts, records of pedigrees, photographs of runners, newspaper clippings and cuttings of their occasional winners.[47] The producer and actor Tom Walls, who also trained horses at Epsom, had reduced his string to a mere four after a hunting accident. He won the Derby with his own horse April the Fifth in 1932, exclaiming in his excitement, 'By gad! I've lived for this'. The three thousand plus begging letters he received subsequently were not unusual.[48]

Some owners entered racing for the social prestige and cultural capital it offered, and to an extent could target these attempts since different races and courses offered different levels of prize money, upper-class attendance and associated prestige. Racing at upper-class Ascot was very different to racing at the more artisan-attended Manchester course. The prize money offered for the Classic races at Newmarket, Epsom and Doncaster was far higher than prize money at Yarmouth or Beverley. Flat racing was more prestigious than National Hunt meetings, while within National Hunt the Aintree Grand National was far more prestigious than Tenby or Sedgefield. Prestige of winning had to be managed, and some paid highly for social advancement.

Top owners had opportunities to socialise at a number of formal occasions during the year, even if they were not members of the sport's governing organisations. Winning a Classic could involve the owner in a wide variety of 'society' associations, ceremonial and presentational aspects. For example, the Jockey Club Epsom Derby celebration dinner in 1935 was held in Buckingham Palace, with the table decorated with the winning owner's colours. He was congratulated by the king and queen, and the king proposed the toast. Another key event was the Derby lunch at the London Press Club, where owners would often discuss publicly their views of the chances of their horses, although often denying any real knowledge. The sixth earl of Rosebery claimed that he 'always turned to the newspapers when he wanted to know what chance any of his horses had of winning'.[49] Another social occasion was York's November or December Gimcrack dinner. Speeches for such events show that it was expected that winning owners of the Gimcrack race would accept their success modestly, ascribing it to the horse, trainer and jockey, or to 'good luck', rather than claiming it personally.

Most owners had great respect for leading trainers and jockeys and their expertise. When Lord Stanley won his Ascot Gold Cup, even in the heat of the moment he told reporters, 'Whatever you say, do not forget to give full credit to Leader for turning the mare out in such wonderful condition and to Perryman for riding such a grand race'.[50] The 'luck' theme, and the respect shown for jockeys, emerges clearly in interviews given by the Aga Khan after Bahram won the 1935 St Leger, in which he not only praised the horse and jockey, but also mentioned Freddy Fox, who was to have ridden the horse but was injured the previous day: 'I cannot forget Fox in our hour of victory. I am so sorry at the bad luck which prevented him riding, I am going to the nursing home to see him'.[51]

Over-boastful, cocky or smug behaviour by owners was always seen as inappropriate. If possible winning and losing had to be treated just the same, and winning had to be celebrated modestly. When, for example, Mrs G. B. Miller became the first woman owner of a Derby winner (Mid-day Sun) in 1937 she was interviewed by the *Daily Sketch* reporter who asked her what it felt like. She reportedly simply replied that it was all 'an awful fuss'. When it was pointed out to her that it was a national event and millions of people were celebrating, she asked, 'Celebrate? Does one celebrate? We are having dinner in the ordinary way'.[52]

Most owners did not expect to make money out of racing. At the same time, however, there was always concern to reduce its costs. Most owners always hoped for some financial return. The jockey Snowy Shepherd remembered one millionaire owner whose horse won the Birmingham Cup and 'sent it back and had the money' instead.[53] Owners made constant complaints about miserly prize money and exorbitant costs in the press, at dinners and elsewhere. In a letter read at York's Gimcrack dinner in 1936, for example, Sir Abe Bailey complained that owners spent their own money to provide racing for the public. He compared the entrance and forfeit money English owners had to pay with South Africa, where it cost £1 to race for a stake of £400 or £500.[54] Lord Harewood's 1937 Gimcrack speech also focused on the high cost of racing to owners. 'If', he said, 'they could do anything to assist the small owner who has got to make both ends meet it would be an advantage to racing.' He went on to say that 'rich races, which alone will enable you to take a high place in the list of owners, involve you in very high costs'. He wanted the expenses of owners to be reduced, and the business of owning horses to be made much cheaper.[55]

There had been many middle-class owners even in the nineteenth century, but increasing numbers of successful owners were now industrialists, financiers or businessmen, and many were much keener to win than simply to race. Wartime millionaires, such as Sir Arthur Black with his Grimsby trawler fleet, or shipping and meat magnate Sir William Nelson, came into racing in large numbers. Successful untitled, upper-middle-class owners also entering included the miller J. V. Rank, the two Liverpool cotton brokers David Goold and W. H. Midwood, the international financier A. Lowenstein, the Dublin match manufacturer Alex Maguire, the Belfast corn trader Mr Barnett and the Shanghai bill broker Mr Morriss.[56] The pages of memorial biographies in the *Bloodstock Breeders' Review* provide details about their occupations, involvement in ownership, and successful horses but are less clear about motivations. We know only that George Hands, for example, was 'interested in the motor industry in Birmingham, and in one of the big hotels in Torquay', and had been 'an owner of racehorses for many years and also a breeder in a small way'.[57] Officers in the armed services, turf commissioners, sporting journalists, brewers, bookmakers and trainers were other significant groups owning just a few horses but running them in the most efficient way possible. For those who could not afford the full costs of ownership, partnerships were already emerging. Buckshee, for example, trained by Vasey at Doncaster, was the property of five owners.[58] The hope of the smaller owner was always 'useful horses at moderate prices'.[59] It was reasonably common for owners to have horses with several trainers simultaneously, matching horses to trainers. R. D. Eddleston built stables at Gainford for his horses in 1910, and bred there, but had them trained at Redcar, Ellington and Neasham.[60] Bert Drage, a horse dealer and breeder, had had horses with seven or more trainers.[61]

National Hunt racing rarely attracted the wealthier owners, and middle-class owners were even more common here, although many owners only owned only one or two horses, sometimes bred themselves. Prize money was lower, and there was less incentive for rich owners to patronise the sport. Farmers were more likely to be involved in 'chasing than the flat.

Owners from overseas were also playing a more significant role in racing. Rich American owners increasingly bought steeplechasers as well as horses for flat racing. The Grand National was a particular target, perhaps because of the transatlantic shipping links with Liverpool. As early as 1923 the race was won by Sergeant Murphy, a horse owned by Stephen Sandford, a wealthy American Cambridge undergraduate. Other Americans included the 1926 National winner's owner, A. C. Schwartz, who had bought the horse at a very high price only three weeks before in an attempt to win the race. Owners from the British Empire also played a significant role. A key group here came from the Indian sub-continent. The Aga Khan, the most successful owner-breeder of the period, with studs in Ireland and France as well as in England, raced on a huge scale, and was regularly leading owner and leading breeder. He had a commercial approach to racing. He spent huge sums, but may well have profited overall. The maharajah of Kolhapur (1874–1922) spent money freely on racehorses, while Major His Highness Maharajah Vijaysinhji Chhatrasinhji (1890–1951) was a keen patron of the turf and owned the 1934 Derby winner, Windsor Lad.[62] The wealthy maharajah of Rajpipla was particularly popular with race-course crowds, partly because of his playboy lifestyle, while Ranji, the former cricketer and maharajah of Nawanagar, had a few horses in training at Newmarket.[63]

Racehorse ownership was not monopolised by men. Women had owned horses even in the nineteenth century, but most observers felt that the increasing numbers of women owners after 1918 was a significant change. Lord Zetland, for example, accepted that 'after the war ladies, who until that time had for the most part been content to participate … as spectators only, took their courage in both hands and registered themselves as owners'.[64] Sidney Galtrey felt that their entry had 'been on such a scale as to be stupendous'.[65] By the 1930s between a fifth and a quarter of all those who had registered colours with the Jockey Club were women. The percentage of female winning owners rose from 9 per cent in 1920 to 21 per cent in 1938.

Table 7.3 Social background and gender of winning flat-race owners, 1920–38

	No. of winning military and titled males	No. of titled females	Other winning males	Other winning females
1920	107	10	351	35
1926	123	15	357	53
1932	133	18	296	96
1938	139	25	376	116

Source: Ruff's Guide to the Turf

Some women were titled. Many came from traditional racing families, or had married into them. Lady James Douglas both bred and raced, winning the Oaks in 1919 with Bayuda. Lady Barbara Smith inherited her father Lord Coventry's stud. The rich owner Lady Zia Wernher was the daughter of Grand Duke Michael of Russia. There were others who lacked titles but were from similar backgrounds. One of the more famous owners of the period was the eccentric and heavy-betting Miss Dorothy Paget, whose inherited American chain-store wealth was spent on both flat and National Hunt racing. She was a daughter of Lord Queenborough.[66] Viscountess Torrington, who loved horses and would do anything for their welfare, invested a fortune in a failed attempt to develop a successful racing stud.

Biographies suggest that a shared interest in racing, breeding and ownership was a feature of some middle-class marriages during the period. There were couples such as the Whitburns who had separate colours, each racing their own horses. Others were joint owners. Major J. C. Lewis and his wife 'took the keenest interest in breeding' and shared the ownership of Glenhazel, who won the 1928 Queen's Prize in her colours.[67] Many women remained in racing after their husband's death. Some women, such as Mrs Beatty, the energetic wife of an American financier and mining engineer, raced even though their husbands were uninterested in the sport. Mrs Beatty's lavish expenditure was not repaid by racing success. In steeplechasing Mrs William Partridge won the Grand National with Sprig in 1927. She possessed great affection for the horse and steadfastly refused all offers to purchase him. Mrs Ambrose Clark, well-liked and respected, won the Grand National with Kellsbro' Jack in 1933, after being sold the horse by her husband for the token sum of £1.

Some owners rarely or never bet. The excitement of the course, hope of success and the occasional thrill of winning were enough. As 'The Scout' pointed out, 'it often happens that the leading owners are not concerned with betting at all'.[68] He cited Lord Astor, Lord Derby and the Aga Khan as leading examples, although the latter had in earlier years been a punter. Owners were part of the racing world, and most were not immune from the excitement of betting on all horses, not just their own. Probably the majority of owners bet on their own horses when they thought they had a chance. It added spice and excitement to their racing. But few bet large amounts, although winnings could be large when odds were long. Jack Burnley, a well-known advertising industry figure, won £1,000 when his horse won the Cesarewitch in 1921 at odds of 33-1, but more normally wagered around £10. The financier Jimmy White won more than £100,000 on his horse Irish Elegance in the Royal Hunt Cup of 1919.[69] The Yorkshire owner H. F. Clayton backed his horses many months before to win the Cesarewitch and Cambridgeshire in 1931 to win £100,000 to £100, and nearly succeeded. Winning a major race involved 'presents' to jockey and trainers, and other such disbursements, so the risk of backing one's horse often seemed to make sense. There were still those who ended up plunging and losing vast fortunes. White eventually went bankrupt. The marquis of Breadalbane had racing debts which forced much of his Scottish estates to be sold in 1921.[70]

But there were also calculating owners who viewed horses as an instrument of speculation, backing their horses when they were expected to win, and laying them when they could be made sure to lose. Such gambling owners were least likely to be breeders. C. R. Acton suggested that local publicans in particular often ran their horses in selling plates or at small local low-status 'flapping tracks' not recognised by the Jockey Club where results could be more easily manipulated.[71] In fact, however, owner-gamblers of all classes had similar attitudes. Sir Charles Butt, for example, was 'more interested in a coup than in the development of a racehorse', and held his trainer personally responsible for the success of his betting.[72] At the small Pershore steeplechase course a jovial owner-trainer of a few insignificant horses had his 'ideal race' – 'Four runners, two I knew weren't trying, one was my own and the other I backed'. His own horse was (naturally) held back to ensure the 'right' result.[73]

Notes

1 1923 Select Committee on Betting Duty, report p. 50, Minutes of Evidence, QQ7590ff.

2 *Sporting Chronicle*, 29.3.1935; *ibid.*, 22.6.1935.

3 *Bloodstock breeders' review* (London: British Bloodstock Agency, 1938), p. 163.

4 Lady Wentworth, *Thoroughbred racing stock and its ancestors* (London: Allen and Unwin, 1938).

5 William Fawcett, *Thoroughbred and hunter: their breeding, training and management from foal to maturity* (London: Eyre and Spottiswoode, 1934), p. 84.

6 Arthur FitzGerald, *Royal thoroughbreds: a history of the royal studs* (London: Sidgwick and Jackson, 1990), pp. 182–97.

7 Durham Record Office, D/Lo/F652 (9–10) Wynyard Park Stud; D/Lo/F654 accounts; D/Lo/F599 (1–10) statements of racing and other accounts.

8 *Bloodstock breeders' review* (1938), p. 157.

9 Fawcett, *Thoroughbred and hunter*, introduction, p. 73.

10 Sidney Galtrey, *Memoirs of a racing journalist* (London: Hutchinson, 1934), p. 250.

11 Quoted in Jack Fairfax-Blakeborough, *Northern turf history vol. 3: York and Doncaster* (London: J. A. Allen, 1950), p. 460.

12 Stanley Jackson, *The Aga Khan: prince, prophet and sportsman* (London: Odhams Press, 1952), p. 132. The Aga Khan, *The memories of Aga Khan: world enough and time* (London: Cassell, 1954), p. 198.

13 C. R. Acton, *Silk and spur* (London: Richards, 1935), p. 46.

14 For detailed discussion of such theories see Sir Charles Leicester, *Bloodstock breeding* (London: J. A. Allen, 1983).

15 Captain Heath, *News Chronicle racing annual* (London: News Chronicle, 1938), p. 10.

16 See, for example, Miss F. M. Prior, *Register of throughbred stallions* (London: Horse and Hound, 1931).

17 *Bloodstock breeders' review* (1937), p. 227.

18 Suffolk Oral History Project, OHT 68, Mr Lancaster.

19 *Daily Telegraph*, 29.6.1938.

20 Alfred Watson, *A great year: Lord Glanley's horses* (London: Longmans Green, 1921).

21 M. J. Huggins, 'Thoroughbred breeding in the North and East Ridings of Yorkshire in the nineteenth century', *Agricultural History Review*, 42: 2 (1994), 115–25.

22 Wray Vamplew, *The turf* (London: Allen Lane, 1976), p. 191.

23 Fawcett, *Thoroughbred and hunter*, p. 63.

24 For Tattersall's history see V. Orchard, *Tattersalls* (London: Hutchinson, 1953); P. Willett, *The story of Tattersalls* (London: Stanley Paul, 1987).

25 *Bloodstock breeders' review* (1931), pp. 1–3.

26 Vamplew, *The turf,* p. 195.

27 Willett, *The story of Tattersalls,* p. 56.

28 V. R. Orchard, 'The bloodstock industry', in Ernest Bland (ed.), *Flat racing since 1900* (London: Andrew Dakers 1950), p. 63.

29 See the comments in 'Bloodstock sales', in *Bloodstock breeders' review* (1938), pp. 124–5.

30 *Sporting Chronicle*, 27.6.1935.

31 Michael Seth-Smith *et al.*, *The history of steeplechasing* (London: Michael Joseph, 1966), pp. 105–6.

32 Louis Wulff, 'Royalty and racing', in Bland (ed.), *Flat racing*, pp. 1–14. FitzGerald, *Royal thoroughbreds,* gives fuller details.

33 See Duke of Portland, *Memories of racing and hunting* (London: Faber and Faber, 1935).

34 Jack Fairfax-Blakeborough, *The turf who's who* (London: Mayfair Press, 1932), p. 476.

35 Arthur J. Sarl, *Horses, jockeys and crooks: reminiscences of thirty years' racing* (London: Hutchinson, 1935), p. 20.

36 Acton, *Silk and spur*, p. 173.

37 Jackson, *The Aga Khan*, p. 140; Captain X, *Tales of the turf* (London: Partridge Publishers, 1943), p. 22.

38 Obituary by John Hislop, *The British racehorse* (1974, p. 8.

39 Vamplew, *The turf,* p. 174; Eric Rickman, 'Tests imposed by classic races', in Bland (ed.), *Flat racing*, p. 124. Eric Rickman, *Come racing with me* (London: Chatto and Windus, 1951), p. 65.

40 *The Times*, 11.12.1919.

41 Seth-Smith *et al.*, *The history of steeplechasing*, p. 119.

42 H. S. Persse, 'Training', in Earl of Harewood and P. E. Ricketts (eds), *Flat racing* (London: Seeley Service and Co., n.d.), p. 315.

43 Kenneth Young, *Harry, Lord Rosebery* (London: Hodder and Stoughton, 1974).

44 *Bloodstock breeders' review* (1938), p. 162.

45 Quintin Gilbey, *Fun was my living* (London: Hutchinson, 1970), p. 146.

46 *Bloodstock breeders' review* (1937), p. 113.

47 Durham Record Office, D/Lo 1251 (D) Vol. 22 racing records; D/Lo 1750 (D) Boxes 43/8–9 Wynyard Racing Paddock.

48 *Bloodstock breeders' review* (1932), pp. 16–18.

49 *Bloodstock breeders' review* (1931), p. 17.

50 'The Scout' (Cyril Luckman), *The Scout's guide to racing 1937* (London: Daily Express, 1937), p. 54.

51 Quoted in Fairfax-Blakeborough, *York and Doncaster*, p. 475.

52 *Daily Sketch*, 3.6.1937.

53 Suffolk Oral History Project, OHT 355, Snowy Shepherd.

54 *Bloodstock breeders' review* (1937), p. 272.

55 *Bloodstock breeders' review* (1938), p. 282.

56 *Daily Telegraph*, 26.3.1925; 24.3.1939. Seth-Smith, *History of steeplechasing*, pp. 128, 133.

57 *Bloodstock breeders' review* (1938), p. 166.

58 Nottingham's *Post Tissue*, 26.3.1932.

59 John McGuigan, *A trainer's memories* (London: Heath Granton, 1946).

60 Durham Record Office, D/Ed 17/93–102.

61 Bert Drage, *Reminiscences of Bert Drage* (London: David Green, 1955), p. 60.

62 Kusoom Vadgama, *India in Britain: the Indian contribution to the British way of life* (London: Robert Royce, 1984), pp. 121, 147.

63 Marcus Marsh, *Racing with the gods* (London: Pelham Books, 1968), p. 38; *Bloodstock breeders' review* (1933), p. 130.

64 Lord Zetland, 'Preface', in Fairfax-Blakeborough, *The turf who's who*, p. xix.

65 Galtrey, *Memoirs of a racing journalist*, p. 241.

66 Quentin Gilbey, *Queen of the turf: the Dorothy Paget story* (London: Barker, 1973).

67 *Bloodstock breeders' review* (1928), p. 167.

68 'The Scout', *The Scout's guide to racing, 1937*.

69 S. Theodore Felstead, *Racing romance* (London: Werner Laurie, 1949), p. 130; George Hamlyn, *My sixty years in the ring: a racing and gambling autobiography* (Hungerford: Sporting Garland, 1994), p. 82.

70 F. M. L. Thompson, *Gentrification and the enterprise culture: Britain 1780–1980* (Oxford: Oxford University Press, 2001), p. 112.

71 Acton, *Silk and spur*, p. 259.

72 Marsh, *Racing with the gods*, p. 41.

73 Seth-Smith, *History of steeplechasing*, p. 107.

Conclusion

The vast majority of ordinary people in Britain between the wars paid far more attention to sport, and the doings of 'society', than to the interests of the country's intellectual elite. Racing was one of Britain's leading national sports, and the media gave it more prominence than football or cricket, its main competitors. Involvement in or opposition to it were integral factors in British cultural life. Previous pages have explored its place in detail, and discussed social and economic changes in racing between the wars, power and control in racing, the relationship between racing and the media, the status of trainers and jockeys, owners and breeders, betting, bookmaking and its policing, and the experience of actually attending the races in a period supposedly characterised by economic hardships and depression, unemployment and misery. In exploring such topics, it becomes clear that a study of racing also adds a vital dimension to debates amongst historians about the extent of social harmony, the political and social predominance of conservatism, the construction of gender identities, national sentiment, and the relationship between the economy and sport.

Racing was not immune from wider social and economic changes. Rail strikes affected numbers attending meetings in the early 1920s and most especially during the General Strike. Death duties cut back some of the involvement of the landed classes, although such losses were constantly replaced by new money. In the areas of high unemployment, the troubles of the local economy were mirrored by indices such as the numbers of bookmakers, betting turnover, or crowd size at meetings. National economic difficulties impacted more widely. Crowd numbers at meetings were hard hit in 1926 and 1927, and again in the early 1930s, a period when prices of thoroughbreds also dropped, and breeders suffered.

The study has shed new light on gender roles during this period. Men still dominated state, society and sport. Both rugby and soccer were male-dominated.

They projected masculine values, and discouraged women's involvement. In racing, in 1939 women were still unable to be professional jockeys or trainers, or be members of the Jockey Club or NHC. Yet, perhaps because of its sociability, women were far more involved in racing than in other mass sports. Wider changes in gender relationships did have an effect, albeit slowly, and in turn racing affected women's leisure lives. Women entered racing as owners and breeders in significant numbers, and this allowed them opportunities for success, achievement and some fame, offering more than the beginnings of challenge to male social power. They were well able to compete with men on equal terms, playing their part in the post-1918 'new feminism'. Numbers of women book-makers were small but were growing. Women jockeys rode in point-to-point races. Race meetings of all kinds attracted large numbers of women spectators, not only in the club stands but in most sections of the course. The course was a liminal social zone, yet one where women were treated respectfully and courte-ously, and could dress up, bet and socialise. Popular newspapers provided articles which catered for this new interest. Women's betting was a hobby providing interest, thrills and potential financial independence. Many of the customers of the racecourse Tote were women, while, off-course, women were well known to bet with illegal cash bookmakers.

Racing acted back on British society in other, more complex ways. In part it contributed to the essential harmony and cultural conformity of broader society. It also underpinned and sustained economic and social inequalities and snobberies. Major studies of interwar leisure have argued strongly for leisure's clear differentiation on class lines and racing was no exception.[1] Yet it was never a site of resistance, of class-ridden battles. It had an appeal to all classes, and played a part in uniting them. Through the constantly reinforcing images in the sporting press, cinema, radio and other media it aided the invention and main-tenance of a particular image of Britain, an image which showed respect and deference for the monarchy and upper classes. Recent revisionist analysis of the effects of the First World War has shown how elites and their institutions stayed firmly in place afterwards, and in the 1920s and 1930s had the support of the great majority of the middle class.[2] In part a study of racing supports such an analysis. Racing both symbolised and reflected the undemocratic nature of British society. The general acquiescence by followers of racing in its inequality and snobbery may have helped them acquiesce in society's wider inequalities, ensuring that gentlemanliness remained embedded in normative models of Britishness. The popular and racing press, as we have seen, only rarely attacked racing's ruling bodies. Crowds at race-meetings were shown as having a sense of tradition and history and as sharing in the delight of the Aga Khan, Lord Derby or the royal family at their successes. The doings of 'society', with its glamour, smartness, and apparent modernity, focused on Ascot, York or Epsom as much as the smart London clubs. McKibbin has noted the hold of the monarchy on public opinion, and racing was associated in the public mind with the royal family and aristocracy.[3] The cinema newsreel and press accounts of the ceremony and glamour of Ascot, and the conscious archaism of the course parade, with its scarlet and gold-uniformed, plumed and epauletted figures, helped that hold. This was also presented and sensationalised as a 'society' occasion legitimating the privilege, honour and wealth of its members. It is perhaps therefore unsurprising that racing was in part a force for conservatism.

Like cricket, racing made very obvious the inequalities found in English society.[4] In racing the upper classes only too clearly seemed to continue to exercise authority, power and prestige. The Jockey Club and NHC, undemocratic and socially exclusive, helped to legitimate the amateur ideology which dominated British sport, and supported a broader assumption that it was 'natural' for such elites to rule. Attitudes to power in British racing showed an acceptance of the status quo, an unwillingness to change established procedures, but also an expectation that power should be exercised only reluctantly, an attribute also found more broadly in British opposition to all forms of political extremism, whether from left or right. Racing was a socially ranked and ordered microsociety which made clear to individuals their place in the social hierarchy, from the Royal Enclosure, to the Club stands, or the stands and enclosures further down the rankings. But such divisions, embedded within racing, generated very little evidence of resentment or antagonism between classes. There was only limited criticism of the amateur authorities, and racing autobiographies by jockeys and trainers did not stress the social gap between amateur and professional jockeys, but responded to individuals as individuals, rather than as members of a particular social class.

There were also counter-currents, which placed limits on the extent to which racing supported the established, conservative order. In part betting could be fatalistic, reliant on luck rather than business expertise. In part too it could be anti-authoritarian, with street betting becoming either a working-class leisure diversion allowing attempts to outwit the class enemy, the police, or informal collusion between 'bobby' and 'bookie' to ensure that it ran smoothly. At racecourses jockeys were seen as working-class heroes, and their successes celebrated, while some at least of the extra crowds of 'expectant onlookers' who went to watch the Prince of Wales riding in point-to-points were there in hopes of his fall.[5] Within racing itself not all horses ran to win, while others might be doped to increase their speed. The 1920s moral panic associated with the race gangs prefigured 1930s concerns over the cinema and youth. The Jockey Club and NHC could be seen as in effect puppet rulers, unable as much as unwilling to intervene unless they had the support of those within racing, slow and reluctant to act against those with power, and only tough on the weak.

The respect accorded to amateurism in cricket, and resistance to the greater commercialism of the game, it has been argued, lends support to the views of Martin Weiner, Corelli Barnett and others in suggesting that English culture did not encourage a spirit of bold, risk-taking entrepreneurship or a belief that the principle of making profit should be extended to all forms of activity, and that these attitudes, stemming most of all from the public schools, were a vital factor in Britain's relative economic decline.[6] Racing provides a less simplistic model. On the one hand it should be clear that racing was never a profit-maximising industry dominated by commercial values. With only rare exceptions, racecourses never tried to maximise dividends. Most owners and some breeders lost money each year. Authority was exercised by amateurs, and there was great resistance to increasing racing's commercial appeal. Yet at the same time most owners and breeders wanted to make money, and both racing and betting were dominated by profit-seeking and risk-taking, attitudes that in the economic and business vocabulary could be seen as manifestations of entrepreneurship. As F. M. L. Thompson has pointed out, this can be viewed as 'a kind of application of business methods to leisure interests'.[7] It should be stressed too that some at least of those owners who lost money on racing had been and often continued to be highly entrepreneurial and successful in the business sphere. They were simply making their own choices about spending their money. Collecting art gave pleasure to those of an artistic bent. Racing too provided pleasurable spending. Both were at least potentially profitable and in the process both gave pleasure to the general public, even if they were of different ethical and moral persuasions. A more profit-pursuing approach can be seen in the aggressive attitude of some top jockeys, moving from owner to owner for the best offer, 'jocking off' other jockeys in the process. Stable lads were prepared to strike to increase wages and improve conditions.

Racing also helped to sustain a wider national belief in the superiority of British sport. Britain had long experience and tradition in most sports, and racing had been in existence far longer than most. Britain's success and leading role in international breeding was yet another example of such superiority. People took pride in the fact that the thoroughbred was an English creation.

England had given it to the world and still enjoyed the respect of racing else-where. Top races were still largely won by British-bred thoroughbreds, but Britain had been breeding for speed rather than stamina for some time. Increasingly French, Irish and American horses could compete successfully in the fewer middle-distance events, although Britain still enjoyed the key position at the heart of a global racing culture.

There has been increasing interest amongst historians in the effects of sport on local, regional and national identity. Welsh rugby union and football, sport and the political affiliations of religious groups in Northern Ireland, sport and the making of the Scottish nation, and sport and northern England have all found their historians.[8] Such works have shown too a recognition of competing versions of nationalism, regionalism and locality. Racing affected identity at a number of levels. The point-to-points and steeplechases still functioned as ways of bringing the local community together, providing a sense of local identity and purpose, with the social elite playing its part as stewards and in the grand-stands. Most race-meetings catered for racing insiders and spectators from the surrounding region. The great events like Ascot, the Derby or the St Leger were national, collective occasions, bringing people together from throughout Britain and the Empire.

In that respect racing demonstrates the strength of British cultural con-formity and cohesion. Support for racing crossed the boundaries of class, gender and locality. In racing there was no major divide or strong sense of com-petition between England, Ireland, Scotland and Wales, although English training and breeding dominated, and horse-racing was least strong in Wales. Amongst jockeys there were still North–South rivalries. But Britain largely saw itself as united in racing terms, although Eire's political actions meant that obstacles to Irish horses and breeders were being set up. Racing articulated ideas of Britishness rather than of a divided state. At a time when England was eco-nomically declining, and relations with the Empire were less close, racing pro-vided the British with a powerful, reassuring and comforting myth, reaching back to the past for ideas about sportsmanship, sporting standing, and sporting flair and skill, as well as about social relationships. The emphasis on breeding, for example, and the 'best' blood, might perhaps apply to people as well as ani-mals, a celebration of the hereditary principle.[9] The stress on etiquette, pro-priety and following traditional procedures, on the course or in the stables, reflected similar social preoccupations, and has clear parallels with cricket.

Racing also offered a repertoire of identities from which to choose. Betting could be rash and risk-taking or careful and rational, punters could be regular or occasional. Racing even privileged different forms of masculinity. The two most high-profile household names of racing were arguably Donoghue and Richards, stars who might be seen as representing different British characteristics. Both appeared 'natural' jockeys and were hugely popular. Donoghue was naive, charming, impulsive, kindhearted, and likeable, but could be over-generous, unbusiness-like and disloyal to his employers. Richards was shyer, more hard-working, with unquestionable integrity and a natural intelligence, and deferential to his employers.

Racing played its part too in the wider reshaping of public attitudes to leisure during the interwar period. These were shifting from the brisk and purposeful recreations of the mid-nineteenth century to a more frank and indulgent enjoyment of leisure in an expanded leisure world.[10] Of course the carefully constructed images of Victorian middle-class respectability built up by historians such as Geoffrey Best and F. M. L. Thompson were always somewhat overdrawn.[11] Only some of the Victorian middle classes actually internalised the 'respectable' habits of deferred gratification, self-control and continence, and pursued only rational recreations. Many others, in particular leisure contexts, found the appeal of at least occasional hedonism, gambling and other temptations much too strong to resist.[12] The same was true of the twentieth century. Recently John Lowerson has pointed out that a singularly unexplored twentieth-century theme in social and cultural history has been that of the 'naughty fringe' of middle-class life.[13] Whilst such behaviour may have been unexplored, his comment pushes it to the margins of bourgeois life. As the middle classes increased their access to a wider popular culture, 'respectable' values had more limited relevance than he supposes. A study of racing supports a view that by the interwar period some of the middle classes were playing a full part in leisure's more hedonistic excitements, whilst in other contexts maintaining a respectable front. The middle classes attended meetings as spectators and placed bets in large numbers. They were also owners, trainers, bookmakers and investors, and occupied professional roles in racing's administration.

Across all classes this reshaping of attitudes was seen most clearly in changing attitudes to gambling, from the football pools to greyhounds and horses. Betting on horse-racing was extremely popular and general public opinion showed few taboos about it. It was treated sympathetically in films, books and the theatre as well as at work and in many homes. It was acceptable to much of society, both in its more calculative forms and in the sweeps, which give the lie to the claim that betting was commonly characterised by rationality and reserve. Cash betting, like Class C drug possession today, attracted strongly-held and emotional opinions. Like use of such drugs, the illegality of betting inevitably shaped cultural attitudes and practice, and may have added to the excitement. There are further parallels in that betting was rarely and usually lightly policed, the frequency varying according to local personnel, while attitudes of magistrates also varied. Indeed police action against betting caused widespread resentment in working-class communities. Yet because betting generated an oppositional discourse from bastions of disapproval like the Home Office or the Nonconformist churches, governments were unwilling to do anything which might disturb this status quo. Such groups were still able to take a moral high ground, and there were only very limited attempts to present an alternative rhetoric of sportsmanship and the moral value of racing and betting by its followers. Even without a case for betting's special moral worth the betting laws were almost entirely ineffective. Opposition to betting was falling away. The reasons for this are not totally clear, but probably lie at least in part in the decline in formal religious observance from the early twentieth century, alongside the decline of political Liberalism which had strong temperance and anti-gambling sections. Certainly the National Anti-Gambling League and other formal anti-betting organisations were much less well supported between the wars.

The falling attendance of the 'respectable classes' at churches, the growth of leisure alternatives to Sunday church- or chapel-going, and the growing urbanisation of Britain, all contributed to a failure to recruit, and the major forcing ground for anti-betting campaigns became seriously weaker.[14]

A belief that the sportmanship of cricket expressed Christian teaching and the strength of the churches' role in recreational cricket may have sustained the role of organised Christianity in English social life. By contrast most sporting writers accepted that 'racing is certainly not [the sport] that brings most good, either bodily or spiritually to its devotees. It is not on the racecourses . . . that are to be sought those benefits and qualities that we prize'.[15] Popular betting aided secularisation. If commentators plausibly saw football as an emotional substitute for religion, providing a key source of social identification and cultural consolation, so too was racing and betting. Although some of its followers were Christians, Jews or Muslims, racing did not generally utilise the language of religion. More often it used the commonplace residual language of other, more ancient beliefs – in luck or ill-luck, fortune and misfortune. In the cases of failure this was coupled with an emphasis on Nature – horses breaking down, a virus, the wrong weather.[16] Sporting newspapers sometimes advertised lucky charms, and even astrology was sometimes called upon in the service of breeding.

Betting had become commonplace. Indeed, unemployment probably increased rather than decreased the numbers of its adherents. It provided a compelling world of alternative loyalties to class and politics. Cunningham has emphasised the 'participant competitiveness' of small-scale localised urban culture and this applied to betting too.[17] Betting drew people together, not against capitalism, the establishment, the factory owners or just 'them', but against the bookie. Cash betting was an integral part of a working-class identity that helped to define that class. Interest in racing was a key part of working-class sociability, at work, at home or in the pub. Yet interest in racing was far wider. By 1939 it could be found amongst both sexes at all levels of British society, right across the country and the age range. And finding a winner was a key source of pleasure and delight both on and off the course.

Notes

1   S. G. Jones, *Workers at play: a social and economic history of leisure 1918–1939* (London: Routledge, 1986); Ross McKibbin, *Classes and cultures: England 1918–1951* (Oxford: Oxford University Press, 1998).

2   David Rubenstein, 'Britain's elites in the interwar period', in Alan Kidd and David Nicholls (eds), *The making of the British middle class? Studies of region and cultural diversity since the eighteenth century* (London: Sutton Publishing, 1998), pp. 186–202.

3   McKibbin, *Classes and cultures*, p. 7.

4   Jack Williams, *Cricket and England: a cultural and social history of the inter-war years* (London: Frank Cass, 2000).

5   Michael Williams, *The continuing story of point-to-point racing* (London: Pelham, 1970).

6   Williams, *Cricket and England*, p. 179. See M. E. J. Weiner, *English culture and the decline of the industrial spirit 1850–1980* (Cambridge: Cambridge University Press, 1981); Corelli Barnett, *The audit of war* (London: Macmillan, 1986); W. D. Rubinstein, *Capitalism, culture and decline in Britain, 1750–1990* (London: Routledge, 1993). For an opposing view see F. M. L. Thompson, *Gentrification and the enterprise culture: Britain 1780–1980* (Oxford: Oxford University Press, 2001),

7   Thompson, *Gentrification and the enterprise culture*, p. 112.

8   Dai Smith and Gareth Williams, *Fields of praise: the official history of the Welsh rugby union 1881–1981* (Cardiff: University of Wales Press, 1980); Martin Johnes, *Soccer and society: South Wales, 1900–1939* (Cardiff: University of Wales Press, 2002); Grant Jarvie and Graham Walker (eds), *Scottish sport in the making of the nation: ninety minute patriots* (Leicester: Leicester University Press, 1994); Jack Sugden and A. Bairner, *Sport, sectarianism and society in a divided Ireland* (Leicester: Leicester

University Press, 1993); Jeff Hill and Jack Williams, *Sport and identity in the North of England* (Keele: Keele University Press, 1996).

9 An idea developed further by R. J. Moore-Colyer, 'Gentlemen, horses and the turf in nineteenth century Wales', *Welsh history review,* 16 (1992), 308–23.

10 For a good overview see Peter Bailey, 'The politics and poetics of modern British leisure', *Rethinking history,* 3:2 (1999), 131–75.

11 Geoffrey Best, *Mid-Victorian Britain 1851–1875* (London: Weidenfeld and Nicholson, 1971); F. M. L. Thompson, *The rise of respectable society: a social history of Victorian Britain, 1830–1900* (London: Fontana, 1988).

12 See Mike Huggins and J. A. Mangan (eds), *Disreputable pleasures: less-virtuous Victorians at play* (London: Cass, 2003).

13 John Lowerson, 'Starting from your own past? The serious business of leisure history', *Journal of contemporary history,* 36: 3 (2001), 517–30.

14 Doug A. Reid, 'Playing and praying', in Martin Daunton (ed.), *Cambridge urban history of Britain Vol. 3* (Cambridge: Cambridge University Press, 2000), pp. 800–5.

15 Bernard Darwin, *British sport and games* (London: Longmans Green, 1940), p. 41.

16 Similar explanations were used about Denis Compton's 1950 test failures. See Jeff Hill, 'The legend of Dennis Compton', *Sports historian,* 18:2 (1998), 22.

17 Hugh Cunningham, 'Leisure and culture', in F. M. L. Thompson (ed.), *The Cambridge social history of Britain 1750–1950 Vol. 2* (Cambridge: Cambridge University Press, 1990), pp. 279–339.

Select bibliography

Manuscript sources

Too many record offices were consulted during this study to credit them fully. Doncaster Archives, Durham Record Office, East Sussex Record Office, Leicestershire County Record Office, Northumberland Record Office, Surrey History Service and West Sussex Record Office receive acknowledgement in the text. The Suffolk Oral History Project contains a number of useful interviews.

Newspapers

Cleveland Standard
Daily Express
Daily Graphic
Daily Mirror
Daily Sketch
Daily Telegraph
Doncaster Gazette
Evening Standard
Film Weekly
Hartlepool Daily Mail
Liverpool Daily Post
Liverpool Echo
Liverpool Post
London Evening News
North-Eastern Daily Express
North-Eastern Daily Gazette
Northern Daily Mail
Nottingham Post Tissue
Racing World and Newmarket Sportsman
Sporting Chronicle
Sporting Life
Sportsman

Strand Magazine
The Times
Yorkshire Evening Press
Yorkshire Herald

Printed primary sources

Acton, C. R., *Silk and spur* (London: Richards, 1935).

Aga Khan, *The memoirs of Aga Khan: world enough and time* (London: Cassell, 1954).

Bakke, E. Wight, *The unemployed man: a social study* (London: Nisbet, 1935).

Bebbington, W., *Rogues go racing* (London: Good and Betts, 1947).

Bird, T. H., *Admiral Rous and the English turf 1795–1877* (London: Putnam, 1939).

Bird, T. H., *A hundred Grand Nationals* (London: Country Life, 1937).

Bloodstock breeders' review (annually, 1919–39).

Booth, J. B., *Sporting Times: the Pink Un world* (London: Werner Laurie, 1938).

Bretherton, J., *Why gambling is wrong* (Manchester: Purpose Publications, 1936).

British Board of Film Censors, *Annual report of the British Board of Film Censors* (London: British Board of Film Censors, 1933).

Brown, Billie, *Also ran: the life story of Billie Brown, owner, trainer and jockey* (London: E. Hulton, 1920).

Browne, T. H., *A history of the English turf 1904–1930: vol. 2* (London: Virtue and Co., 1931).

Captain X, *Tales of the turf* (London: Partridge, 1943).

Darwin, B. R. M., *John Gully and his times* (London: Cassell, 1935).

Dawson, Elizabeth, *Mother made a book* (London: Geoffrey Bles, 1962).

Donoghue, Steve, *Donoghue up!* (London: Collins, 1938).

Donoghue, Steve, *Just my story* (London: Hutchinson, 1923).

Dorling, E. E., *Epsom and the Dorlings* (London: Stanley Paul, 1939).

Drage, Bert, *Reminiscences of Bert Drage* (London: David Green, 1955).

Ewen, C. L'Estrange, *Lotteries and sweepstakes* (London: Heath Cranton, 1932).

Fairfax-Blakeborough, Jack, *The analysis of the turf* (London: Philip Allan, 1927).

Fairfax-Blakeborough, Jack, *Northern turf history, volume III: York and Doncaster* (London: J. A. Allen, 1950).

Fairfax-Blakeborough, Jack, *Paddock personalities: being thirty years of turf memories* (London: Hutchinson, 1935).

Fairfax-Blakeborough, Jack, *The turf who's who?* (London: Mayfair Press, 1932).

Fawcett, William, *Sporting spectacle: a cavalcade of sports in England's yesteryear* (London: Methuen, 1939).

Fawcett, William, *Thoroughbred and hunter: their breeding, training and management from foal to maturity* (London: Eyre and Spottiswoode, 1934).

Fletcher, J. S., *The history of the St. Leger Stakes, 1776–1926* (London: Hutchinson, 1927).

Galtrey, Sidney, *Memoirs of a racing journalist* (London: Hutchinson, 1934).

Gilbey, Quintin, *Fun was my living* (London: Hutchinson, 1970).

Gilbey, Quintin, *Winners and Losers Vol. 1, 1928* (London: Welbecson Press, n.d.).

Good, Meyrick, *Good days* (London: Hutchinson, 1941).

Green, Peter, *Is gambling morally wrong?* (London: Friends Book Centre, 1926).

Green, Peter, *Betting and gambling*, (2nd edn, rev. C. H. Rose (London: Student Christian Movement, 1935).

Greenwood, Walter, *Love on the dole* (London: Jonathan Cape, 1938).

Gulland, John, *Gambling: the modern problem* (London: National Anti-gambling League, 1932).

Gulland, John, *Youth and gambling* (London: British Christian Endeavour Union, 1936).

Hamlyn, George, *My sixty years in the ring: a racing and gambling autobiography* (Hungerford: Sporting Garland Press, 1994).

Harewood, Earl of and P. E. Ricketts (eds), *Flat racing* (London: Seeley Service, 1937).

Heath, Captain, *News Chronicle racing annual 1934* (London: News Chronicle, 1934).

House of Commons, *Select Committee on Betting Duty, and minutes of evidence* (London: 1923).

Jarvis, Jack, *They're off: an autobiography* (London: Michael Joseph, 1969).

Jayne, Leonard, *Pony racing, including the story of Northolt Park* (London: Hutchinson, 1949).

Johnstone, Rae, *The Rae Johnstone story* (London: Stanley Paul, 1958).

Lambton, George, *Men and horses I have known* (London: Thornton Butterworth, 1924).

Leach, Jack, *A rider in the stand: racing reminiscences* (London: Stanley Paul, 1970).

Liverpool Council for Voluntary Aid, *Report on betting in Liverpool* (Liverpool: Liverpool Council for Voluntary Aid, 1926).

Luckman, Cyril, aka 'The Scout', *The Scout's guide to racing* (London: Daily Express, 1937).

Lyall, J. G., *Round goes the world* (Stamford: Haynes, 1937).

Lyle, R. C., *Brown Jack* (London: Putnam, 1934).

Macey, A., *The romance of the Derby Stakes* (London: Hutchinson, 1930).

Marsh, Richard, *A trainer to two kings* (London: Cassell, 1925).

McGuigan, John, *A trainer's memories: being 60 years' turf reminiscences and experiences of home and abroad* (London: Heath Ganton, 1946).

Moorhouse, Edward, 'The racing year', *Bloodstock breeders review*, 1938.

Munroe, D. H., *The Grand National, 1839–1931* (London: Heinemann, 1931).

National Anti-gambling League, *The great waste and the cure: 31st annual report* (London: National Anti-gambling League, 1921).

National Anti-gambling League, *Gambling and the state: 43rd annual report* (London: National Anti-gambling League, 1933).

Newton, Edward, *Derby Day and other adventures* (Boston: Little, Brown, 1934).

O'Sullevan, Peter, *Calling the horses: a racing autobiography* (London: Hodder and Stoughton, 1994).

Perkins, E. B., *Betting facts* (London: Wesleyan Methodist Church and SCM, 1925).

Perkins, E. B., *Gambling and youth* (London: Sunday School Union, 1933).

Perkins, E. B., *The problem of gambling* (London: Epworth Press, 1919).

Pilgrim Trust, *Men without work* (Cambridge: Cambridge University Press, 1938).

Porter, John, *John Porter of Kingsclere* (London: Grant Richards, 1919).

Prior, Charles Matthew, *The history of the Racing Calendar and Stud Book from their inception in the eighteenth century* (London: Sporting Life, 1926).

Prior, F. M., *Register of thoroughbred stallions* (London: Horse and Hound, 1931).

Richards, Gordon, *My story* (London: Hodder and Stoughton, 1955).

Richardson, Charles, *Racing at home and abroad: British flat racing and breeding, race-horses and the evaluation of the thoroughbred* (London: London and Home Counties Press Association, 1923).

Richardson, Charles, *Racing at home and abroad, vol. 3: British steeplechasing and racing in Ireland* (London: London and Home Counties Press Association, 1927).

Rickman, Eric, *Come racing with me* (London: Chatto and Windus, 1951).

Rickman, Eric, *On and off the racecourse* (London: Routledge, 1937).

Rose, Cecil H., *Gambling and Christian ideals* (London: Epworth Press, 1930).

Rowntree, B. Seebohm, *Poverty and progress: a second social survey of York* (London: Longman, Green, 1941).

Royal Commission on Lotteries and Betting, 1932/3.

Royal Commission on Police Powers and Procedures, 1929.

Ruff, *Ruff's guide to the turf*, (London: Ruff, annually 1919–1939).

Sarl, Arthur J., *Horses, jockeys and crooks: reminiscences concerning thirty years' racing* (London: Hutchinson, 1935).

Shadwell, Arthur, *Industrial efficiency: a comparative study of industrial life in England, Germany and America* (London: Longman, Green, 1920).

Sporting Chronicle, *Racing up-to-date: a complete record of flat racing* (Manchester: Sporting Chronicle, 1938).

Temple, W. and Perkins, E. B., *Gambling and ethics* (London: Pilgrim Press, n.d.).

Turf Guardian Society, *Directory of turf accountants and commission agents* (London: Turf Guardian Society, 1921).

Watson, Alfred, E. T., *A great year: Lord Glanley's horses* (London: Longman, Green, 1921).

Wentworth, Lady, *Thoroughbred racing stock and its ancestors* (London: Allen and Unwin, 1938).

Weston, Tommy, *My racing life* (London: Hutchinson, 1952).

Secondary sources: books

Abelson, Edward, and Tyrrel, John, *The Breedon book of horseracing records* (Derby: Breedon Books, 1993).

Bevan, R. M., *The Roodee: 450 years of racing in Chester* (Northwich: Cheshire Country Publishing, 1989).

Birley, Sir Derek, *Playing the game: sport and British society 1910–1945* (Manchester: Manchester University Press, 1995).

Bland, Ernest (ed.), *Flat racing since 1900* (London: Andrew Dakers, 1950).

Blaxland, Gregory, *Golden Miller* (London: Constable, 1972).

Brady, Terence and Felton, Michael, *Point-to-pointing: a history, an introduction and a guide* (London: Pelham, 1991).

Briggs, Asa, *Social thought and social action: a study of the work of Seebohm Rowntree 1871–1954* (London: Longman, 1961).

Brock, D. W. E., *The racing man's weekend book* (London: Seeley Service, n.d.).

Brown, Callum, *The decline of Christian Britain* (London: Routledge, 2000).

Burnett, John, *Idle hands: the experience of unemployment* (London: Routledge, 1994).

Cannadine, David, *Class in Britain* (New Haven: Yale University Press, 1998).

Cannadine, David, *Rituals of royalty: power and ceremonial in traditional societies* (Cambridge: Cambridge University Press, 1987).

Chinn, Carl, *Better betting with a decent feller: bookmakers, betting and the British working class 1750–1990* (London: Harvester Wheatsheaf, 1991).

Clapson, Mark, *A bit of a flutter: popular gambling in England c.1823–1961* (Manchester: Manchester University Press, 1992).

COPEC, *A report of the meetings of the conference on Christian politics, economics and citizenship held in Birmingham, April 5–12, 1924* (London: Longman, Green, 1924).

Cross, Gary (ed.), *Worktowners at Blackpool* (London: Routledge, 1990).

Curling, Bill, *The Captain: a biography of Captain Sir Cecil Boyd Rochfort, royal trainer* (London: Barrie and Jenkins, 1970).

Davies, Walter Haydn, *Blithe ones* (Bridgend: Bridgend Printing, 1979).

Devereux, Edward, *Gambling and the social structure* (New York: Arno Press, 1980).

Dixon, David, *From prohibition to regulation: bookmaking, anti-gambling and the law* (Oxford: Clarendon Press, 1991).

Downes, D. M., Davies, B. P., David, M. E. and Stone, P., *Gambling, work and leisure: a study across three areas* (London: Routledge and Kegan Paul, 1976).

Fairfax-Blakeborough, Noel, (ed.), *J. F-B: the memoirs of Jack Fairfax-Blakeborough* (London: J. A. Allen, 1978).

Felstead, S. Theodore, *Racing romance* (London: Werner Laurie, 1949).

Fishwick, Nicholas, *English football and society, 1910–1950* (Manchester: Manchester University Press, 1989).

Fiske, John, *Reading the popular* (London: Unwin Hyman, 1990).

Fiske, John, *Television culture* (London: Methuen, 1987).

Fitzgerald, Arthur, *Royal thoroughbreds: a history of the royal studs* (London: Sidgwick and Jackson, 1990).

Fowler, David, *The first teenagers: the lifestyle of young wage-earners in inter-war Britain* (London: Woburn Press, 1995).

Fox, Kate, *The racing tribe: watching the horsewatchers* (London: Metro Books, 1999).

Gifford, Dennis, *The British film catalogue, 1875–1970: a guide to entertainment films* (Newton Abbot: David and Charles, 1973).

Gilbey, Quintin, *Champions all: Steve to Lester* (London: Hutchinson, 1971).

Gilbey, Quintin, *Queen of the turf: the Dorothy Paget story* (London: Barker, 1973).

Good, Meyrick, *The lure of the turf* (London: Odham, 1957).

Green, Reg, *A history of the Grand National* (London: Hodder and Stoughton, 1987).

Herbert, Ivor and Smyly, Patricia, *The winter kings* (London: Pelham, 1968).

Hill, Jeffrey, *Sport, leisure and culture in twentieth century Britain* (Basingstoke: Palgrave, 2002).

Hill, Jeff and Williams, Jack (eds), *Sport and identity in the North of England* (Keele: Keele University Press, 1996).

Hillenbrand, Laura, *Seabiscuit: three men and a racehorse* (London: Fourth Estate, 2002).

Hislop, John, *Far from a gentleman* (London: Michael Joseph, 1960).

Hislop, John, and Swannell, David, *The Faber book of the turf* (London: Faber and Faber, 1990).

Huggins, Mike, *Flat racing and British society 1790–1914* (London: Frank Cass, 2000).

Huggins, Mike and Mangan, J. A. (eds), *Disreputable pleasures: less virtuous Victorians at play* London: Frank Cass, 2003).

Jackson, Stanley, *The Aga Khan: prince, prophet and sportsman* (London: Odhams Press, 1952).

Jarvie, Grant, and Walker, Graham (eds), *Scottish sport in the making of the nation: ninety minute patriots* (Leicester: Leicester University Press, 1994).

Johnes, Martin, *Soccer and society: South Wales, 1900–1939* (Cardiff: University of Wales Press, 2002).

Jones, Michael Wynn, *The Derby* (London: Croom Helm, 1979).

Jones, Stephen G., *Workers at play: a social and economic history of leisure 1918–1939* (London: Routledge and Kegan Paul, 1986).

Kaye, Richard with Peskett, R., *The Ladbroke's story* (London: Pelham, 1969).

Laird, Dorothy, *Royal Ascot* (London: Hodder and Stoughton, 1976).

Landy, Marcia, *British genres: cinema and society, 1930–1960* (Princeton, NJ: Princeton University Press, 1991).

Lane, Charles, *British racing prints 1700–1940* (London: Sportsman's Press, 1990).

Leicester, Sir Charles, *Bloodstock breeding* (London: J. A. Allen, 1983).

LeMahieu, D. L., *A culture for democracy: mass communication and the cultivated mind in Britain between the wars* (Oxford: Clarendon Press, 1988).

Low, Rachael and Manvell, Roger, *The history of the British film 1929–1939: films of comment and persuasion in the 1930s* (London: Allen and Unwin, 1979).

Marsh, Marcus, *Racing with the gods* (London: Pelham, 1968).

Mass Observation, *The pub and the people: a worktown study* (London: Hutchinson/Mass Observation, 1987).

McKibbin, Ross, *Classes and cultures: England 1918–1951* (Oxford: Oxford University Press, 1998).

McKibbin, Ross, *The ideologies of class* (Oxford: Oxford University Press, 1990).

Morgan, Kenneth O., *Rebirth of a nation: Wales 1880–1980* (Oxford: Clarendon Press, 1981).

Morley, David, *Television, audiences and cultural studies* (London: Routledge, 1992).

Mortimer, Roger, *The Jockey Club* (London: Cassell, 1958).

Mortimer, Roger, Onslow, Richard, and Willet, Peter, *Biographical encyclopaedia of flat racing* (London: MacDonald and Janes, 1978).

Munnings, Sir Alfred, *The second burst* (London: Museum Press, 1951).

Munting, Roger, *An economic and social history of gambling in Britain and the USA* (Manchester: Manchester University Press, 1996).

Munting, Roger, *Hedges and hurdles: a social and economic history of National Hunt Racing* (London: J. A. Allen, 1987).

Orchard, V., *Tattersalls* (London: Hutchinson, 1953).

Pain, Rollo, *Why Cartmel: survival of a small racecourse 1856–1998* (Kendal: Lakeland Health, 2001).

Parker, Tim FitzGeorge, *Ever loyal: the biography of Neville Crump* (London: Stanley Paul, 1987).

Pegg, Norman, *Focus on racing* (London: Robert Hale, 1963).

Pitt, Chris, *A long time gone* (Halifax: Portway Press, 1996).

Plumtre, George, *Back page racing: a century of newspaper coverage* (London: MacDonald/Queen Anne Press, 1996).

Portland, Duke of, *Memories of racing and hunting* (London: Faber and Faber, 1935).

Pyke, J. K., *A Grand National commentary* (London: J. A. Allen, 1971).

Rasmussen, Leo, and Napier, Miles (comp.) *Treasures of the Bloodstock breeders' review* (London: J. A. Allen, 1990).

Richards, Jeffrey, *Age of the dream palace: cinema and society in Britain 1930–1939* (London: Routledge and Kegan Paul, 1984).

Richards, Jeffrey (ed.), *The unknown 1930s: an alternative history of the British cinema 1929–1939* (London: I. B. Tauris, 1997).

Richards, Jeffrey and Sheridan, D. (eds), *Mass-Observation at the movies* (London: Routledge and Kegan Paul, 1987).

Rickaby, Bill, *First to finish* (Gateshead: Northumberland Press, 1969).

Rickaby, Bridget, *About Bill* (Newmarket: R and N Publications, 1990).

Rickman, John, *Old Tom and young John: stories from a horseracing family* (Cambridge: Allborough Press, 1990).

Rose, Jonathan, *The intellectual life of the British working classes* (New Haven: Yale University Press, 2001).

Rowe, David, *Sport, culture and the media* (Buckingham: Open University Press, 1999).

Runciman, W. G., *A treatise on social theory: volume III, applied social theory* (Cambridge: Cambridge University Press, 1997).

Russell, Dave, *Football and the English* (Preston: Cicerone press, 1997).

Seth-Smith, Michael, *The head waiter: the biography of Harry Wragg* (London: Michael Joseph, 1984).

Seth-Smith, Michael, *Steve: the life and times of Steve Donoghue* (London: Faber and Faber, 1974).

Seth-Smith, Michael (ed.), *The history of flat racing* (London: New English Library, 1978).

Seth-Smith, Michael and Mortimer, Roger, *Derby 200: the official story of the Blue Riband of the turf* (Enfield: Guinness Superlatives, 1979).

Seth-Smith, Michael, Willett, Peter, Mortimer, Roger and Lawrence, John, *The history of steeplechasing* (London: Michael Joseph, 1966).

Shafer, Stephen C., *British popular films 1929–1939: the cinema of reassurance* (London: Routledge, 1997).

Sidney, Charles, *The art of legging* (London: Maxline International, 1976).

Sim, Andrew, *English racing stables* (Addlestone: Dial Press, 1993).

Smith, Vian, *Point-to-point* (London: Stanley Paul, 1968).

Stevenson, John, *British Society 1914–1945* (Harmondsworth: Penguin, 1984).

Tanner, Michael and Cranham, Gerry, *Great jockeys of the flat* (Enfield: Guinness Publishing, 1992).

Thompson, A. H., *Censorship in public libraries in the twentieth century* (Epping: Bowker, 1975).

Tyrell, John, *Running racing: the Jockey Club years since 1750* (London: Quiller Press, 1997).

Vamplew, Wray, *Pay up and play the game: professional sport in Britain 1875–1914* (Cambridge: Cambridge University Press, 1988).

Vamplew, Wray, *The turf* (London: Allen Lane, 1976).

Verney, J. H. (ed.), *Steeplechasing* (London: Seeley Service, 1954).

Walker, John, *Halliwell's film and video guide* (London: Harper Collins, 1998).

Walker, Michael B., *The psychology of gambling* (Oxford: Pergamon Press, 1992).

Walton, John K., *Lancashire: a social history 1558–1939* (Manchester: Manchester University Press, 1987).

Welsh, Phil, *Stable rat: life in the racing stables* (London: Eyre Methuen, 1979).

White, Sidney H., *I gotta horse: the autobiography of Ras Prince Monolulu as told to Sidney H. White* (London: Hurst and Blackett, 1950).

Wigglesworth, Neil, *The evolution of English sport* (London: Frank Cass, 1996).

Willett, P., *The story of Tattersalls*, (London: Stanley Paul, 1987).

Williams, Jack, *Cricket and England: a cultural and social history of the interwar years* (London: Frank Cass, 1999).

Williams, Michael, *The continuing story of point-to-point* (London: Pelham, 1970).

Young, Kenneth, *Harry, Lord Rosebery* (London: Hodder and Stoughton, 1974).

Secondary sources: articles and chapters in edited collections

Bailey, Peter, 'The politics and poetics of modern British leisure', *Rethinking history*, 3: 2 (1999), 131–75.

Bourdieu, Pierre, 'The aristocracy of culture', *Media, culture and society*, 2: 3 (1980), 235–53.

'Britain's betting industry – II', *The Economist*, 7.3.1936, 517.

Clapson, Mark, 'Playing the system: the world of organised street betting in Manchester, Salford and Bolton c.1880–1939', in Andrew, Davies and Steven Fielding (eds), *Workers' worlds: cultures and communities in Manchester and Salford 1880–1939* (Manchester: Manchester University Press, 1992).

Corrigan, Philip and Willis, Paul, 'Cultural forms and class mediations', *Media, culture and society*, 3: 2 (1980), 306.

Cunningham, Hugh, 'Leisure and culture', in F. M. L. Thompson (ed.), *The Cambridge social history of Britain 1750–1950, Vol. 2* (Cambridge: Cambridge University Press, 1990).

Dyer, Richard, 'Entertainment and utopia' in Rick Altmann (ed.), *Genre, the musical: a reader* (London: Routledge, 1981).

Graham, Clive, 'The pencillers', in 'The Scout' (Cyril Luckham), *The Scout's guide to racing* (London: Daily Express, 1937).

Hermes, J., 'Gender and media studies: no woman, no cry', in John Corner, Philip Schlesinger and Roger Silverstone (eds.), *International handbook of media research* (London: Routledge, 1997).

Hill, Jeff, 'The legend of Dennis Compton', *Sports historian,* 18: 2 (1998).

Huggins, M. J., 'The first generation of street bookmakers in Victorian England: demonic fiends or decent fellers?', *Northern history,* 36: 1 (2000).

Huggins, M. J., 'Thoroughbred breeding in the north and East ridings of Yorkshire in the ninteenth century', *Agricultural history review,* 42: 2 (1994), 115–25.

Huggins, Mike, 'Culture, class and respectability: racing and the middle classes in the nineteenth century', *International journal of the history of sport,* 11: 1 (1994), 19–41.

Huggins, Mike, 'More sinful pleasures? Leisure, respectability and the male middle classes in Victorian England', *Journal of social history,* 33: 1 (2000), 585–600.

Huggins, Mike, 'Nineteenth century racehorse stables in their rural setting: a social and economic study', *Rural history,* 7: 2 (1996), 177–90.

Melling, Alethea, 'Wicked women from Wigan and other tales: licentious leisure and the social control of working-class women in Wigan and St Helens, 1914–1930', *North-west labour history,* 24 (1999/2000).

Munting, R., 'Social opposition to gambling in Britain', *International journal of the history of sport,* 10: 3 (1993).

Reid, Doug A., 'Playing and praying', in Martin Daunton (ed.), *Cambridge urban history of Britain, vol. 3* (Cambridge: Cambridge University Press, 2000).

Rubenstein, David, 'Britain's elites in the interwar period', in Alan Kiddand David Nicholls (eds), *The making of the British middle class? Studies of regional and cultural diversity since the eighteenth century* (London: Sutton Publishing, 1998).

Stanley, Edward George Villiers, Earl of Derby, 'Foreword' to Rickman, Eric, *In and out of the saddle* (London: Routledge, 1937).

Vamplew, Wray, 'Still crazy after all those years: continuity in a changing labour market for professional jockeys', *Contemporary British history,* 14: 2 (2000), 115–45.

Williams, Jack, 'A wild orgy of speed: responses to speedway in Britain before the Second World War', *Sports historian,* 19: 1 (1999), 1–15.

Unpublished theses and papers

Hall, James Russell, 'The racing media in Britain from Prince Charlie to Zafonic: some neglected perspectives', MA dissertation, University of Lancaster, 1993.

Harris, George, 'Street betting in the twentieth century: its social significance in the working-class community', MA dissertation, University of Lancaster, 1978.

Jones, Steve, 'The British labour movement and working class leisure 1918–1939', PhD thesis, University of Manchester, 1983.

Khan, Paull, 'The sport of kings: a study of traditional social structures under change', PhD thesis, University of Wales, Swansea, 1980.

Index